When the
Stars Begin
to Fall

When the Stars Begin to Fall

Overcoming Racism and Renewing the Promise of America

Theodore R. Johnson

Atlantic Monthly Press
New York

"Let America Be America Again" from *The Collected Poems of Langston Hughes* by Langston Hughes, edited by Arnold Rampersad with David Roessel, Associate Editor, copyright © 1994 by the Estate of Langston Hughes. Used by permission of Alfred A. Knopf, an imprint of the Knopf Doubleday Publishing Group, a division of Penguin Random House LLC. All rights reserved.

FIRST EDITION

Published simultaneously in Canada
Printed in Canada

First Grove Atlantic hardcover edition: June 2021

This book was designed by Norman E. Tuttle of Alpha Design & Composition. This book was set in 12-pt. Adobe Caslon Pro by Alpha Design & Composition of Pittsfield, NH.

Library of Congress Cataloging-in-Publication data is available for this title.

ISBN 978-0-8021-5785-0
eISBN 978-0-8021-5787-4

Atlantic Monthly Press
an imprint of Grove Atlantic
154 West 14th Street
New York, NY 10011

Distributed by Publishers Group West

groveatlantic.com

21 22 23 24   10 9 8 7 6 5 4 3 2 1

CONTENTS

PART IV   A PATH TOWARD NATIONAL SOLIDARITY

An Introduction

Race and Solidarity in the United States

I was twelve years old the first time someone called me a nigger.

It happened one autumn morning as I and my friends—four white boys and Marcus, a black kid who had just moved to an adjoining neighborhood—trekked through our predominantly white suburban community nestled in the Piedmont plains of North Carolina. We walked the same route to school every morning past colonial homes with brick facades, plush green manicured lawns tucked between sidewalks and country porches, and small house dogs bravely yipping from bay windows. A small, nasally voice hurled the slur from behind a hedge of evergreen bushes as we crossed the trodden-grass clearing adjacent to our school. I immediately knew it was Cameron.

The air around eleven-year-old Cameron was spoiled and self-obsessed, a characteristic that felt uncommon among the children in our subdivision. His signature tic was flipping his blond-frosted skater bangs over a head of brown hair—a peacock gesture that added some heft to his slight build. Sometimes his hotheaded ways caused him to spit fire that would eventually consume him in the backdraft. This was such a moment. The songs of the morning birds were interrupted as the n-word landed like a grenade in the middle of our unit. It had barely settled into the dirt beneath us when its heat singed the air between us. *All black people are niggers!* The last syllable bounced around the trees behind us until it was rushed away by the breeze.

The unblinking eyes of my white friends all fell on me, their mouths agape. These were guys with whom I'd camped out, played basketball, traded baseball cards, and talked with endlessly about girls and professional wrestling. But they were not angry. They were not offended. They did not rush to my defense or to reassure me, as friends often do as a display of solidarity in moments like this. The only thing they had for me were slack-jawed expressions dotted with darting eyes that seemed to ask, *What's our black friend Teddy gonna do?* Standing there in my frail, prepubescent body, attempting to shoulder this new burden, I felt isolated and smothered, as if no one around could hear my muffled struggling. It was the first time I saddled the silent weight of being black in America.

Then, in a flash of relief and with an oddly timed sense of joy, I remembered that I was not alone. The new kid! Marcus! In a single heartbeat, I turned to find him already moving toward Cameron's hiding place in the hedges with choppy strides that quickly extended into a sprint. My instincts took over, and I launched with him. For some reason, it suddenly felt important to me that the two black people within earshot acted together, in solidarity. Even though Marcus and I were only newly acquainted, in the face of racial hatred we found common cause and unified action. Running with him—my heart racing and my breath short and shallow between long strides—I still remember feeling strong . . . vibrant . . . affirmed.

Thirty years later, on a crisp October morning in 2017, I slide into a beige-and-burnt-orange subway seat, rattling along the blue path of Washington, D.C.'s color-coded Metro line, deep in thought. If twelve-year-old Teddy stepped into that train and eyed this older version of himself, he would have sneaked a steady stream of glances in search of something that felt familiar, trying to decide if he liked the man he had become. He would have recognized the puffs of skin around the eyes that his mother's family passed down like recipes and old wives' tales; the prominent nose from his father's lineage, born in a place where *haints* lurk in the crossings of darkened country fields; and his pigeon-toed mien that made his feet look as if they were continuously leaning in to whisper to each other, whether seated or in motion. He would have noted the gold on the left hand and smiled to know that he would one day have a girl and find love. He never would have predicted the titles Commander and Doctor now preceding his last name, the receding hairline where there were once waves he brushed into uncooperative hair laden with pink lotion and pomade, or that he had traveled the world in suits and uniforms, from Johannesburg to Japan, war zones to the White House. He definitely would have sensed the same melancholic insecurity that often grasps his adult pinky finger and tags along on all his life's pursuits, little and large. And he would have noted that the burden he felt that one morning with Marcus and Cameron had doubled and transformed—the weight of race had evolved into a responsibility to America and to the dignity of its black citizens. Had I caught his glance, perhaps I would have smiled, or simply just looked away. I was distracted. I had a speech to give.

There on the subway, I closed my eyes and mouthed the words of an address about the fate of our country. Five decades of alumni from the prestigious White House Fellowship program had gathered for the annual leadership conference in the U.S. Chamber of Commerce's august Hall of Flags, and I was one of the many speakers lined up to offer some thoughts on the state of our Union. Ben Carson, previously a Republican presidential candidate and secretary of the U.S. Department of Housing and Urban Development, began the morning by assuring us that the nation was on the right track. Later, H.R. McMaster, then President Donald Trump's national security advisor and a three-star Army general, took to the podium and sought to give us all confidence that the nation was safe. Others ascended the stage and opined on the evolving nature of media and the impact of globalization on international economies. And then, when it was my turn, I looked the audience in the eye and told them America was in danger.

I began with the well-traveled story of Benjamin Franklin in 1787 emerging from the summer-long convening in Philadelphia, where our Constitution was put to paper. As Franklin stepped outside and took in a breath of fresh air, a woman approached and asked what sort of government the state delegates had created. Franklin responded wryly with a challenge: "A republic, if you can keep it."[1] *Can we keep it?* Racism, I told the room, was the only thing that has ever proved strong enough to break up the nation. If we fail to keep our republic, it will be because we allowed racism to swipe it from us once more.

I struggled through listing a sampling of racial incidents pointing to the fissures in our republic: protests and riots in black communities after lethal confrontations between unarmed black people and police officers; white nationalists marching with Nazi Germany and Confederate battle flags declaring America belongs to them alone; black athletes and white politicians at war over appropriate displays of patriotism and free speech during the national anthem; and increased vitriol between political parties accompanied by the racial sorting of party membership. But I also needed my audience to understand what racism felt like—how it shaped a different reality for one of their black peers. So I told them: America is where I have achieved dreams that would have been impossible elsewhere, but it is also a haven for my deepest disappointments. It is where the color of my skin enters the room before I do, crashing the party and casting a shadow over conversations. It is where military men who are supposed to be my brothers in arms tell me that my promotions are affirmative-action handouts. It is where I have been yanked from my car, handcuffed, searched, and tossed in jail because two cops thought a black guy with a blown headlight was suspicious. It is where I raise sons who cannot escape airings of shaky smartphone videos showing black people's deadly encounters with law enforcement: George Floyd. Philando Castile. Eric Garner. Walter Scott. And so many others. And it is where I have had to explain to them why their brown skin and dreadlocks make them prime candidates to be excluded from the full rights and protections of citizenship.

Despite maddening contradictions, I love America. I simply cannot help it. I told the room that there is an undeniable and admirable strength in a nation that slowly but steadily groans toward the incorporation of those it used to exclude. It is a country founded on high-minded ideals with an aspirational, hopeful orientation propelled by a people who believe it will be better tomorrow than it is today. For two decades, I wore a military uniform, proudly pulling the cloth of the nation over my shoulders each morning with the full understanding that many people suffered and died for me to have the honor. An appreciation of how far the United States has come, coupled with the vision of what it can become, should inspire us to do our part so that future generations can experience a more perfect union than we have. It is imperfect, but it is ours.

I should not have been startled when a sudden and familiar force tugged at the corners of my face after I asked the room if our republic was one that we could keep. My throat tightened, choking off the words trying to push through. My eyes warmed. My vision blurred. Drawing from my last ounce of composure, I told the mostly white, mostly conservative, and mostly middle-aged audience that racism was an existential threat to America. If we could not muster the bravery to figure out and confront our racial issues, there would be no United States worth saving to leave to our children.

Then a tear fell. And then another. I bowed my head, ashamed of the public surrender to emotion. After a couple of seconds and some deep breaths while pinching at the bridge of my nose, I lifted my head to find, much to my surprise, that many in the chamber were in tears, too.

My tears were the product of a lapse of optimism and faith in the American idea. A naive revelation, perhaps, for a grown black man. But for the first time in my life, it dawned on me that the nation might be more wedded to racial hierarchy than to the founding principles I had sworn to support and defend as an officer in the U.S. Navy. And I realized that the feeling sweeping through me was the polar opposite of the strength and purpose that had flooded my twelve-year-old body after an eleven-year-old called me the n-word. Race is at the root of both the empowering connections and the debilitating disconnections that characterize our American experience. Sitting with these two feelings in the same moment on a stage one block from the White House, I worried that we may not be capable of overcoming the effects of racism or the animus it pollinates. I worried that we may not be truly committed to keeping the republic.

The weeping faces that October morning in the nation's capital were proof that I was not alone. Americans of all races, ages, and political leanings share the deep concern that an inability to resolve our racial issues may be our undoing. All of our tears carried a question: *What is to be done?* My tears, however, also contained an answer—an answer that has been passed down through generations of black experiences in America and that has slowly but relentlessly pushed the nation closer to its professed ideals: solidarity.

EVEN THE MOST HOPEFUL and optimistic among us sense the negative shift in our racial climate over the last decade. Nearly two in three Americans believe that racism remains a major problem.[2] Approximately three in four of us say race relations are bad, and more than half think they are getting worse.[3] And that's the good news. Here's the bad: 80 percent of us think incivility will lead to violence, and the average American voter believes that the United States is two-thirds of the way to the edge of a civil war.[4] Hate crimes are on the rise, and black Americans are victims of nearly half of them, despite being less than 14 percent of the population.[5] The feeling that race relations have worsened is further fueled by an increasingly divisive brand of politics, viral videos transcribing violent and heated interracial confrontations, changing racial demographics that some perceive as a threat to the American identity, and a more vocal and visible black population that is not bashful about pointing out how the nation has excluded them from the Promise.

And just what is the Promise? It is that all men and women are inherently equal, that each of us will respect and defend the rights and liberty of others, and that the state will not deny or unjustly hamper our equality or our exercise of liberty. The Promise is not the American Dream. The Dream is a question of opportunity and economic attainment. The Promise, however, is about a person's basic value and the state's fundamental obligation to protect one's rights. The United States and Americans have fallen short of the Promise, and racism has been the primary cause. We should have no delusions about how intractable the problem is or how invested some are in its preservation. The steps toward the Promise are not crystal stairs—they are splintered, tacked, and rickety in spots, and the well is dark. The climb is perilous, but we cannot afford to turn back or rest to admire the laurels.[6]

And yet, amid all this angst, a majority of Americans believe the nation's best days are ahead of it[7]—and optimism is particularly high among poor black Americans.[8] There is a growing sense among all Americans that today's youths will have better lives than we have had, a particularly important measure in American culture. We agree on the ideals that are important to American democracy, and we know that the country falls short of many of those ideals. For example, five in six of us maintain a fierce desire for a nation in which the rights and freedoms of all people are respected, but less than half of us think this accurately describes the country today.[9] The problem this demonstrates is that the nation we have and the nation we want are separated by a vast sea, and racism marauds any who would dare attempt the crossing. We wonder aloud how a country that has inarguably become more aligned to its founding principles over the last couple of centuries remains confounded by racial injustice and conflict at every turn. We are hopeful, yes, but we are tired.

This paradoxical mix of passion and pessimism, of energy and exhaustion when it comes to confronting racial inequality, is part of what makes us American. The nation's air has always danced with the tension between these fevered emotions. For as long as there has been a United States of America, there has been a racial hierarchy that has threatened its very existence, marshaled its citizens in different directions, and tested the national narrative. At the outset, the humanity and rights of black people were the subject of heated debates in those austere settings where the Declaration of Independence and the Constitution were formulated. Some of our nation's founders recognized the dangers in the inherent hypocrisy of permitting slavery to persist while declaring "all men are created equal" with unalienable rights to life, liberty, and the pursuit of happiness. And yet they tabled the issue—a tactic for which we have developed quite a propensity—so that a new country could emerge. For the founding generation, and those that followed, creating and establishing a nation based on the idea of equality and liberty was more important than immediately extending those rights to all the country's inhabitants. Many of them believed that slavery would eventually run its course anyway and that its end was inevitable. In due time, they thought, the evils of slavery would wither and give way to our better angels. This view is what makes solidarity possible but frustratingly always just out of reach. This approach, too, is quite American: *It'll all work out somehow*—an optimistic phrase that has long been our unofficial national motto.

The working out, however, is exceptionally hard. It is an endeavor for the ages that is never complete. For all the founding generation's expedient blind faith that the institution of slavery would naturally devolve over time and be accompanied by America's welcoming embrace for the newly freed, emancipation did not descend coolly over a grateful nation—instead it came with the raging fire of muskets, cannons, and racial fervor. The argument over the humanity of black people in the United States accomplished what nothing else has: the fracturing of the Union. When the first mortars exploded at Fort Sumter marking the beginning of the Civil War, Charles Francis Adams, grandson of national founder John Adams, observed with sorrow, "We the children of the third and fourth generations are doomed to pay the penalties of the compromises made by the first."[10]

The longer we allowed racism to live, the harder it became to kill. Slavery did indeed die, but its offspring—racial hierarchy and injustice—live on. Not even the blood sacrifice of hundreds of thousands of Civil War soldiers, sailors, Marines, and enslaved black people managed to cleanse the nation of its original sin, which is that a nation founded on the high-minded ideals of liberty and equality enslaved human beings. And though two decades of presidential executive orders, Supreme Court rulings, and transformational civil rights legislation during the mid-twentieth century began the dismantling of Jim Crow, black Americans still experience a lesser form of citizenship than their white fellow citizens. For a nation that rightfully prides itself on the racial progress realized over the last two centuries, this is an uncomfortable truth. We are still falling short of the Promise.

Now, time has settled on us. It is our turn to attempt the crossing and take on the leviathan. This challenge—whether we face it, disregard it, or willfully steer clear and wait for better people in a different era to fight it—joins us to previous generations that have each shaped, and been shaped by, America's defining struggle with race, an issue that clarifies the national character like no other. Fortunately, we do not need to start at the beginning. We get to pick up the baton from the courageous ones who came before us. But we also pick up the burden of the mistakes, malice, and maladjustments left by those lesser spirits who sought to hoard the Promise for the few. Both are our inheritance. Taken together, how racism is exercised has changed, but its presence remains constant. It is this latter point that makes us weary. As much as we may wish it so, racism, like the institution of slavery, will not just die off on its own and be carried quietly into the past by the winds of change. We have to believe we can forge new ground and then do the work to make it so. We would be equally foolish to think that we are incapable of making our Union more perfect as we would to think that there is nothing more that can be done. So then, what exactly *can* be done to finally overcome racism in the United States? Is it even possible to strip away its impact given how much our history is infected with it and how much of it still courses through the nation's veins?

The answers to these questions, and some that naturally spring from them, are in the chapters that follow. *When the Stars Begin to Fall* suggests that the well-being of America and its future generations rests on our ability to establish a national solidarity. This sounds straightforward enough but risks tripping us up before we can even get out of the gate. Depending on whom you ask, solidarity can mean different things. Some perceive it as standing in agreement with others or showing support for a cause. There are those who attach it to socialism or large labor movements. And there are others who will point out its religious and philosophical connotations. Such varied meanings can make it impossible to take the next step. How can we create a thing if we cannot agree on what it is?

Herein, national solidarity is a combination of political and civic solidarities—the moral relationship among citizens in response to injustice and the obligations the country has to each citizen, respectively.[11] That is, national solidarity is the political unity of a people demanding, on moral and principled grounds, that the country address wrongs suffered by some of its members so that the rights and privileges prescribed in the social contract are equally available to all. This is especially important for a nation founded on the principles of equality and liberty—ideas that are supposed to be the basis of our shared identity. National solidarity is founded on a set of common civil beliefs, not based on race, culture, ethnicity, theistic religion, region, social hierarchies, or similar attributes. It requires each of us to acknowledge the diverging paths ahead: actively champion the right to equality and liberty for yourself and your fellow citizens, or accept that your professed love of America is only skin-deep. Either we believe the principles inscribed in our national sacraments apply equally to us all, or we do not.

Naturally, this sort of solidarity is not easily created. It requires those who benefit from the status quo to be resolved to some disruption of it. And it requires those who suffer under the status quo to practice civic forbearance while compelling the state to undertake significant reforms. No one can exercise solidarity without sacrifice. Because of the restraint of self-interest that national solidarity requires, some think it can occur only following the onset of a sudden national catastrophe. This is an unnecessary, self-imposed constraint, and it has routinely proved insufficient. Solidarity across lines of race, class, and ethnicity can only be formed when a convincing case is made that it is in the people's and the nation's best interest to do so. To create a national solidarity in response to racism requires that the nation sees racism as a threat to its interests. Both are our charge. How can we make them so? What does such an endeavor look like?

Fortunately, we have a blueprint of the solidarity we desperately need, and black America is the architect. The same solidarity that sustained black Americans through the horrors of slavery and the violence of Jim Crow, that energized their quest for increased access to civil rights and economic opportunity, and that fosters the group's political unity to compel the nation to become a better version of itself contains lessons for a multiracial national solidarity to confront the race problem head-on. This should not be all that surprising— who better to model our political efforts after than those people who have made substantial, if incremental, gains against racism since the nation's inception? Racial progress in the United States was not a gift to black people or the product of sporadic deluges of white magnanimity; it is the result of black work energized by the same revolutionary spirit of independence that created America in the first place. The solidarity found in black America is a uniquely American creation and, as such, has especial utility in addressing the country's racial challenges. This is not to say that black people exclusively hold the key to beating back the threat posed by racism; they do not. Every group that has fought for access to the Promise has something to contribute and must be part of the effort. But black America offers a particular set of experiences that highlight attributes of solidarity the nation would be wise to adopt. And if we are to be the same America in our reality that we claim to be in our mythology, adopt them we must.

THIS BOOK UNFOLDS in a series of stories and ideas to help us rethink how to approach the race question in the United States. It begins by declaring that racism is an existential threat to America. While the geopolitical entity known as the United States may limp along with entrenched racial inequalities, American ideals cannot coexist with any hints of racial revanchism. And if the idea that we are all created equal with certain unalienable rights dies, it will not make much difference what the shell of a nation left behind is called—America will be dead, too. Black America knows this precipice well and has developed strategies to survive and manage racism, as well as endure the broken promises of a tepid nation that have accompanied it through the years. Black solidarity teaches us about superlative citizenship, the necessity but inadequacy of laws and policies, unity in a common cause, and how to exercise solidarity in a heterogeneous society.

It then suggests that a national solidarity can be formed through a recommitment to civic virtue and our civil religion, by recognizing that racism is more usefully understood as a crime of the state than as solely a matter of people's hearts, and by understanding that a color-conscious society—not a colorblind one—is the true fulfillment of the Promise. The American experiment is a novel undertaking. As Harvard political theorist Danielle Allen has written, "The simple fact of the matter is that the world has never built a multiethnic democracy in which no particular ethnic group is in the majority and where political equality, social equality and economies that empower all have been achieved."[12] Either we will meet the challenge and pass to future generations a nation that is one step closer to living up to its founding ideals, or we will fall short and our legacy will be defined by a historic missed opportunity. If we fail, America will be the blessing that almost was—and then spectacularly was not. But if we manage to strike another critical blow to racism, our progress will be a message to posterity and an example for the ages.

This book necessarily approaches the threat of racism from the black American perspective. But it does not suggest that racism in the United States is solely a black-and-white phenomenon. The experiences of other racial and ethnic minorities cannot be discounted in the larger narrative about race relations. It must not be lost on any of us that even in those moments of immense national unity, racial discrimination found its way to nonblack communities of color. In the immediate aftermath of the September 11 terrorist attacks, Arab Americans and mosques—and, due to a deep ignorance in segments of the American citizenry, even Sikhs—were subjected to hate crimes. Within months of the bombing of Pearl Harbor, Japanese Americans were forcibly confined in internment camps on American soil.

Historically, racism and violent oppression directed at other groups now part of the American story are older than the nation itself. The brutality and injustice experienced by Native Americans are defining features of the nation's founding and existence—so much so that indigenous peoples were not legally recognized as citizens until 1924, nearly sixty years after enslaved black people were constitutionally granted citizenship. Hispanic Americans and immigrants of various national origins are the targets of particularly concerted efforts to delegitimize their citizenship and question their value to the nation. Muslim Americans and immigrants endure undue social scrutiny and national security surveillance. Asian Americans suspected of being from East and Southeast Asia were harassed and violently assaulted during the coronavirus pandemic of 2020. And none of this is new. In the landmark lone dissent in 1896's *Plessy v. Ferguson*, Supreme Court justice John Harlan argued that the "separate but equal" doctrine aimed at black Americans was unconstitutional while also stipulating, "There is a race so different from our own that we do not permit those belonging to it to become citizens of the United States. Persons belonging to it are, with few exceptions, absolutely excluded from our country. I allude to the Chinese race."[13] The list continues, to include discrimination faced by those Americans who are now considered "white," like citizens of Irish, Italian, and Jewish descent, among others. But because this is a book specifically about the lessons black America has for national solidarity, the experiences of these groups are not explored here, though they, too, have messages for the nation.

Ultimately, this book makes the case that policy is just a way to manage how racism is experienced and expressed, not whether it exists. No matter what promises politicians make or prescriptions scholars suggest, no statute or policy agenda will straighten out what racism has wrought. The tools of our democracy—elections, institutions, laws, judiciary oversight—are all necessary, of course; I am thankful to live in the United States of today rather than the United States of a century ago. But our democratic processes and institutions are wholly insufficient to eradicate racial hierarchy on their own—the people must find solidarity for that to happen. We will never become the nation we profess to be by implementing a set of laws and regulations, clapping the dust off our hands, and thinking we can walk off into the horizon to live happily ever after. This is not just a matter of better laws but of better character.

Overcoming racism honors the very idea of America, and, importantly, is not just for the benefit of racial minorities—white Americans will gain substantially from it as well. A lot of the concerns white citizens have—economic security and stability for their families, affordable health insurance, safe neighborhoods and good schools, and their future in America's changing demography—can be better addressed if racism is sufficiently mitigated and disempowered. Their economic grievances and anxieties remain unresolved as long as political and economic elites can convince some number of them that racial and ethnic minorities are the source of their misery. Their desire for policy solutions for out-of-control healthcare costs, exorbitant college tuition, and unaffordable housing goes unaddressed because they are fed a narrative about lazy and inept people of color cutting in line and hogging precious resources. And racism attempts to convince white Americans that their place in the racial hierarchy is a result of the incompetence and cultural inferiority of others.

Stoking racial tensions is one of the easiest and most effective tools to distract some white Americans from how economic and political elites undermine their access to the Promise. Governments and businesses will be less responsive to the demands of average white Americans as long as racial and ethnic minorities can be made into scapegoats. This is not mere supposition. Lee Atwater, a prominent political strategist in the 1970s and '80s, declared forthrightly in an infamous interview detailing the strategy to win over white segregationists that certain economic and social policy positions— like states' rights, forced busing, and tax cuts—were intentional distractions and that "a byproduct of them is blacks get hurt worse than whites."[14] The subtext is clear: white Americans, too, are harmed, and their ability to grasp the Promise is hindered by these politics of expedience. Racism not only puts the Promise out of reach for minorities, but it also ensures white Americans taste only a watered-down version of it, and some of them are denied even that.

The truth is, realizing the Promise will require us all to bear some of the cost. It will require abandoning sanitized conceptions of a colorblind society. It will require understanding that racism is a crime of the state, which is when a nation actively promotes or implicitly accepts violations of its own laws. It will require accepting that race will always be a primary feature of American life and society. And it will require that we bind together as one people vested in the idea of equality and hold the government accountable when it fails to deliver it in full to any one of us. We, the people, can and should have the deciding say in the future and fate of our country.

THE IDEAS IN THIS BOOK are incomplete if they are not explored alongside the people that constitute the nation. The stories of Americans are the Promise's barometer. They trace the ebbs and flows of the Promise's reach. My family story over the course of the last couple of centuries will provide contours for the argument that black solidarity is a suitable model for national solidarity. It will be supplemented by narratives of black Americans who model what the fight for full citizenship for all looks like. Generations of these men and women have lived and gone to their graves wanting nothing more than for their children and children's children to have the opportunity to live a life of dignity and be accepted as truly American. You will meet us in great detail over the course of the book and undoubtedly recognize parts of the larger American story found in yourself and your own family. Let us begin here . . .

I am Theodore Roosevelt Johnson, III, a Southern black man named after a turn-of-the-century rich, white Republican from New York. A familial faith in the Promise led to my name and quietly shaped the path my life has taken. When Teddy Roosevelt ascended to the presidency following the assassination of William McKinley in September 1901, one of his first actions was to invite educator and influential political leader Booker T. Washington to dinner at the White House. This was the first time a black man had dined there in such a capacity, and reactions across the nation were fevered. Many white Southerners felt Roosevelt had disgraced the office. Others thought something worse had occurred. A reader of Jacksonville's *Evening Metropolis* sent in a letter to the editor asserting, "Eating at the same table means social equality . . . When the white race yields social equality with the negro, it has defied the laws of God, and he will sweep them from the earth."[15] James Vardaman, who would become the governor of Mississippi, said that the dinner had left the White House "so saturated with the odor of the nigger that the rats have taken refuge in the stable."[16]

But my sharecropping great-grandparents Will and Annie Johnson, like many other black Americans in the South, caught a glimpse of the promise of racial equality reflected by the dinner. When their third son was born just as Roosevelt's health spiraled after losing his son in World War I, they named him Theodore Roosevelt Johnson in honor of the Promise that the White House dinner symbolized. If Will and Annie were alive today, they would be quite proud of how far the family has come thanks to their sacrifices and belief. They would also be disappointed, but not surprised, to know that more than a century after their American stories began, their offspring generations later would still have racist insults hurled at them for no other reason than being black in America.

Back on that autumn morning of my youth when the n-word knocked the wind out of me, Marcus and I chased Cameron, but we did not catch him before he reached the school grounds. That afternoon, however, saw a different result. Cameron and Marcus crossed paths on the way home and immediately engaged in a profane war of words, calling each other everything but a child of God until the kindling caught fire in a series of blows. The two fought their way through the subdivision: throwing punches in a neighbor's yard and trampling her tulips, swinging wildly at each other in the street and up into driveways like a caravan of chaos, and even knocking an American flag to the ground—the stars falling and settling in the dirt to be trampled by an adolescent interracial conflict.

Decades later in the Chamber of Commerce's Hall of Flags, I tearfully concluded my address to a room of White House Fellows by recalling the gold sun etched into the back of the chair that seated George Washington during the 1787 Constitutional Convention. The sun was bisected by an imagined horizon, giving the illusion that it was either on its way up into the sky or descending to give way to the stars. As the delegates made their way to sign what would become our Constitution, Benjamin Franklin remarked, "I have often looked at that behind the President without being able to tell whether it was rising or setting: But now at length I have the happiness to know that it is a rising and not a setting Sun."[17]

Under the sweltering suns of an America unrealized, many black people toiled under the lash to help build a nation. Forbidden to sing of the freedom their souls demanded, they turned to Christian themes to cloak their hearts' desire. Substituting visions of a heavenly rapture for their dreams of emancipation, they devised spirituals that famed sociologist and historian W.E.B DuBois called the nation's first original music—the "sorrow songs."[18] One such song chronicled the rising sun, symbolizing the end of one day and the beginning of another:

> *My Lord, what a morning*
> *My Lord, what a morning*
> *My Lord, what a morning*
> *When the stars begin to fall.*

When I descended the stage, I stumbled a bit. After I awkwardly took a few steps to regain my balance, David, a white retired Air Force pilot with silver hair, caught me in a bear hug next to the

American flag that bordered the stage. I could not help thinking of what the generations before us would have thought of this fleeting moment of connection and unity, especially the generations of my family filled with sturdy men and women from the red clay of Georgia and the tobacco fields of South Carolina who had endured the nation's worst impulses just so I would have a fighting chance at the Promise. If my name is any indication, they would have seen a rising sun—a reason to continue hoping that racial equality lies ahead. Whether it is indeed setting or rising, however, will depend on our ability to find the solidarity charted in the pages ahead.

PART I

The Challenge
for America

O, let my land be a land where Liberty
Is crowned with no false patriotic wreath,
But opportunity is real, and life is free,
Equality is in the air we breathe.

(There's never been equality for me,
Nor freedom in this
"homeland of the free.")

Say, who are you that mumbles in the dark?
And who are you that draws your veil across the stars?

I am the poor white, fooled and pushed apart,
I am the Negro bearing slavery's scars.
I am the red man driven from the land,
I am the immigrant clutching the hope I seek—
And finding only the same old stupid plan
Of dog eat dog, of mighty crush the weak.

. . .

O, yes,
I say it plain,
America never was America to me,
And yet I swear this oath—
America will be!

—*Langston Hughes, "Let America Be America Again"*

CHAPTER I

The Primary Threat to America

Six months after the inauguration of the nation's first black president, a small skirmish in Cambridge, Massachusetts, dimmed the lights of our shining city on a hill. Famed black Harvard professor Henry Louis Gates, Jr., returned home from a trip abroad to find his front door jammed. A neighbor observed him trying to push his way into the house and alerted police that there appeared to be a burglary in process. James Crowley, a white sergeant in the local police department, responded to the call and a verbal spat quickly ensued. Gates was beside himself that the police were questioning his right to be in his own home; Crowley was a bit shocked by the reaction he received for simply verifying that no crime was taking place. Gates became increasingly agitated as more police arrived on the scene, and he was soon arrested and charged with disorderly conduct. Handcuffed on his front porch and being led to the back seat of a squad car, Gates repeatedly posed a rhetorical question to Crowley and to everyone within the sound of his voice—a question well traveled in places where black men, a red-blooded indignation forcing them to the balls of their feet, vent to one another beyond the public eye—"Is this how you treat a black man in America?!"

Gates's profile and his friendship with new president Barack Obama carved the local incident into pieces that soon populated the national chessboard. And almost instantly, Americans took sides, each hoping to keep the other in check. On one side were citizens who sympathized with Gates and saw his arrest as a result of racial profiling, a practice that too often preordains black people with criminality. On the other side were those who believed Crowley behaved professionally in carrying out his duties and was unfairly labeled a racist. The police officers' association lawyer commented that "this had nothing to do with race and everything to do with Gates's behavior."[1] It became painfully clear almost immediately that race colored one's perception of the incident—nearly 60 percent of white Americans felt Gates was in the wrong, while the same number of black Americans felt Crowley was at fault.[2]

When President Obama weighed in, the nation not only further polarized; it changed. Asked about the incident at a news conference, Obama remarked that the police had "acted stupidly" and cited the nation's long history of racially discriminatory law enforcement practices. His comments raised the temperature of the public and intensified the debate about the role race played in the confrontation. The country came down with that old fever once again. Obama quickly offered a mea culpa and encouraged the nation to see this as a teachable moment on race relations. To tamp down the controversy, he held an informal "beer summit" with Gates, Crowley, and Vice President Joe Biden in hopes that the visual of the two black men and two white men enjoying a few brews together would be a symbolic gesture of racial reconciliation. Perhaps, it would even inspire the ever-elusive national conversation on race, encouraging dialogue across racial lines and beginning to restore the pride the nation felt after the historic presidential election just a few months earlier.

It did not. And most importantly, the nation never viewed Obama the same. While most Americans thought holding the beer summit was a good idea, the majority of black and white citizens felt it was not a teachable moment that would improve race relations. Moreover, the president took a major hit from which he and his presidency would not recover. The month preceding his comments on the incident, 53 percent of white Americans and 95 percent of black Americans approved of the job he was doing. Immediately after, black Americans' approval held steady, but white Americans' approval dropped by 7 points and stayed there, or lower, for the remainder of his presidency.[3] Over a decade later, some white Americans still explicitly point to Obama's comments on this incident as the turning point in their personal politics—one, who had voted for Obama, said the incident demonstrated the president "was prejudiced against white people."[4] We learned then that when a black president of the United States talked about race, Americans retreated to their respective partisan corners and dug into their racial-group positions. Not even high-fives over a couple of beers could get us to shake hands in the middle of the ring. That old fever is hell to break.

The truth is we, the people, simply see the world differently. We are indeed having a national conversation on race; it is transpiring in thousands of places in millions of small discussions—over lunches, during commutes, in text messages and social media circles. But these interactions are most often taking place between people of the same race instead of with people of other races. Black men in barbershops and black women in churches are having a national conversation about race. White men at happy hours and white women during playdates are having a national conversation about race. Native, Hispanic, and Asian Americans are all having a national conversation about race. We are all talking about it, but we are not talking about it with one another. Social science research shows that 75 percent of white Americans and 66 percent of black Americans have social networks that do not contain a single person of another race.[5] Overall, white Americans' social networks are 91 percent white, and black Americans' networks are 83 percent black.[6] As a result, rarely do these groups engage each other on the topic in open and honest discussions with the objective of learning more about the experiences of their fellow citizens and with an eye toward compassion. The cumulative effect is that we emerge from our intimate conversations with more rigid views that are only hardened as the competing narratives flood the public circle.

Not surprisingly, then, even the most minor race incidents still prove particularly contentious. That the nation was immediately divided along racial lines, and the view of a historic presidency forever changed, over a confrontation in Professor Gates's home illustrates just how deep the issue of race in the United States runs. How we responded to a small, civil misunderstanding between two people who are now friendly to each other is an indication of the challenge we face to create a truly united America.

THERE ARE FEW THINGS Americans want to be true more than the vision outlined by a young black preacher in 1963 at the foot of the Lincoln Memorial. With a melodic cadence etching divinely inspired prose into the nation's conscience, he told us of his dream for a country that judges people based on the content of their character and not by the color of their skin. Today, most Americans want his dream to be true because it aligns with the nation's founding principles, which assert that we are all created equal with rights to life, liberty, and opportunity. We want to realize his vision because it would mean that we have finally managed to put the nation's less-than-admirable record on race behind us. We want his words to become reality so that we no longer have to talk about racism and its effects on the United States and the Promise. If only we could skip forward to King's dream, our democracy would be more complete—it would finally become closer to the vision of what it means to be truly American.

Yet while we want the dream badly, we do not agree on exactly what it is. Some of us believe the dream depicts a colorblind meritocratic society full of citizens who no longer see race. Others of us think it describes a nation where racial diversity is embraced as an invaluable feature of American culture without being determinative of our American experience. And we do not see eye-to-eye on the exact problem that this vision for America is supposed to resolve: Does it remove racism as an overused excuse employed by people dissatisfied with the nation, or does it now free up the efforts and ingenuity of the many who have been bridled by its presence? That is, some want the dreamed America because it means racism can no longer be used as a crutch, while others will be glad that it can no longer be used as a cudgel. Those many who agree that racism divides us cannot seem to find common ground on what it is, what it does, how it is used, or even, somewhat surprisingly, who is harmed by it most.

Some have a sense that accusations of racism are used to guilt the nation into providing unearned assistance and favors to black people. An elderly white man in Akron, Ohio, griped to National Public Radio, "If you apply for a job, they seem to give blacks the first crack at it . . . Basically, you know, if you want any help from the government, if you're white, you don't get it. If you're black, you get it."[7] Further to the point, a supermajority of Americans oppose using race as a factor in college admissions—including 78 percent of white Americans, 65 percent of Hispanic Americans, 62 percent of black Americans, and 58 percent of Asian Americans.[8] Two-thirds disapproved of the Supreme Court's 2016 decision in *Fisher v. Texas* that determined an affirmative action program to increase student-body diversity was constitutional.[9] In this view of race relations in the United States, black activists are perceived to employ strategic claims of racism to jimmy resources and opportunity away from white people. Indeed, half of white millennials believe discrimination against white Americans is just as big a problem as discrimination against people of color.[10] As Congressman Peter King of New York said at a town hall while discussing lethal encounters between police and the public just before the November 2018 midterm elections, "If anyone can say they're being discriminated against, it's whites."[11]

And then some assert that racism is not only alive and well; it is an oppressive force that perpetually squeezes us out of opportunity, access to justice, and full inclusion in America. By nearly every socioeconomic measure, black Americans lag behind the rest of the nation. Black unemployment, for decades, has consistently been twice the rate of white unemployment, no matter how strong or weak the economy is. Schools and neighborhoods in the United States remain racially segregated—a study by education scholar Erica Frankenberg found that "more than 40 percent of black and Latino students attend intensely segregated schools, where at least 9 in 10 students are people of color."[12] Half of all black Americans live in neighborhoods with no white residents.[13] It helps explain why black citizens earn less income for doing the same job as their white coworkers and are arrested and incarcerated more for drugs though usage rates are about the same as those for white citizens. It is why black Americans have poorer health outcomes and higher death rates—from heart disease and diabetes to maternal mortality and the 2020 coronavirus pandemic—even when accounting for their economic status. It is why mortgages and small-business loans are harder to come by for black Americans, why standardized test scores are consistently uneven, and why stereotypes persist of black people as being lazy, irresponsible, prone to criminality, and harboring a preference for government dependence.

This sort of injustice and inequality is baked into the systems that govern all aspects of our society, and it is distinct from the interpersonal racial prejudice we typically associate with the word *racism*. In this structural form, "Whites Only" signs are replaced by a system that appears to be colorblind but erects substantial barriers along the path that black Americans must travel to access equality and opportunity. This kind of discrimination painfully reveals an ugly truth to a country justifiably proud of its progress: one does not have to be called a nigger to be treated like one.

Such disparate perceptions of what racism is and who is truly harmed help explain why racial tensions and conflicts are felt most deeply when they become public and emblazon our television screens, newspapers, and social media. There, we see black women scaling the Statute of Liberty in New York City and snatching down the Confederate battle flag in South Carolina. We watch as white women from Oakland, California, to Washington, D.C., make national news summoning law enforcement to minor interracial conflicts in public parks and coffee shops. We watch as shirtless black men confront heavily armored police officers in the dark of night, lit only by helicopter spotlights and burning cars. We observe white men with torches marching in ranks across university campuses screaming, "White lives matter!" and "You will not replace us!"—flames illuminating their faces as they hold a candlelight vigil for the nostalgic conception of the country of their fathers and grandfathers. And the nation gasps in disbelief as a riotous horde storms the Capitol Building to prevent presidential election results from being certified, questioning the validity of votes cast in predominantly black communities and undermining democracy in the process.

Instead of attempting to understand each other better, we quickly choose to take sides based on who we believe was wronged and who was justified in their actions or responses. And then, just as quickly, we move on. These incidents are viewed as unfortunate flare-ups of race relations instead of as symptoms of some deeper, enduring national problem with racism that should command our attention after the latest fire has been extinguished. But a few strong political winds fan the flames of some other issue that grabs our attention, and the nation leaves the glowing embers of racial discord unattended, only to feign surprise that it remains an issue the next time we find ourselves ablaze.

OUR CURRENT DISAGREEMENTS, disparate perceptions, and differing approaches to race relations in the United States belie the danger in the ether: racism is an existential threat to America. This claim may seem alarmist and unwarranted at first blush. After all, if racism presents such peril to the country, then why is the United States still in existence? How has the nation managed to survive and grow stronger for nearly 250 years? Claiming that a difficult problem is an existential threat can be seen as a trite proclamation. However, regarding the question of whether racism is really capable of causing America to cease to exist, there can be no doubt of the seriousness of the inquiry or the certitude of the answer—it is yes.

When the end of America is discussed, our minds conjure scenes of calamity and chaos. We suspect that it would encompass a military coup against elected officials in Congress or the White House, with tanks rolling end to end down Pennsylvania Avenue, an economic collapse and the pillaging of the nation's wealth by twenty-first century robber barons, and urban areas swimming in broken glass as elected officials, the military and heavily armed police, and the people trade haymakers. It summons visions of Hollywood's postapocalyptic doomsday movies wherein widespread violence carried out by and against the public fills ungoverned spaces, and the blatant trampling of constitutional rights is done for sport. And though some of these scenes have visited our towns and cities on occasion, the likelihood that the ultimate collapse of the United States would play out with such chaotic immediacy, and that racism would be the impetus, is quite low.

Instead, the fact that racism is an existential threat is less about the durability of the United States as a sovereign entity and more about the death of the American idea. The United States is a geographical polity with borders and a government, but America represents an aspiration and the embodiment of our principles, ideals, and beliefs. America is the Promise of citizens' equality, liberty, and solidarity. Together, the United States of America is championed as a nation-state founded on a radical idea—a view espoused by both political parties. In 2012, Barack Obama proclaimed during his reelection-night victory speech, "I believe we can keep the promises of our founders, the idea that if you're willing to work hard . . . you can make it here in America if you're willing to try."[14] When he was Speaker of the House, Republican Paul Ryan sought to comfort the public ahead of the contentious 2016 presidential election, saying, "America is the only nation founded on an idea—not an identity. That idea is the notion that the condition of your birth does not determine the outcome of your life."[15]

The nation's history demonstrates that this idea was a vision of what is possible and not a description of reality. The enslavement of black people in a country founded on such an idea exposed a deep hypocrisy. The suffragist and civil rights activist Mary Church Terrell noted in 1906, "The chasm between the principles upon which this Government was founded, in which it still professes to believe, and those which are daily practiced under the protection of the flag, yawn so wide and deep."[16] But over time, belief in the idea—and the sacrifices of millions—delivered moral energy to the abolition of slavery, the installation of civil rights safeguards, and the proposition of a more perfect Union. Racism, however, resists the American idea and the progress it demands. The idea can survive alongside declining racism so long as the nation inches away from racial hierarchy and toward equality. But once racial backsliding begins, America is in danger. And should the United States step into a double-armed embrace of racial revanchism, the life will be squeezed out of the American idea.

The threat is a result of a basic truth: our founding principles of equality, liberty, and opportunity cannot coexist with racial hierarchy. We cannot believe that all of us are created equal while also subscribing to the view that white citizens are "more American" than black ones. Racism undercuts our ability to ensure equal access to all the rights, protections, and responsibilities of citizenship. It suggests that there is an American caste system in which freedom in its fullest form is available only to some, while others are permitted to taste only a lesser, diluted version of it. Racism threatens to undermine the ideals at the foundation of our country—and at the core of what is supposed to unite us—and relegates them to little more than a ruse meant to placate those for whom the Promise remains out of reach and to justify the superior position of others who enjoy it in its fullness. The soul of America is steeped in aspirations set forth in our founding documents, and racism robs us of those ambitions. It laughs at the Dream, scoffs at the Promise, and chastises our professed values. And if the light ever goes out of our ideals, the potential of the United States will be diminished, devolving from a shining city on a hill to a gloomy burg on a bluff.

This threat of racism has been clear and present since our inception. The nation's first political leaders crafted the Declaration of Independence as a list of grievances that outlined the unjust practices of a distant monarch and explained why the colonies deemed it necessary to separate from Great Britain. An early draft contained a passage authored by Thomas Jefferson—himself a slaveholder—on the evils of the slave trade, but it was deleted at the insistence of representatives from South Carolina and Georgia, which owed much of their economy to an enslaved labor force and the human trafficking that fed it.

Though many of the founders enslaved black people, and all of them benefited from the institution of slavery, some of them were not comfortable with the hypocrisy and expressed a desire for abolition. John Jay wrote, "The honour of the States, as well as justice and humanity, in my opinion, loudly call upon them to emancipate these unhappy people. To contend for our own liberty, and to deny that blessing to others, involves an inconsistency not to be excused."[17] George Mason noted the threat slavery posed to the new nation, saying, "The augmentation of slaves weakens the state; and such a trade is diabolical in itself, and disgraceful to mankind."[18] And yet, though they recognized that slavery was incompatible with the newly declared self-evident truths, the nation's framers allowed it to persist. They believed that a practice so inconsistent with the American idea could not endure and destiny would dissolve it. *Patience*, they implored, *the ugly thing will die an ugly death on its own,* as though Providence had already inscribed the incantation on America's bedrock. As Jefferson wrote in his autobiography, "Nothing is more certainly written in the book of fate than that these people are to be free."[19] This is, perhaps, one of the earliest allusions to our country's unofficial motto of blind faith: *it'll all work out somehow.*

With national independence secured, the framers of the Constitution convened in the summer of 1787 to articulate the structure of our democratic government. But the issue of the status of black people reared its head again and almost sank the Union before it could set sail. James Madison explained that the greatest danger to the new nation was the conflict between the Northern and Southern states over slavery and congressional representation. When Maryland delegate Luther Martin argued that the slave trade was "inconsistent with the principles of the revolution and dishonorable to the American character,"[20] he was met with fierce resistance led by South Carolina delegate John Rutledge.

Revered in the state, and its former governor, Rutledge, who enslaved black people, was an ardent supporter of the system and defended South Carolina's interest in it throughout the Continental Congress. "Religion and morality have nothing to do with this question," he said. "Interest alone is the governing principle with nations. The true question at present is whether Southern states shall or shall not be parties to the Union."[21] It was either slavery or the end of the Union. The framers of the Constitution made their choice. "Great as the evil is," lamented Madison, "a dismemberment of the union would be worse." But Madison also recognized that this choice placed the nation at risk: "As nations cannot be rewarded or punished in the next world, they must be in this. By an inevitable chain of causes and effects Providence punishes national sins by national calamities."[22]

The nation descended into a catastrophic civil war just decades later, an occurrence prophesied by Alexis de Tocqueville when he wrote, "The most dreadful of all the evils that threaten the future of the United States arises from the presence of blacks on its soil."[23] The Union indeed broke in two, and the issue that split the nation was the status of black people and the racial order. The deadliest conflict to ever visit the United States consumed the countryside in a massive bloodletting that resulted in more than one million casualties. Abraham Lincoln knew that the United States' only chance of long-term survival and security required the nation to be one, that a balkanized continent would be susceptible to the same frequent internecine clashes that plagued Europe. Racism cleaved one set of states from the other—and one race of people from the other—and threatened the Union and, by extension, the entire American experiment. It is the only threat the United States has ever faced that succeeded in severing a part of the Union from the whole.

Writing to Horace Greeley, the editor of the *New-York Tribune*, in 1862, Lincoln declared, "My paramount object in this struggle *is* to save the Union, and is *not* either to save or destroy slavery ... What I do about slavery, and the colored race, I do because I believe it helps to save the Union."[24] And yet, in Lincoln's hands, the Declaration and the Constitution were transformed, evolving from pragmatic proclamations into national invocations. Though abolishing slavery was not the result of a moral epiphany or a divine inclination to champion racial equality, he trumpeted a spiritual call to arms to take the boldest action on race relations the nation has ever seen. He understood that the race question needed resolution if America was to survive. "In giving freedom to the slave, we assure freedom to the free—honorable alike in what we give, and what we preserve," he told Congress in 1862.[25] "We shall nobly save, or meanly lose, the last, best hope of the earth."

Despite the sacrifice required to renew the American idea, including Lincoln's martyrdom, within a decade racism regained its political prominence, preventing freedoms extended to black Americans from gaining a foothold. In a strategic move to ensure that the Ohio Republican governor Rutherford B. Hayes would win the presidential election of 1876, Republican leaders arranged a compromise with Democrats, whose nominee had won the popular vote, that would allow Hayes to take office via the Electoral College in exchange for the removal of federal troops from the Southern states. This effectively ended the Reconstruction period of civil rights reforms toward racial equality and ushered in an era of racial terrorism and rampant violence against black citizens. Torturous lynchings of black workers, adolescents, military veterans, small-business owners, and prospective voters over the next several decades provided a high-definition and three-dimensional illustration of just how little black Americans were valued and respected as fellow countrymen.

Lawful racial segregation became the order of the day, but prescient thinkers noted how it was incompatible with the American idea and, as such, unsustainable. In his famous 1896 dissent in the case of *Plessy v. Ferguson*, Justice John Harlan wrote, "The destinies of the two races in this country are indissolubly linked together, and the interests of both require that the common government of all shall not permit the seeds of race hate to be planted under the sanction of law."[26] He went on to say that if the nation permitted these racial divisions, it conferred an unconstitutional condition of racial inferiority on black Americans and would cause the highest degree of harm to the nation.

Decades later, the country approached another precipice. This time, domestic politics and national security interests brought about a new tranche of progressive race policy. President Harry Truman helped kick off a generation of transformational civil rights gains by desegregating the military in 1948. Giving a special address on racial equality to Congress, he described the features of structural racism and told the nation that "there is a serious gap between our ideals and some of our practices."[27] Truman believed closing the gap was essential to the nation's stability and well-being, and to his election chances. Two decades later and in the midst of the century's biggest steps toward mitigating racism, President Lyndon Johnson told Congress that racial equality was "an issue that lays bare the secret heart of America itself." He argued it presented a challenge "to the values and the purposes and the meaning of our beloved Nation," and if we did not confront it head-on, "then we will have failed as a people and as a nation."[28]

So the threat racism poses to America has been well chronicled through the nation's history by its founders, its elected leaders, and its stalwart citizens. From the Revolutionary Era through to the Civil Rights Movement, an appreciation existed of the danger racial hierarchy and inequality presented. But in the intervening years between the elections of Richard Nixon and Barack Obama, the less abrasive expressions of racial injustice and inequality gave us a false sense of comfort that the hardest part was behind us and that we would have a much easier go of it in the days ahead. Following Obama's election, there were even claims that the United States had embarked on a post-racial period and that any lingering racial inequalities could be overcome with grit and elbow grease.

Martin Luther King, Jr., warned in a 1967 speech at Stanford University that while civil rights legislative gains were important, the real aim of genuine equality—to realize the Promise in its fullest form—would be a much more difficult struggle.[29] He cautioned that even those who believe racism is wrong and black citizens' rights should be granted and protected will balk at genuine equality because it requires national sacrifice and comes at a personal cost for all Americans. Nearly a year to the date after he shared these thoughts, he was pierced by the bullet of an assassin who could not bear to live in an America that extended its promises to black people. King died on a cool blue Memphis evening in April 1968, but the picture of America he painted one humid August afternoon in the nation's capital five years prior remains framed and hung.

JOE HUMPHREY PASSED AWAY in 1966—living long enough to hear King's dream but not to see him killed. Joe—or Daddy Joe, as he was affectionately called—was my mother's grandfather. He was gone before I was born, and I knew him only through the pictures in my grandparents' small country house, which hovered above the earth on sets of paired cinder blocks. There is a photograph of him surrounded by twenty of his grandchildren, my barely school-age mother in a short-sleeve bib dress among them. There is one of him on a dirt path next to a row of corn with a wide-brimmed hat pulled down low over his face, a pipe in one hand and the hand of a small child in the other. And then there is the one forever etched into my memory—the one I recall from my childhood, when I spent many summers under my grandmother's watchful eye. On the wall hung a picture of Daddy Joe standing with his hands pocketed, as if waiting patiently for something, knee-high work boots with white pants stuffed into the collars, and a pipe hanging out of the corner of his mouth—two American flags, one angled over each shoulder, framing his self-assured stance.

Bundled up in that photo of Daddy Joe is the journey of an American family. Thirty-three years after his death—six months before the turn of the millennium—five of his six daughters gathered relatives around to trace the trail our blood blazed in the little corner of the nation's history that marked our inception. At our biennial family reunion, the Sisters, then in their seventies and eighties, held court in a Georgia state park where the heat was thick enough to choke the devil, occasionally bowing to a sticky breeze off the adjacent lake named after a staunch white segregationist. The red clay for which the state is known was rolled out in front of us like a royal carpet, awaiting the procession of ancestral celebrities who were the stars of the story and would descend in turn to light the path. The soil's hue comes from iron, the same element that makes our blood red and that constitutes the will of those testifying old souls who grew up with the clay underfoot. These women—my mother's mother among them—sang the family history in a key that only the attuned ear could comprehend, filled with *yondas*,

*Lawwud hammercy*s, and *reckenso*s amid glideless vowels and saunter-
ing intonations. Serving as our guides, the Sisters took the family on
a 120-mile and 175-year ride. They retold our American story in the
same way it had been told to them, and it begins with an enslaved
African man given the name Kincey.

Family lore has it that Kincey was purchased by a plantation
owner with the last name Humphrey in Lamont, Florida, probably
at some point in the 1830s. We will never know Kincey's birth name,
where he was born, how much he was sold for, how he spent his days,
or where he's buried. And if not for his and his wife Patsy's names
on their daughter's 1939 Florida death certificate, there would linger
the haunting possibility that snakes through the family trees of many
black Americans: that perhaps he was not real at all, the man existing as little more than a personification of those distant memories
of various loved ones whisked away from their families and given a
name so that future generations would have one to call and a wisp
to grasp. But for all we do not know about him, we know he lived.
We know that the average price for an enslaved person in Jefferson
County, Florida, was about $1,000—that's approximately $30,000 in
today's money. We know that land there was plentiful and that the
main agricultural product was cotton. We know that enslaved black
men and women were the fuel and the engine for this industry. And
we know that while all the land and cotton in the county in 1860
was valued at $3 million, the value of all the enslaved black people
there was more than $6 million.[30] Kincey had one type of value to
America and another kind to us, his descendants.

As was the custom in those terrible days, his children were sold
away from him, trafficked northwest to the Fain plantation in Bluff-
ton, Georgia, twenty miles to the east of where the five Humphrey
sisters had gathered the family that warm afternoon to exhume our
history. But the Civil War and emancipation soon came, and all
but one of his kids, Bill, returned to Florida. Bill decided to make
his home in Georgia, a decision that probably centered on a young

woman named Rena who operated the plantation cotton gin. They married and tried to start a family, but their first four children were all born deceased. And when the fifth child shared the same fate, Rena did, too, dying in childbirth. The Sisters say they are not sure where Rena and her children were laid to rest, but the belief is they were settled among the pine along the way to a nearby church. To get to that church today, one must travel on a rural highway called Fains Hatchery Road. The name of the plantation is memorialized, but the names of the children are forever lost to time.

After some years, Bill married a lady named Ella, the offspring of a white overseer and a black woman who was a plantation cook. Bill and Ella had fifteen children, but only ten made it to adulthood—the youngest five all passed away between infancy and the age of fourteen. Joe—Daddy Joe—was one of the surviving kids, and on Christmas Eve 1907, at the age of twenty-two, he married Eula. This is where the Sisters' memories began to jump and jostle, recalling their father and the life he breathed into their childhoods. They say he was a farmer who loved to hunt and fish. They speak of the pride the family takes in maintaining his shotgun. They say their mother, Eula, loved sewing, reading, and directing programs at church. The 1910 Census tells us Joe could read but could not write—Eula could do both. And while it describes Eula as a black woman, it says that Joe was a mulatto man, the blood of a white overseer etched into his federal record. A decade later, in the 1920 Census, however, this was no longer the case—the government changed its mind, and now Joe was just black.

But he was something else, too—something beautifully stitched onto his soul: an American. In the picture where Daddy Joe is framed by two flags of the United States, pressed to the wall of my grandparents' home brimming with love and remembrance, I saw an American man. He could just as easily trace his blood to an African man as to a white plantation overseer. In black and white was a man born just as lynch mobs began using public torture and death as instruments to pry any notions of liberty away from black American souls—a man who died two years after the passage of the Civil Rights Act of 1964, experiencing both the prejudice and potential of America over the course of a rugged lifetime. And here was a man with a countrified and knowing simper dancing in the corners of his face as he stood, almost defiantly, flanked by the nation's flags and laying claim to the courage, ideals, and justice its colors are intended to represent.

Daddy Joe and the Stars and Stripes seemed at once wholly compatible and yet tragically ill-fitted. It was as if the idea of America was big enough, but the United States refused to accommodate him or his hopes and dreams. Reading his face in the picture, I imagine he could not help being amused that he came from a people who knew the same thing some of the nation's founders, presidents, and leaders had long known and prophesied: the belonging and value of black Americans cannot be denied or discounted without also endangering the nation. If America is to endure, it must make room for all its people—or the whole experiment risks failure. So Joe Humphrey, like many before him, stood there insisting on being fully acknowledged, slightly tickled by the folly of it all but acutely aware of the situation's gravity.

CHAPTER 2

The Veiled Threats Exposed

Memorial Day is a day set aside to honor military personnel who have died in service of the country. In 2020, however, it was the death of an everyday civilian that would force the nation to pause and consider the values it holds dear. That holiday evening, George Floyd, a forty-six-year-old black man, was apprehended by police outside a Minneapolis neighborhood grocery store on the suspicion of using counterfeit money. Within minutes, Floyd was handcuffed and facedown on the street—a police officer's knee squeezed firmly into the back of the neck where the officer's body weight could be focused to pinch the air out of Floyd's body. For eight minutes and forty-six seconds, the officer casually smothered a man whose body was grasping at the last tendrils of his spirit—smartphone cameras of onlookers recording every second of the assault and every plea Floyd made for his life before falling silent. By the time the encounter was over, an ambulance was on the scene and George Floyd's last conscious breaths were left pressed into the asphalt. The video of the disinterested policeman kneeling on the disjoining neck of George Floyd struck the country like a bolt of lightning. The public first bowed to honor George Floyd and then collectively lifted its head with an eye toward justice, resolute that his death would energize the cause of racial equality, in memoriam.

In the days and weeks that followed, a nationwide movement was born that saw protests blossom in every state in the country and several nations around the world. Conditions were ripe for this response: just days before Floyd's killing, media outlets were broadcasting video of white vigilantes accosting and killing black jogger Ahmaud Arbery, and the nation was confronted by reports of the police shooting of Breonna Taylor. Moreover, the public was a captive audience, with most of the nation sequestered indoors due to stay-at-home orders in place to halt the spread of the highly contagious coronavirus that has killed hundreds of thousands of Americans. The national gaze could not be averted; it was forced to confront racial injustice and the illiberal application of violence against black Americans. The combination of righteous indignation, death on instant replay, and an isolated populace craving social interaction contributed to hundreds of protests and demonstrations that continued for months.

As usually happens when the passions that accompany racial conflict are not tempered by appropriately responsive leaders and institutions, looting and violence paired themselves with the protests. Day and night, on television stations and social media outlets, sensational images of militarized police, raucous crowds, broken glass and cars ablaze, and the disorienting mix of smoke, tear gas, and rubber bullets filled our screens and bruised the American psyche. The violence by agents of the state who were deployed to be keepers of the peace soon reached those who had assembled peaceably. As incidents of law enforcement using excessive force against protesters piled up, topped off by the June 1, 2020, scene outside the White House, where federal agents surged with questionable intentions and nonlethal munitions against protesters to clear President Trump's path across Lafayette Square, it became clear what the protests were really oriented toward—unwarranted violence sanctioned by the state against its own people.

The killing of George Floyd and the ensuing national reaction demonstrate the challenges that racism presents and the problems the presence of racism reveal. It spoke directly to the longstanding tensions between many black communities and law enforcement, modeling in a single encounter the historical practice of overpolicing black Americans and complaints of abuse of power. And when those victimized in decades past sought accountability and redress, they were left wanting. But racial injustice also illuminates a broader question the state and its citizenry cannot avoid: What is the proper balance between the powers of the state and the liberty of its people? If citizens' First Amendment rights are being curbed by agents of the state in the name of security, the resulting tension places principles at the core of America—equality, security, and liberty—squarely in its sight. When infringements of this sort occur, they typically find fullest expression in communities historically excluded from many of the rights and protections of citizenship. And in the United States, black Americans have received more than their fair share of injustice, and the violence of enforcement never trails too far behind. In this way, racism exposes flaws in our systems of democracy and justice, and, accordingly, demonstrates it is not just a problem that requires national attention, but a means to lift the veil of other threats to the well-being of the United States and the sanctity of the American Promise.

George Floyd's public death changed the nation. Just years earlier, the phrase "black lives matter" was divisive and polarizing—one could get a strong sense of others' politics based solely on whether they would utter the phrase at all. But after a few suns had set following Memorial Day 2020, people and politicians from across the ideological spectrum were not shy about proclaiming the value of black life. And in a presidential election year when partisan rancor and unprincipled leadership seemed to place any prospect of good governance beyond the nation's reach, both parties agreed that racial discrimination remains a problem in law enforcement institutions and that measures to reform police departments across the country were necessary and overdue. The truth of the moment shines brightly through: addressing racism tackles issues that extend far beyond basic race relations and, in the process, tempers other national threats, helping to create a more equitable and just country to everyone's benefit.

ALL THE WARNINGS from previous generations of Americans about the threat racism poses to the United States make the danger feel outmoded rather than contemporary. Instead of inciting us to action to mitigate the range of racism's effects today, they serve to make the threat part of an unfortunate and inconvenient, but largely settled, history. We take pride in the nation's leaps of progress following our leaders' words of caution: the framers of the Constitution lived to see the cessation of the legalized slave trade in 1808, Lincoln's generation brought about the abolishment of slavery and national reconstruction, post–World War II Americans witnessed a civil rights reformation that recast the nation in a mold closer to the ideals in its sacraments, and we elected and reelected a black man to the White House. Because of such gains, some contend that for whatever racial bigotry and violence existed in the past, racism today mostly survives in a lesser, interpersonal form—predominantly surviving in the realm of bad apples and lone wolves.

We spend less time, however, acknowledging the reason there are multiple inflection points that spur a new generation of racial progress. After every blow we strike against racism, backlash to our progress lands a counterpunch. Yes, the slave trade ended, but slavery continued. And the Supreme Court soon declared that the words in our Declaration of Independence and Constitution did not pertain to black people because the United States was born of a European tradition that was more than clear on the matter. Chief Justice Roger Taney infamously wrote in the 1857 opinion in the case *Dredd Scott v. Sandford* of black people:

They had for more than a century before been regarded as beings of an inferior order, and altogether unfit to associate with the white race either in social or political relations, and so far inferior that they had no rights which the white man was bound to respect, and that the negro might justly and lawfully be reduced to slavery for his benefit.[1]

While the Civil War ended slavery, it was followed by the terrorizing of black Americans who dared try to vote or eke out a living. The Civil Rights Movement rid the nation of de jure segregation, but it was soon followed by a politics of racial division explicitly exercised to maintain a social hierarchy and secure election victories at the expense of national unity. We have progressed, but we have not yet arrived.

The primary obstacle to recognizing and addressing racism today is that its expression has undergone a fundamental evolution. It is precisely because of the nation's progress on race that the old forms of racism, now largely taboo and socially unacceptable, lurk in the darker corners of society and only occasionally bound into the spotlight. The resulting issue is that any inequality or injustice that black Americans disproportionately experience is too often reduced to questions of personal, cultural, intellectual, or even biological deficiencies. This line of thinking asserts that racism is not the thing holding black people back, but rather any perceived unfairness is a result of an individual unwillingness or inability to capitalize on all the United States has to offer. This sleight of hand also casts racism as a lamentable trait of backward individuals instead of as a structural flaw in our society that still requires remedy. When conceived of in the interpersonal form, racism is a matter of the heart—and in the United States, there is rarely a place for civic or governmental intervention in matters of the heart. But just because the nation may no longer wear racial discrimination on its sleeve does not mean racism no longer pollutes our bloodstream.

The fluctuations of racism from headline to national subtext mask the role it plays in what are often perceived to be the real threats to the nation and our democracy today. For a few years now, there's been no shortage of opinions offered by scholars about why American democracy is in decline and headed for a messy demise. We feel it, too. Slightly less than 60 percent of citizens say the nation's democracy is working well.[2] We blame a lot of the dysfunction in our political system on wealthy donors and the flood of money in politics. Just about two in three of us think the design and structure of our government need significant change if our democracy is to survive. And, perhaps most telling, we are not happy with what our democracy has become. Since 2002, the number of Americans who are not proud of our system of government has quadrupled from 9 to 36 percent. Gene Gardner, a retiree in southwest Virginia, describes our democracy as being reduced to a "rock-throwing contest," observing, "It seems like the country is being divided on so many topics on so many fronts at one time."[3]

Why we sling stones at one another depends on whom you ask, but few believe that racism is the motivating rationale. One of the more prevalent beliefs is that hyperpartisanship is the true threat to the nation. More than seven in ten Americans believe partisan disagreement has reached a dangerous low point.[4] Forty-one percent of Democrats view the Republican Party as a threat to the nation's well-being, and 45 percent of Republicans view Democrats as such.[5] There are wide partisan differences in what the most pressing issues facing the nation are, including climate change, gun violence, immigration, and racism. Not only do we disagree on what the issues are or how to best resolve them, but each political party also believes the other is actively engaged in the subversion of the country. Such views fueled the riotous insurrection at the Capitol on January 6, 2021, when elected officials were targeted for violence. This makes good-faith engagement and compromise virtually impossible, bringing good governance to its knees and weaponizing politics in a way that ultimately paralyzes democratic processes and institutions.

Scholars have shown how membership in a political party has become more central to our personal identity. This causes partisan disagreements on issues to feel like personal attacks. And it makes us more uncomfortable to be around those who do not share our same political views and party affiliation. It is not just that we do not want to engage with our fellow citizens on the other side of the aisle; we view them and their entire families with contempt. It is rare to come across someone who does not have an anecdote of falling out with a relative or longtime friend over political bickering on social media that descended into a deeply personal attack and a virtual shunning. One especially revealing statistic sums up the problem up quite nicely: Only 4 percent of Democrats and 5 percent of Republicans in 1960 said they would be displeased if their child married someone belonging to the other party. But by 2010, those numbers swelled to 33 percent and 49 percent, respectively, making interparty unions more undesirable than interracial or same-sex marriages today.[6] University of Maryland political scientist Lilliana Mason notes that anger accompanies this intense political sorting, finding that "the more people who feel angry, the less capable we are of finding common ground policies, or even treating our opponents like human beings."[7]

American democracy cannot survive if it is composed of parties that view each other as the enemy. They will each attempt to entrench political advantages into democratic processes and systems, thereby undermining them and making them less responsive to the people's voting choices. If they begin to question the legitimacy of their opponents or election results, the resilience of our government may be insufficient to manage the collapse of a fundamental aspect of American democracy—the peaceful transition of power. For those who subscribe to this ominous view of hyperpartisanship, there is no greater threat to the nation today.

Another increasingly common view is that economic inequality is the greatest threat to the United States. This is reflected in Americans' view that money has a terribly corrosive effect on our democracy. Generally, economic inequality refers to the distance between the haves and have-nots in society based on wealth and all forms of income. And that gap is massive. In 2015, the average household income for the top 10 percent of U.S. households was $312,536; for the rest of the nation it was just $34,074.[8] And the top 1 percent now earn an average of $719,000, which is the highest wage level in American history and a 157 percent increase over the last thirty years. We are familiar with how much more chief executives make than their employees do—in 1965, the ratio of CEOs' compensation to that of their workforce was 20 to 1; today it is 312 to 1.[9] The top 0.1 percent saw an annual growth of 8 percent in that same time period and reached $2,757,000 in 2017.[10] Meanwhile, Americans' paychecks have stagnated, and they possess no more purchasing power today than they did forty years ago. This means our income has barely kept pace with inflation, and American workers effectively have not gotten a raise in four decades.

Economic inequality is a problem for democracy because our system is more responsive to elites than to average citizens. Martin Gilens and Benjamin Page, two professors who study politics and public policy, released an oft-cited study that showed "economic elites and organized groups representing business interests have substantial independent impacts on U.S. government policy, while average citizens and mass-based interest groups have little or no independent influence."[11] As money becomes more of a factor, our elected officials are less responsive to the people. Of course, their findings do not suggest that the public never gets what it wants, as other scholars have pointed out. But there is little doubt that the increased amount of private money circulating in our democratic processes does not amplify the public's will. More economic strength increases access to power. And our democracy is bruised, if not broken, when the voice of the people is muted by the policy demands of the well resourced. As the nation's founders set forth in the Declaration of Independence, government's legitimacy and power are derived from the consent of the governed. When moneyed interests tip the scale, they are undermining the central pillar of American democracy.

Growing economic inequality also skews the American idea. We are a nation that claims any of us can rise as high up the economic ladder as our individual talents and efforts will take us. But economists have determined that our parents' incomes are the strongest predictor of our own future earnings as well as our life path. Economic mobility has stagnated in the United States—just 7.5 percent of those born into households in the bottom fifth making less than $23,000 a year will ever make it to the top fifth, where household income begins at $200,000. In Canada, that number is 13.5 percent, which means the American Dream is being deported north, as it is almost twice as likely to happen there than it is in the United States.[12] More than 90 percent of Americans born in 1940 ended up better off than their parents, while only half of Americans born in 1980 will be able to say the same.[13] Economic inequality allows those at the upper end to hoard resources to improve their future generations' chances at maintaining and increasing their economic status, and it often comes at the expense of those on the lower end.

Americans have rejected exorbitant economic inequality in the past. A number of monopolies and trusts, or organized business interests, sprouted up in the late nineteenth century, dominating the railroad, steel, oil, sugar, and tobacco industries. These corporations owned large chunks of the American economy and employed large numbers of citizens. This permitted them to set prices wherever they liked while ensuring workers' rights remained as limited and weak as possible. Former Supreme Court justice Louis Brandeis wrote that these trusts had concentrated so much economic power that they were behaving like a state within state, thereby weakening the United States by holding its economy at risk.[14] President Theodore Roosevelt and later his cousin President Franklin Roosevelt enacted significant antitrust reforms to reduce these monopolies' influence on the nation's course and on our political freedoms.

In an attempt to rebalance the nation's economy and shift power away from corporations and toward the protection of the American people, Teddy Roosevelt laid out a comprehensive socioeconomic agenda in his New Nationalism speech in Osawatomie, Kansas, in 1910, one of the most famous orations of the twentieth century. Returning to that location just over a century later, Barack Obama offered a vision for economic justice that struck the same chord. Obama lamented the unfairness of teachers, nurses, and construction workers being forced to pay higher tax rates than multimillionaires. He told a rapt audience, "This kind of inequality—a level we haven't seen since the Great Depression—hurts us all." He went on to say that such large economic disparities "distort our democracy" and attack the "promise at the very heart of America: that this is the place where you can make it if you try."[15] Teddy Roosevelt would not have had much quibble with this sentiment. Economic inequality presents a danger to the stability of the United States and the integrity of the American idea.

Yet another threat to our democracy that is receiving lots of attention is populism, a concept that Donald Trump's campaign and presidency brought to the fore of the nation's conscience. Populism is an ideology that pits two groups against each other, where one is depicted as virtuous and like-minded and the other is portrayed as a bastion of elites and dangerous "others" who threaten the rights, prosperity, and well-being of the righteous group. Trump's rhetoric on race has tapped into the grievances of many Americans and cast his supporters as the virtuous ones who are attempting to stave off attacks from the elites and establishment politicians who populate the swamp he promised to drain. At various points in his political ascendancy, he has gone after media elites, political elites, the elites who raise money for global corporations, and the elites responsible for foreign policy problems. Once president, however, he reclaimed the term, declaring that he and his supporters were the true elites[16]—smarter and more successful than the others who are "stone cold losers" and "slobs." But this sort of rhetoric alone is not sufficient to threaten our longstanding democracy. In fact, in its strictest construction, it is entirely possible for a democracy, where the will of the majority directs the activities of government, to also be populist. The problem arises when considering the specific form of American democracy, which does not allow for a simple majority to run roughshod over every other citizen.

Our democracy is liberal—a loaded word sometimes used as a partisan pejorative. In political science, *liberalism* refers to a doctrine that espouses the freedom of individuals as its most important aim and requires government to acknowledge and protect that freedom. The United States is a liberal democracy, which, according to public policy scholar William A. Galston, can be defined as a "political order [that] rests on the republican principle, takes constitutional form, and incorporates the civic egalitarianism and majoritarian principles of democracy."[17] That is, our democracy's power is derived from the people, who are equal and who select representatives to advocate for them through agreed-upon political institutions and processes. Importantly, liberal democracies temper majoritarian impulses, limiting the power of the majority while ensuring the rights of citizens in the minority are shielded.

In this context, then, illiberalism is a direct threat to America. An illiberal democracy does not protect the rights of individual citizens, does not consider all citizens equal, and tolerates the abridgement of civil liberties. It is the opposite of the American idea that we are all created equal with inalienable rights to life, liberty, and the pursuit of happiness. The appeal of this system of government can increase when a society is undergoing significant change and the majority's power is threatened. In an attempt to hold on to its status and priority access to resources, the majority or those who hold the most power may allow a slide toward illiberalism. And if an illiberal democracy rises, the American idea will be fundamentally altered to the point that its current form necessarily will perish.

MARLBORO COUNTY, SOUTH CAROLINA, is a locality nestled atop the rich soil of the Pee Dee River. The body of water and the region itself are named after the small agrarian Native American tribe that still calls the area home and for the river that patiently ushers water from the Appalachians to a Lowcountry Carolina estuary. The origins of my paternal family are buried in this land, forever lost amid the hardscrabble lives of a people whose interactions with white residents forced them to navigate the thin line between sex and violence—sometimes finding the two were bedfellows with no line of demarcation. For this reason, like much of black America, but unlike my maternal side, which can trace its blood back to an enslaved African man, my father's family seemed to arise out of nowhere, cropping up as a product of the postbellum mishmash of formerly enslaved black people, the Scots-Irish descendants, exploitative farming arrangements, and virulent racism.

Will Johnson, my father's grandfather, was biracial, the offspring of an illicit coupling between a white man and a young black woman—whether it was consensual or something more sordid is likely forever unknowable. Annie Stevenson, my father's grandmother, was also multiracial; her strawberry-brown hair, green eyes, and rose-beige skin publicized her black, white, and Native American constitution. The two were reared in the shadow cast by state's most revered politician, former governor and U.S. senator Ben "Pitchfork" Tillman—an irascible man who saw value in lynch mobs and viewed black Americans as an unfortunate lot that the nation had foolishly "inoculated with the virus of equality."[18]

Before Will and Annie met, they were schooled in the arts of injustice, inequality, and the violent suppression of any urge black citizens might have to express themselves as equals. In the years of their birth, 1893 and 1894, respectively, Governor Tillman ruled on a very straightforward principle: "The whites have absolute control of the State government, and we intend at any and all hazards to retain it."[19] And then, as if reading from the playbook on how to run an illiberal democracy, Tillman declared that the right to vote was beyond the mental capacity of black Americans and that the founding proposition that we are all created equal "is not true now, and was not true when Jefferson wrote it."

My great-grandparents were born into a stretch of land where the light of the Promise did not reach, blotted out by the darkness of racism. Moreover, it was a corner of the country where the central American ideal of equality was cast as little more than a poetic lie, and where the man making the charge was rewarded for the critique with years of state power and national influence. It is a wonder that Will and Annie—coming of age in a place and time when Southern breezes were weighted with racial injustice and the imminence of malice—managed to hold on to a belief in America, adhere to a faith in the Promise, and snatch some small measure of freedom from the air around them.

Their experience is instructive of how racism both compels and reveals subversions of a well-ordered democratic republic. A closer look at the threats that hyperpartisanship, economic inequality, and illiberalism pose to the United States reveals that racial inequality is a common thread through each. While it is certainly true that both parties are moving further apart ideologically, they are also dividing along lines of race. Over the last twenty-five years, the partisan divide between the two parties has more than doubled.[20] Not coincidentally, in that same time frame white Americans have left the Democratic Party in a slow and steady stream. Scholars have found that the ideological polarization is accompanied by a particular racial phenomenon: as the number of nonwhite Americans increases, white Americans find themselves right of center on a number of issues.[21]

Meanwhile, black voters have long been clustered in support of the Democratic Party, and more Hispanic and Asian Americans are joining them. Politicians seized on this occurrence and began tailoring more-conservative messages for white voters and more-progressive policies for nonwhite audiences. The result is partisan animus significantly driven by differences in our racial identities. Further, the increasing overlap between partisan and racial schemas suggests that racial animosity is a defining feature of American politics.[22] The reality is that one cannot discuss the dangers of hyperpartisanship without considering racial tensions and polarization.

Similarly, economic inequality has deep ties to racial inequality. Though the American Dream is more difficult for us all to achieve, upward economic mobility is especially challenging for black Americans. While 10.6 percent of white Americans will make it from the lowest income levels to the highest, only 2.5 percent of black Americans will accomplish the same feat.[23] Median income for black households is only 60 percent of that of white households, and median black household wealth—a term for net worth that represents the total value of assets minus the total value of liabilities—is $11,030, compared with $134,230 for white households.[24] And black Americans are the only racial group whose real-dollar income has not risen in two decades.[25] In addition to the economic distance between black and white Americans, there is a significant and growing economic disparity among black Americans, which means they are increasingly stratified along lines of income and wealth into haves and have-nots. If economic inequality is going to be Americans' undoing, black Americans are the canary in the coal mine who will be undone first, suffocated by the lack of opportunity.

And when considering the risk of illiberalism, the United States already knows it quite well. For the vast majority of the nation's first two hundred years of existence, it was an illiberal democracy. It denied the right to vote and other civil liberties to black and indigenous people, women, and most immigrants. The nation's illiberal tendencies almost always occurred as a means to disenfranchise or subjugate large swaths of the population. And its populist inclinations usually occurred in response to a challenge to the racial social order. Taken together, the danger of succumbing to illiberalism is intimately tied to the nation's racial composition and expansion of the full rights of citizenship to racial minorities.

This is not to say that if we manage to overcome the effects of racism, the problems presented by hyperpartisanship, economic inequality, and populism will suddenly dissipate. Each of these issues can disassemble our democracy if left unattended. However, as long as racism remains a viable virus in the American ecosystem, it will infect and erode the public will to take on other pressing issues. Sparking racial resentments and inciting racial animus are tried and true tactics to ensure that the American people do not develop a collective will and political solidarity across lines of race and class. Therefore, living up to our professed ideals will require a dismantling of the racial hierarchy. Failure to do so leaves our biggest vulnerability completely exposed and readily accessible to those who will exploit it for their own purposes.

We are a country established from sea to shining sea, but we have clustered ourselves on opposite shores, leaving a vast expanse between us that is mainly traversed by arrows and barbs when the race question is raised. The current political landscape and climate provide exceptional growing conditions for a bumper crop of pessimism about the future of the United States and American democracy. And when the words *race relations* and *racism* are layered on, the outlook can appear bleak. But our nation, like most, has a mythology that is essential to our national identity. If we can agree that our national story—bound up in the veracity of the Promise—is worth fighting for and preserving, we can weaken the effects of racism. But it will require work, sacrifice, and prioritizing the well-being of something bigger than ourselves.

America is indeed a massive project and a daunting undertaking. But we are fortunate to have among us a model of the solidarity that we will need to ensure the nation's continued progress, viability, and prosperity. To determine how we can finally become the next version of a more perfect Union, we can turn to those people pressed down and shaken together who managed to ascend anyway: black Americans.

PART II

American, But Black: Lessons for National Solidarity

It is a peculiar sensation, this double-consciousness, this sense of always looking at one's self through the eyes of others, of measuring one's soul by the tape of a world that looks on in amused contempt and pity. One ever feels his two-ness,—an American, a Negro; two souls, two thoughts, two unreconciled strivings; two warring ideals in one dark body, whose dogged strength alone keeps it from being torn asunder.

The history of the American Negro is the history of this strife,—this longing to attain self-conscious manhood, to merge his double self into a better and truer self. In this merging he wishes neither of the older selves to be lost. He does not wish to Africanize America, for America has too much to teach the world and Africa. He wouldn't bleach his Negro blood in a flood of white Americanism, for he knows that Negro blood has a message for the world. He simply wishes to make it possible for a man to be both a Negro and an American without being cursed and spit upon by his fellows, without having the doors of opportunity closed roughly in his face.

—*W.E.B. DuBois,* The Souls of Black Folk

CHAPTER 3

Superlative Citizenship

In the lengths to which they have gone just to be accepted in the United States, black citizens are animated by the same spirit living within Americans of all races and ethnicities who have refused to accept anything less than liberty and equality. And though many were never permitted to complete the journey, they heel-and-toed their way through the tangled underbrush without pause, etching a path to the Promise that future generations could continue clearing. Such striving in the face of the meanest of odds is the mark of citizen exemplars. It is also the first attribute of black America that the nation could adopt to help trample the ugliness of racism underfoot.

No greater story of superlative citizenship can be told than that of Jehu Grant, which sings its gospel truth beautifully and tragically.[1] Jehu was a simple but remarkable man who desperately wanted to be an American. Well into old age, he could vividly recall the swell of emotion that consumed him as an adolescent whenever he imagined the day that he could finally taste freedom. Two significant problems stood in the way of his dream becoming reality in the year 1777, when Jehu was about twenty-five years old. First, the newborn United States was still working out with Great Britain whether there would be an America at all, negotiations usually occurring amid volleys from smoothbore muskets and naval carronades. Second, and even more daunting, Jehu was black and enslaved in Narragansett, Rhode Island, tagged as the property of Elihu Champlen.

Champlen was a Tory who traded with King George III's ships, floating sentries that paced the territorial waters in need of Champlen's sheep and cattle to remain fit for duty. Once the Revolutionary War began, Jehu feared that Champlen would contract him out, or perhaps sell him outright, to the British navy. Since a number of black men in Rhode Island were enlisting in George Washington's Continental Army, a Loyalist might be inclined to simultaneously help Great Britain and hurt the United States by sending his enslaved black people to support the British side. Feeling this might be his fate, and desiring the same independence that the young nation did, Jehu walked 125 miles away from his enslavement in August 1777 to Danbury, Connecticut, where he joined the United States' fight for nationhood and freedom.

In going off to fight for independence, Jehu became one of nine thousand black people to serve in the Continental Army, constituting about 4 percent of the military's total strength. Danbury was an important supply depot and manufacturing center for the army, and shortly before Jehu's enlistment, the British had burned much of it to the ground. So though he wanted to see action on the battlefield, Jehu's duties were to help reestablish Danbury. He was put to work as a teamster, responsible for managing supply wagons and the animals that hauled them. At the onset of winter about four months into his enlistment, he became a waiter to the wagon master general. Jehu's experience was typical—only about half of the black men who served in the Continental Army were permitted to take up arms, amid widespread fear that providing enslaved black men with guns would give them the means to revolt or, worse, the audacity to believe engaging in combat would give them grounds to demand freedom. Therefore, many early black enlistees were put into service jobs. But whether in combat or support roles, the average length of service for black members of the Continental Army was four and a half years, which was eight times longer than that of the average white soldier's enlistment early in the war.[2] In this regard, black military men contributed a disproportionately high amount of service in the cause for independence.

Jehu's enlistment was for eighteen months, and he was sure to extend it if the war was still ongoing when the time came. But he never got the opportunity. In June 1778, ten months into his military commitment, his former master Elihu Champlen found him serving in the army just outside New York City. Champlen accused the army of possessing his stolen property and demanded it immediately return Jehu to enslavement. The army quickly conceded. Jehu was seized and dragged from the bout for national independence—as well as his own—and tossed back into the slavery machine. Shortly after the war ended, Champlen sold him. His new slaveholder promised manumission in exchange for a set period of dedicated enslavement. Jehu complied, and freedom eventually found the faithful servant. Jehu married and had six children, settling in upstate New York and living a long, difficult life.

Some years later, in 1832, the United States was a fully established nation, thanks to the Revolutionary War victory delivered by volunteers like Jehu Grant, who was now about eighty years old, blind, and indigent. In that year, Congress considered an expansive military pension act in response to President Andrew Jackson's persistent urging to provide payments to "every Revolutionary soldier who aided in establishing our liberties, and who is unable to maintain himself in comfort."[3] The law that passed went even further—it granted full military pay for life to veterans who had served in any capacity for at least two years total during the war, and it permitted prorated pay for those serving between six months and two years. In order to receive their pensions, veterans first had to appear before a state court, describe their service under oath, and provide any supporting papers and witness statements. The court would certify the veterans' declarations and petition the War Department for their pensions.

Working with the court, Jehu described being enlisted to an Army captain named Giles Galer, teaming horses and wagons until the winter, serving as a waiter to wagon master general John Skidmore, and marching with the army from Danbury, Connecticut, to Highland, New York, a small hamlet along the Hudson River. His declaration was sent to the nation's capital in 1832, but no response was forthcoming. Finally, two years later, in 1834, the War Department's commissioner of pensions replied, notifying Jehu that his petition had been denied.

The rationale for the rejection was heartbreaking. "Services while a fugitive from your master's service are not embraced by the Pension Act of June 1832," the response read. "Your papers have been placed on file." In other words, a black man who broke an immoral law to fight for independence was undeserving of recognition by a nation that had broken the monarch's laws to fight for its independence. Nothing could be more American than Jehu snatching his personal liberty away from his captor in order to fight for national liberty for all. Yet in the eyes of the U.S. government, a black runaway slave could not be an honorable American soldier—he was worthy of neither the personal independence nor the national independence for which he fought. Revolutionary War veteran Jehu Grant died blind and penniless, denied by the very United States he helped establish.

Only one record survives of Jehu Grant following the rejection of his petition—an 1836 response he sent to the commissioner of pensions. He wrote that his decision to escape enslavement was because the call for national independence was too strong for him to ignore. He remembered how elated he was at the Promise of America: "When I saw the liberty poles and the people all engaged for the support of freedom, I could not help but like and be pleased with such thing." He pleaded for the reconsideration of his pension, saying, "I served my country faithfully," and adding that the men with whom he served were "receiving the liberalities of the government." Jehu atoned for his wriggling free from slavery's clutches prematurely, gave assurances that his master had been justly compensated for the infraction, and remarked that God had forgiven him for trespassing on man's law. But he, like any true American, was compelled to act by "the songs of liberty that saluted my ear, thrilled through my heart."

In his quest to be an American, Jehu did more than most. Knowing full well that racism contaminated the high ideals of our new nation, he still voluntarily served the country and put himself at risk despite the nagging possibility that he would never be permitted to ride the wave of liberty he helped create. This sort of superlative citizenship is not just an accurate description of Jehu's commitment; it is also a deliberate strategy that black Americans have long employed in an attempt to overcome the corrosive effects of racism.

Few questions persistently roil the nation more than this one: Who is truly American? This is not just a narrow legal inquiry about citizenship, which itself has proved quite contentious throughout the nation's history and continues to plague us. Rather, it is a question that forces us to confront the nation's myth and the history, values, and morals it espouses. Myths serve an important function in establishing national identity—they are the stories we tell ourselves about who we are and what we believe. But they tend to do so while casting the nation in an idealized form and simplifying historical complexities. The result is usually a narrative that downplays flaws and missteps in order to forge a more widely acceptable shared understanding of what the nation proclaims to be. America's creation myth is a story about enlightened men who revolted against abridgments of their liberty to establish an exceptional country, ordained with a consecrated civic virtue. This novel nation proclaimed that all are created equal, power is vested in the people, opportunity is available to those who seek it, and the bonds of kinship among the citizenry are based on a set of ideas and principles. The ugly bits of our history, such as slavery, armed domestic conflicts, sex and race discrimination, and greed-induced economic depressions, are portrayed as basic tests of character that the nation passed, challenges that only added moral weight to our national myth.

The answer to the question of who gets to be truly American begins with this story, designating its primary historical actors—the framers of the Constitution—as personifications of the nation. Those who are fashioned after these heroic characters in our national myth—white, male, Christian, English-speaking, economically or politically elite—tend to be the people who are perceived as the truest conceptions of the nation's identity, largely because they are also the economic and political descendants of the myth's authors and benefit the most from its widespread acceptance. This is more than just supposition. Numerous scholars have noted the nexus between race, religion, and national identity that makes a baseline conception of an American to be both white and Christian.[4]

This depiction has rooted itself in all of us. For example, public-opinion polling has shown that half the nation thinks the prototypical American patriot is white, while only 2 percent think a black person is representative of an American patriot.[5] Seventy percent of U.S. citizens across all races and ethnicities say that speaking English is "very important for being truly American."[6] In 2014, more than 70 percent of Americans identified as Christian, and more than half of the nation thought being Christian was important in order to be considered truly American. In fact, two out of three Americans say that God has granted America an exceptional role in human history.[7] As sociology professor Rhys Williams succinctly put it, "There has long been a *sub rosa* association that made 'white Christian American' the baseline, default cultural understanding of this nation."[8] Some 84 percent of us say that sharing our national culture, customs, and traditions is important for being considered truly American.[9] Even as far back as 1786 when the Latin phrase *e pluribus unum*—"Out of many, one"—was stamped on official coinage, and five years later tattooed on the nation's Great Seal, there was little mistaking that it referred to many different states becoming one nation, rather than an affirmation that many different groups should become one people.

The question of who gets to be truly American is deeply associated with who gets the full benefits of citizenship. Notions about which of us are truly American influence whom the nation deems eligible to access all the rights and privileges of being a citizen. In the myth's purest form, all citizens who subscribe to our ideals and practice them are equal to, and just as truly American as, their fellow countrymen, no matter their race, sex, ethnicity, religion, class, or place of birth. But in practice, something significantly less desirable has occurred. Some were treated as Americans and citizens long before the rest could even lay partial claim to those titles. This is quite consequential since a nation is defined not only by who it says belongs, but whom it excludes. And in a nation like ours that was founded on an idea, the implication of exclusion is that some people are actually not worthy of equality or liberty—as if the nation believes that such rights are too much of a responsibility for the excluded to handle, too precious to spend on those who are undeserving, or too sacred to dispense to anyone but a divinely chosen few. For this reason, though the United States has certainly expanded who can become a legal citizen, it has been much more begrudging in whom it considers a real and true American.

Taken together, our national myth tells us who is truly American, and thus eligible to access all the benefits of citizenship. The rest are considered lesser Americans and, as a result, experience the United States as lesser citizens. Our history and the present state of the nation bear this out. And so, the question of who gets to be American is intimately connected to the practice of citizenship.

BLACK AMERICANS HAVE LONG UNDERSTOOD the relationship between being considered a true American and the rights of citizenship that come with it. As enslaved men and women, as the targets of racial violence, and as the segment of society today whose access to rights and opportunities continues to be more constrained than other fellow citizens', they know that these discriminatory experiences were permitted only as a result of being perceived as something less than truly and equally American. But their ideas, their work, and their perseverance have contributed as much to the nation's culture and prosperity as those of others. Because black Americans are indeed American, the incessant striving for liberty and equality courses vigorously through their veins.

The story of black people in the United States is a quest for the title of American and the benefits it confers, things they have touched but have not been permitted to grasp firmly. For them, the question of who gets to be American has always been slightly different and remains a defining and age-old quandary—how to show it is possible to be *truly* American *and* black? The answer to this, to how these Americans can access the full benefits of citizenship, is tied to their practice of citizenship. That is, black people's well-being in the United States is the offspring of being seen and accepted as truly American, which, given the role race plays in the national myth, is heavily influenced by demonstrations of exceptional citizenship.

Superlative citizenship is a deliberate strategy that black Americans have employed for the entirety of the nation's existence. Its primary purpose is to demonstrate how aligned and compatible they are with the principles and ideas proffered in the national myth as a powerful argument for inclusion. It employs the same tools used to cut them out of America to build a place for themselves in it. Importantly, superlative citizenship requires taking on all the responsibilities required of the citizenry even when the nation does not deliver on its promises. The relationship between a state and its citizens centers on the obligations one has to the other, usually set forth in some sort of social contract. In return for the nation ensuring our physical security and the provision of certain goods and services, we citizens agree to fulfill our duties. Americans believe good citizens vote in elections, pay all the taxes they owe, and follow the law, as well as take on social responsibilities like volunteering and respecting the views of others.[10] They believe the best citizens answer the call to serve their country and their community, whether in the military or on jury duty. Superlative citizenship is the performance of these sorts of functions with the understanding that the nation may breach its end of the contract. It exposes the hypocrisy of the breach, which, for the United States, questions how dedicated the nation is to the values it claims to hold dear.

Superlative citizenship gets its power from threatening to expose the nation as being more wedded to the appearance of holding certain truths as self-evident than to a steadfast commitment to ensure every citizen enjoys them. Such an undermining of a nation's core story complicates its ability to achieve its interests. International-relations scholars note that a country's maintenance of a stable self-identity—its ontological security—is as important to world leaders as its national security. Superlative citizenship jabs at the veracity of the national narrative and identity. It forces the nation to reckon with the fact that it may not be what it says it is and demonstrates the shortcoming to the world, thereby weakening its power and influence. Challenging the national identity in this way can compel the nation to correct itself.

Superlative citizenship is also an explicit counterargument to the racist tropes that have been used as justifications for why black people have always experienced a lesser version of America than many others. When black Africans were first brought to the United States, their servitude was explained as a condition of their not being Christian. Then as conversion to Christianity became routine, they were depicted as inferior on multiple dimensions—enslavement, as the propaganda of the day asserted, was good for these substandard

people. After their humanity and personhood were constitutionally acknowledged, portrayals of black Americans as lazy, prone to
criminality, and uncivilized practitioners of a boorish culture leapt
to the fore, undergirding the rationale for excluding them from basic
rights and beneficial public policy. Today, these narratives still find
their way into public discourse in attempts to justify why the group
fares worse than other Americans on a range of issues, from income
levels and incarceration rates to health and education outcomes.

Citizenship is not only a set of rights and responsibilities; it
is also a performance. Our status as citizens is displayed through
engaging in specific collective and individual practices. This has
been the case since the earliest formulations of the concept. For
example, in ancient Greece, one's interactions with the community
(in activities like banquets or hunting expeditions) and individual
behaviors (such as personal etiquette and appearance or owning
a horse) communicated citizen status.[11] This remains true in the
United States today, where collective activities (like community service on Martin Luther King, Jr. Day or military service on Veterans
Day) and individual deeds (such as neighborliness and civic virtue)
are hallmarks of the actions and attitudes that bind citizens one to
another. In those instances when performances of citizenship are
especially strong—when a community supports the lemonade stand
of a child who is raising money for victims of a natural disaster or
when a soldier returning from a combat deployment surprises his
family after the national anthem at a baseball game—the citizenry
glows with pride. Such moments not only feel like the epitome of
citizenship; they also feel intensely American. Thus, commanding
performances of citizenship lend credence to claims on the title
of American, especially when undertaken by historically excluded
groups.

Superlative citizenship, then, is a calculated tactic to improve
one's likelihood of accessing more of the rights and privileges afforded
to citizens and, perhaps, compelling a more inclusive conception of

who is truly American. Black Americans seized on this approach and perfected its employment. Performing exceptional acts of citizenship has been a means of associating black people with the American identity and national values, so as not to be seen as necessary clutter for the lower rungs of the social order. The humanity, dignity, and worthiness of model citizens are more difficult to deny than those of people who are seen as a drag on the nation and assigned to the dregs of society. It is no wonder that the racist stereotypes of black Americans deliberately point to characteristics incompatible with the American identity—selfish instead of self-determining, in dependence instead of independent, mostly contradictory to the national culture instead of major contributors to it. Performances of citizenship are exhibitions of Americanism and rebuttals to stereotypical portrayals.

One of the most well-known historical examples of this strategy can be found in the politics of respectability. This tactic was employed effectively by black civil rights leaders for most of the early twentieth century. Its origins are rooted in the survival tactics black Americans leaned on since the dark days of enslavement, but it crystallized among black churchgoing women in the early 1900s. Harvard professor Evelyn Brooks Higginbotham notes that these black women "rejected white America's depiction of black women as immoral, childlike, and unworthy of respect or protection" and combated it by adopting a "religious-political message drawn from biblical teachings, the philosophy of racial self-help, Victorian ideology, and the democratic principles of the Constitution of the United States."[12] The politics of respectability is a marginalized group's practice of strict adherence to specific cultural norms and practices of the majoritarian society as a means to demonstrate compatibility and sameness with the wider public. It concentrates on the actions and activities within one's control—individual behaviors and attitudes—"both as a goal in itself and as a strategy for reform of the entire structural system of American race relations."[13]

Through an emphasis on morality, proper diction, social etiquette, and dress codes, this politics of respectability was a strategy to counter racist images, disarm arguments of racial inferiority, and make an express claim on citizenship. The intent was to show early twentieth-century white Americans that black people were practitioners of the same national traditions and customs, thereby broadcasting the undeniable truth that there was no difference between the abilities of black and white people to perform citizenship, and thus, be American. Historian Paisley Harris has observed that "respectability was one of the primary bases upon which African Americans claimed equal status and citizenship during the Progressive era," acknowledging that the strategy was both pragmatic and problematic in tying one's worth to a set of behaviors as an "entrance fee" to full citizenship.[14] But in its time, it was a survival technique, a genuine and safety-seeking attempt to facilitate white Americans' recognition of black citizens' unquestionable humanity and instill a sense of black American belonging within the United States and its citizenry.

Though respectability politics was given voice and prominence through Baptist women in black churches, it was not constrained to them alone. Black men in the same era also made appeals for its practice. Prominent sociologist and historian W.E.B. DuBois and nationally renowned educator Booker T. Washington engaged in a well-publicized debate about the best course for advancing black Americans' access to civil rights, but both advocated for respectability politics. DuBois wrote a popular essay about the "Talented Tenth," which described a strategy of educating the best black men in college who would serve as role models and beacons of enlightenment for the rest of black America, to showcase for the nation a people worthy of integration and deserving of full citizenship. He argued that the inequality experienced by black citizens was a result of centuries of racist violence and oppressive governance, so to permit the education and community self-help led by its exceptional men was to show the United States "the capability of Negro blood, the promise of black men."[15]

Whereas DuBois wanted to cultivate the intelligence of a specific segment of black America through higher education in the liberal arts, Washington insisted the more productive approach to securing racial equality was to focus on training black Americans in trades and vocations. Instead of demanding the full balance of civil rights that were due to black citizens, Washington believed it better to allow black communities in the agrarian South and industrial North to practice economic self-sufficiency, display their civic value and virtue to white Americans, and exemplify the grit required to pull themselves up by their bootstraps in alignment with the nation's glorified Puritan work ethic. In his famed 1895 Atlanta Compromise speech, Washington urged black America not to "permit our grievances to overshadow our opportunities" and to focus its energies on the economic security that comes from work because "no race that has anything to contribute to the markets of the world is long in any degree ostracized."[16] Political scientist Byron D'Andra Orey writes, "Washington adopted the position that blacks should assimilate and work from within the system, as opposed to trying to change the system."[17]

Though they viewed the world differently, both DuBois and Washington believed that respectability politics was central to any hope of black people being accepted as truly American and fully citizens. This belief permeated the decades and became a prominent feature of the Civil Rights Movement that would reshape the United States and bring America another step closer to its idealized form. Not coincidentally, the nonviolent marches of the day were filled with black men, women, and children dressed in their Sunday best, peacefully assembled, and imbued with a hierarchal structure that flowed from traditions within the black church. Its public leaders were mostly male, college-educated, and attentive to their appearance and diction. These were deliberate undertakings to showcase the civility of black Americans and the reasonableness with which they staked a claim to the rights promised to all citizens in our Constitution.

When white police officers, buttoned up in licensed violence, unleashed heaving German shepherds at black men in slacks and dress shirts . . . when crowds of angry young white men drenched black women in gorgeous blouses and beautifully styled hair with milkshakes and racist invectives . . . when furious white parents chased black boys and girls down the street while launching stones and sneers at the backs of their freshly pressed first-day-of-school outfits . . . which group was behaving uncivilly and in a manner unworthy of the mantle of American idealism was readily apparent. This was no accident; it was a direct assault on the nation's identity and character. Television cameras and print photographers captured the violent iconography of the Civil Rights Movement and spread the visuals around the world, delivering a gut punch to the national myth and to the notion that black Americans were unsuitable for full incorporation into society.

The politics of respectability was an era-appropriate attempt to activate the benefits of superlative citizenship to bring about the equal and just treatment of black Americans. Debates still rage today about whether it remains a suitable or effective strategy. There is little disputing the fact that better behavior, dress, and diction expressly do not immunize black Americans from racial discrimination or exempt them from being treated as lesser citizens. The tactic has been the object of substantial criticism from younger generations of black America and of full-throated rejections by activists like those in the Black Lives Matter movement.[18] And numerous black writers and thinkers have taken respectability advocates—from Barack Obama to comedian Chris Rock[19]—to task for focusing on black behavior rather than explicitly calling out racism's impact on individual life chances. But it is also true that racial progress in the United States, including and especially Obama becoming the first black president, is a product of the same respectability that black Americans exercised for more than a century. And as noted law professor Randall Kennedy points out in an ardent defense of respectability: "Any marginalized group should be attentive to how it is perceived. The politics of respectability is a tactic of public relations that is, *per se*, neither necessarily good nor necessarily bad. A sound assessment of its deployment in a given instance depends on its goals, the manner in which it is practiced, and the context within which a given struggle is being waged."[20] This does not suggest that a return to respectability is the key to racial equality; only that respectability was once a predominant act of superlative citizenship and played an important, but not a singular, role in the racial progress realized in the twentieth century. Such utilitarian strategies are necessary in the fight against inequality.

JUST AS THE POLITICS OF RESPECTABILITY was being refined in the black church, Will Johnson and Annie Stevenson fell in love in South Carolina and soon provided an example of superlative citizenship in the naming of their sons. The two were teenage sweethearts and wasted no time marrying, tying the knot around 1907 at ages sixteen and fourteen, respectively. They rented a small home and the land it rested on, sharecropped long-staple cotton and bright-leaf tobacco, and survived in a time of rampant racism. But Will and Annie, like black Americans before them and since, managed to find the beauty of love, the joy of family, and the importance of community amid the racial hatred of the day.

I never met Will and Annie, my great-grandparents, but their faith in America and pride in blackness are especially evident in a rather unsuspecting place: the Fourteenth Census of the United States in 1920. It reports that they resided in the Hebron Township of Marlboro County with five children—a sixth would be born a couple of years later. They are listed as being literate, farm laborers, and natives of South Carolina going back a few generations.

Nearly all their neighbors were black, except for two older white households that still rented their home and farmed land. But, most interestingly, the Census reveals the names they gave their children. For their daughters, they chose melodic, floral names that rejected society's degradation of black beauty: Corabelle, Rosa, and Alta. For their sons, they chose names connoting a desire to interrupt the sociopolitical order.

Will and Annie's naming of their sons was as much an exercise in activism as a political performance of superlative citizenship. For their first son, they picked the name James Weldon—coupled with the family name, he became James Weldon Johnson. My great-uncle's name was an eponymous salute to the famed black writer and civil rights activist. Will and Annie knew of the young lawyer James Weldon Johnson, whom President Theodore Roosevelt had appointed to be a consul in Venezuela, a post he secured thanks to a relationship with Booker T. Washington. And most of all, they knew he wrote in 1900 what would become the unofficial black national anthem, "Lift Ev'ry Voice and Sing." I imagine that the song's lyrics, which speak of being "full of the faith that the dark past has taught us" and "full of the hope that the present has brought us," touched Will and Annie to the point that they could see "out from the gloomy past" to "where the white gleam of our bright star is cast."[21] This unyielding hope in America and optimism for their children's future led them to name their first son after the man who had given voice to their hearts' desires.

Will and Annie chose to make their second son a junior, naming him Will. By their doing so, this son became part of an interesting history and a tradition of renaming. Will Johnson's father—my great-great grandfather—was a white man named Will Clark who owned a country store in the neighboring town of Clio. No father-son relationship existed, though the parentage was an open secret that largely went unacknowledged—only noticeable in the slightly favorable treatment young Will received when he ventured into the

Clark family's shop. Will Johnson also had a biracial half-brother named William Henry Clark, evidently the offspring of another of Will Clark's improper pursuits. In fact, my great-grandfather Will Johnson—the son of a white man from the Clark family and a black woman we do not know much about except that her last name was Sinclair—exercised what little liberty was available to black Americans of the day and renamed himself, choosing Johnson for his last name, to be associated with a local family he viewed more favorably and in order to explicitly disassociate himself from the Clark household. So, Will and Annie Johnson's new baby boy shared a first name with his father, his half-uncle, and his white grandfather, but importantly, he was the first one of his name to be born a Johnson in our family's lineage. In this way, his naming represented a merging of what was and what could be—in his first name was the "faith that the dark past has taught us," and his last name was "full of the hope that the present has brought us."

For their third son, Will and Annie left little to the imagination in choosing the name Theodore Roosevelt. Though my grandfather Theodore Roosevelt Johnson was born in 1918, Will and Annie were certainly aware of the historic White House dinner that Booker T. Washington and Roosevelt shared more than a decade prior in 1901. They may have encountered the reaction to that dinner by South Carolina's then recently deceased senator Ben "Pitchfork" Tillman, who said, "The action of President Roosevelt in entertaining that nigger will necessitate our killing a thousand niggers in the South before they will learn their place again."[22] Their son's name would show that they did, in fact, know their place—it was in the United States, in the future of the Promise, maybe even in the White House, but certainly not mired in Tillman's racist visions. That they chose to name their third son after the white president instead of the famed black educator is notable. This was just as much a bold proclamation about who could be truly American and aspire to the highest office as it was a political provocation that explicitly asserted no dissonance in a black child of sharecroppers in Jim Crow South Carolina being named after a rich, white New Yorker who came to be president and a personification of early-twentieth-century American identity. Indeed, it was an extraordinary performance of racial protest cloaked in respectability and superlative citizenship.

In their day, the practice of naming black boys after American presidents was relatively common. Black men in the late nineteenth and early twentieth centuries were disproportionately named after presidents Ulysses Grant, James Garfield, Chester Arthur, Benjamin Harrison, William McKinley, and Theodore Roosevelt.[23] In this way, Will and Annie simply joined, rather than pioneered, this political form of expression and tactical claim on citizenship. "A small brown bowlegged Negro with the name 'Franklin D. Roosevelt Jones' might sound like a clown to someone who looks at him from the outside," Ralph Ellison writes in his book *Shadow and Act*. "There you are, so dazzled by the F.D.R. image . . . and so delighted with your own superior position that you don't realize its [*sic*] Jones who must be confronted."[24] Ellison went on to say that black Americans are often reminded that their names originally belonged to those who enslaved their forebearers, but "we must learn to wear our names within all the noise and confusion of the environment in which we find ourselves." In his view, which was shared by much of black America in the days of Will and Annie, these sorts of names, "sometimes with irony, sometimes with pride, but always with personal investment," represent "a certain triumph of the spirit, speaking to us of those who rallied, reassembled and transformed themselves and who under dismembering pressures refused to die."[25]

They speak of those declaring, through a performance of citizenship, that they are truly American.

THE BLACK AMERICAN DEMAND for full citizenship is a function of a burning desire for racial equality. The early-twentieth-century civil rights activists determined that petitioning the nation for the rights and protections of citizenship was the most appropriate method of fighting for full inclusion in the wider society.[26] Distinguished Virginia historian and educator Luther Jackson viewed citizenship as a path to racial equality because America is premised on notions of civic virtue, public participation, and political activism. And given the dire situation that black Americans faced during a time when Jim Crow presided over the nation clutching rage in one hand and rope in the other, nothing less than superlative citizenship would suffice.

Little else in the United States lays as strong a claim to citizenship as military service. In contrast to the subtle assertions present in the politics of respectability, donning the nation's cloth and risking one's life is a visible and explicit declaration of one's worthiness of full citizenship. This idea is as old as the concept of a republic. The connection between military service and citizenship was evident in the ancient societies of Greece and Rome, and it continued into the twenty-first century, as evinced by President George W. Bush's Veterans Day remarks following the September 11 terrorist attacks, when he declared that military service "represents the highest form of citizenship."[27]

The United States is based on a tradition that asserts military service is the preeminent civic duty and intimately intertwined with notions of what it means to be a good citizen.[28] For this reason, black Americans have a long and storied tradition of serving in the U.S. military even when they could not access the rights which they entered harm's way to defend. As with respectability politics, black American's honorable service in the military was a strategy of superlative citizenship, beginning as a fight for personal liberty every bit as much as a fight for the nation. The nation's security and well-being were essential to black claims on citizenship and equality—if there is no United States, there is no appeal for equality to be made on the basis of its Declaration of Independence or Constitution. Military service bundled the objectives of preserving the nation and insisting on full citizenship, permitting black servicemembers to work toward both aims with a single action.

Of course, black Americans knew their military service guaranteed nothing. Jehu Grant's misfortune was prophetic of how fighting for the nation one day could still result in having the boot of racial discrimination firmly on one's neck the next, sometimes with deadly consequences. But they also knew avoiding war would do nothing to bring about racial equality in America; military service at least demonstrated participation in the nation's aims and provided grounds to stake the demand for full inclusion. If those demands went unheeded, as was usually the case, it forced the United States to make that denial while embracing the barbed hypocrisy in which it was draped. This was a point Frederick Douglass pleaded during an 1865 speech in Boston. He noted that in three specific instances—the Revolutionary War of 1776, the War of 1812, and the ongoing Civil War—the United States accepted black people's military service as citizens of a nation under attack. But once the danger passed, they were returned to subjugation and no longer considered worthy of citizenship. "[The Negro] has been a citizen just three times in the history of this government," Douglass said, "and it has always been in time of trouble. In time of trouble we are citizens. Shall we be citizens in war, and aliens in peace? Would that be just?"[29] The power of these rhetorical questions is a direct result of the incredible dedication to the United States and the cause of liberty that led black Americans to serve in the military.

The service of black Americans at war is well chronicled. During the Revolutionary War, the majority-black First Rhode Island Regiment was raised when the state could not find enough white volunteers to fight for the nation's independence. These soldiers performed especially admirably at the Battle of Rhode Island in August 1778, fighting for two revolutionary causes at once: political independence for the United States and social equality for themselves.[30] The nation again faced severe manpower shortages in the

War of 1812, and enslaved black people volunteered, eventually making up no less than 15 percent of the nation's maritime strength.[31]
Black men and women served in the Civil War, with more than two
hundred thousand men in the Union's forces and women serving as
nurses and spies. When the war was over, forty thousand of them had
given their lives, sixteen Medals of Honor were awarded to them,
and their sacrifices for the abolishment of slavery also helped reunify
the country.[32] The Buffalo Soldiers, two black infantry units, served
on the frontier, where they earned nineteen Medals of Honor, and
black servicemen in the Spanish-American War earned another six.

   When the draft became the primary source of military manpower in World Wars I and II, more than 1.5 million black Americans answered the call despite being unconstitutionally deprived of
basic rights of citizenship and subjected to the violent terrors of Jim
Crow.[33] Because of racial discrimination in the military, however, not
a single one was awarded the Medal of Honor for several decades
until the Department of Defense and Presidents George H.W.
Bush, Bill Clinton, and Barack Obama processed buried recommendations and upgraded lower medals based on files chronicling
heroic actions.[34] Black servicemembers were overrepresented in the
Korean and Vietnam Wars and received twenty-two Medals of
Honor between the two conflicts.[35] And in today's all-volunteer
force, black Americans still constitute a disproportionate amount of
the military's strength. Though black Americans are just 13.4 percent
of the nation's population, they constitute 16.8 percent (more than
350,000) of those serving in the U.S. military—the only large racial
or ethnic group that is overrepresented.[36] Black Americans' service in
the military has always been of two purposes: to claim Americanism
and full citizenship as well as to defend the principles of freedom
and equality that give the claim irrefutable weight.

   And yet, though black Americans helped the nation find independence and security, they often found only injustice upon returning home. Jehu Grant was ripped from service and returned to the

plantation. The black soldiers in the First Rhode Island Regiment were promised their freedom from slavery in return for military service, but in 1778, the state had purchased the freedom of only about 10 percent of black soldiers.[37] Black sailors in the U.S. naval corps during the War of 1812 were not freed at its conclusion, but those who took the British offer of freedom if they served the crown retained their liberty, some of them moving to land set aside for them in southeastern Trinidad after the war.

Black servicemembers in the period between the Civil War and World War I faced deep and enduring racial discrimination by both the Army and the public. Many Americans did not want black servicemen living on the bases in their towns or representing the nation in battles in Europe, so segregated black American military units were sometimes forced to fight under the flags of other nations or serve as the face of the nation's Manifest Destiny philosophy that required them to persecute other racial minorities like Native Americans and Filipinos. Black soldiers in World Wars I and II served in segregated units and were often treated worse than white prisoners of war, enduring humiliating slights such as being forced to sit in colored balcony seating in base theaters while captured white enemy troops were permitted to occupy preferred floor seating. The 369th Infantry Regiment, a black unit known as the Harlem Hellfighters, was assigned to the French army in World War I because white American soldiers refused to serve with them, and the unit was awarded 170 Croix de Guerre medals for heroic individual and unit deeds.

And upon coming home, black servicemembers were denied benefits through the G.I. Bill, such as affordable mortgages and education assistance, that white veterans received. Some were lynched while still in their military uniforms, like Private Charles Lewis, who was honorably discharged after World War I on December 14, 1918, and the next day was hanging from a tree in his olive Army attire courtesy of a local Kentucky sheriff and a mob of vigilantes.[38] Adversarial nations exploited American racism in combat, dropping different sets of leaflets over segregated black units and white units to exacerbate racial tensions within the United States military. For example, in World War II, the Japanese military papered white units with cartoon drawings of beastly black men hitting and sexually assaulting white women in factories, the two thrust together because white men were off fighting. Meanwhile the German military launched leaflets over black units showing pictures of white mobs back home beating black citizens and suggesting the nation valued them as nothing more than cannon fodder.[39]

For black Americans, military service has long been a strategic effort to win racial equality at home by defeating nations abroad. Today, access to the military's economic and social benefits are a strong pull for black citizens, especially since their socioeconomic status lags behind that of the rest of the nation. But for the majority of the nation's history, black Americans' commitment to military service has been aimed at realizing the American rights that are supposed to be inalienable as well as defending America to ensure the preservation of the nation that has promised those rights.

Writing in 1942 to the *Pittsburgh Courier*, the largest black newspaper in the nation at the time, James G. Thompson kicked off a national campaign that accurately captured the reason black people had long served in the U.S. military despite not being considered true Americans and full citizens. He wondered in his letter to the editor, "Should I sacrifice my life to live half American? Would it be demanding too much to demand full citizenship rights in exchange for the sacrificing of my life?" He went on to articulate that if "V is for victory," then black Americans had to adopt a double "VV" for double victory: "The first V for victory over our enemies from without, the second V for victory over our enemies from within. For surely those who perpetuate these ugly prejudices here are seeking to destroy our democratic form of government just as surely as the Axis forces."[40] Even Thompson, a twenty-six-year-old cafeteria worker in Wichita, Kansas, during the thick of World War II, knew that racism was an existential threat to America. Black military service was not just a way to secure a more inclusive nation but a way to save the nation itself.

WHEN THE STORY OF AMERICA was first scribbled onto parchment and narrated to an anxious public, scarcely anyone could have envisioned a woman like Hope Copeland. Even today, when she enters a crime scene and applies her extensive knowledge of forensic science, Americans—and foreigners for that matter—are not quite sure what to think. Hope is a black woman from the Deep South who is also Muslim, a chemist, and a special agent in the FBI— simultaneously the perfect picture of an inclusive America and a citizen so contrary to our preconceived notions of who and what a true American is that she often confounds colleagues, criminals, and onlookers alike. "When I walk in a room wearing my hijab, whether serving a search warrant or guest-lecturing at a university, people are stunned. You can see it clear as day on their faces. Being black, female, and a Muslim—all three of those present challenges day-to-day: my identity is challenged, my expertise is challenged, and, post–September 11, even my patriotism is challenged." Though our current interpretation of the soaring rhetoric in our founding documents suggests that her race, sex, religion, and profession do not disqualify her from being an archetypical American, reality has something else to say on the matter.

Special Agent Hope Copeland was born in Greenville, South Carolina, to college-educated parents saturated with an abiding Christian faith. The family made their home in the Nicholtown area, a parcel of land once part of a Revolutionary War veteran's plantation that became the city's first black community after nine black families acquired portions of it during the 1870s. A century later, when Hope arrived, Nicholtown was like many black American neighborhoods across the country in that it held tremendous socioeconomic diversity—the black poor, working class, middle class, and professionals all lived in the same community, producing leaders that would go on to notable careers at the local, state, and national levels. Thanks to a small-business loan made possible by Senator Strom Thurmond, whose excruciatingly slow and painful evolution on the race question remains an allegory for the nation, the Copeland family opened an early-childhood-development center. As a child, Hope could always be found in one of three places: church, the family school, or in the community bonding with relatives and neighbors.

Just as Hope entered her adolescent years, however, her parents separated. Her father, a military veteran, like most of the men in her family, remained in Greenville, South Carolina, while her mother took her and her siblings to Greenville, North Carolina, about a hundred miles southwest of the historically black Elizabeth City State University, where her parents had met. While at the North Carolina School of Science and Math, a selective residential high school in Durham, away from her family, Hope first visited a mosque.[41] A couple of years later, as an undergraduate student at North Carolina Central University, she converted to Islam. Her dyed-in-the-wool Christian parents were not pleased. One evening, her mother burst into the mosque where Hope worshipped and disowned her in front of everyone, exclaiming, "You can't be in this family and be a Muslim!" Hope was crushed. The next day, Hope was at the mosque in search of comfort and understanding when her mother suddenly appeared again. This time, in tears, her mother apologized profusely and asked Hope for forgiveness: "How can I disown my own child?! I don't agree with this religion, but you're still my child—you will always be my Hope!" Today, her mother sometimes goes to Friday prayers at the mosque with her—Hope facing east with knees, palms, and forehead to the ground; her mother sitting in the visiting section as a show of love and support for her daughter.

Hope's desire for a career in law enforcement mirrored the reason she decided to convert to Islam—justice. After graduating from college, she soon joined the North Carolina State Bureau of Investigations to put her passion for chemistry to good use, and she became a special agent in order to examine crime scenes. As she honed her skills as a forensic chemist, the FBI took notice, and Hope became the first black woman to work in the FBI's Scientific Response and Analysis Unit, a specialized team that investigates crimes involving chemical, biological, and nuclear weapons. "I paid attention to all the injustices around me when I was growing up. There was injustice in the education system, injustice in the judicial system, economic injustice in the communities where I was raised. Everywhere I looked in American society, there was injustice." And in the Copeland family, it isn't enough to believe in something; they are expected to act on their beliefs.

The idea that she is somehow less American and less of a citizen in the United States is laughable to Hope. "Because of my family's deep military background, we grew up believing there is no one more patriotic than our family. Our mantra was 'God, Family, Country.' Period." But this patriotism did not blind her family to the problems in the country, especially those concerning race. Where they saw problems, they saw a requirement to get involved. They have always been faithful voters. They do not skirt debates on politics and religion, but instead jump into them enthusiastically with others as well as among themselves. They have served as first responders and as faithful members of their communities. Her grandmother was so well known in Nicholtown for feeding hungry families that the city set aside a day in her honor after her death. They are a family steeped in a strong belief in participatory democracy.

Like those of countless black Americans across the country, hers is a story of superlative citizenship in the face of unequal treatment, as well as a model of solidarity. Hope and the Copeland family are religiously diverse, have differing political views on a range of issues, and do not always agree on the best way to correct injustice. But her devout Christian father takes his grandchildren to their Muslim school. On Christmas, they share a family dinner, with Hope providing the meat to ensure it is halal. When Hope fasts during Ramadan, some of her Christian relatives will join her. Though they see the world very differently, they exercise a solidarity with one another out of respect and in order to be living examples of what America should be.

To anyone who subscribes to the stereotypes and caricatures of law enforcement officers, black people, women of color, and hijab-wearing Muslims—or who believes that true Americans are white Christians, and any not in that mold are a lesser version—Special Agent Hope Copeland is an impossibility.

And yet, Hope is real.

Superlative citizenship is strategic. It is not a superficial endeavor geared toward white Americans in hopes that they will like their black countrymen better. It is an assertive claim on citizenship exercised within the terms and conditions set by the political and economic elites who hold power. It disputes stereotypical depictions of black Americans and demonstrates that there is absolutely nothing incompatible about being black and being American. It is a deliberate and concerted effort to point out how illogical and unethical it is to exclude black citizens from the full rights and protections of citizenship simply because of racist ideas about their value and dignity.

Superlative citizenship is a people's social, political, and moral claim on America and its professed ideals. It is also a concept that should be adopted and practiced by all Americans if we are to have a nation that can overcome the threat of racism and adhere to its principles. If superlative citizenship is the practice of exceeding one's obligations to the state and society for the purposes of creating a fairer and more equal nation, then the benefits of doing so are clearly universal. Yet, one of our biggest challenges is working toward true equality instead of accumulating advantages for ourselves at the expense of others. It is human nature to want to ensure the security and well-being of oneself and loved ones—superlative citizenship does not require placing those things on the altar for sacrifice. It does, however, require that we go out of our way to extend the reach of equality and justice to those who have too often been excluded. Superlative citizenship demonstrates a belief that all of us are worthy of the American tenets of life, liberty, and the pursuit of happiness.

When black Americans practiced the politics of respectability as a safety tactic and a means to claim civil rights, the ultimate objective was to make America be what it says it is. When black Americans went off to fight in wars for a democracy that treated them as lesser Americans, the goal was to push the country to live its creed. The fulfillment of the Promise means the end of racial inequality. So superlative citizenship has always been about the creation of a more perfect Union through the eradication of a racial hierarchy that excludes and endangers citizens for no reason other than their race.

Importantly, superlative citizenship is an individual decision. It advocates for change one person at a time. The nation's evolution into a more inclusive entity where full citizenship is not abridged because of one's race requires individuals to take actions within the span of their immediate control. And while these things cannot individually reshape America, they are indispensable to the larger project. They provide the characters and narratives that model what it means to be American. And, in the course of doing so, they spotlight a people's humanity and a national commitment to a fair and equitable society, which should be the aim of every citizen no matter their race. As Coretta Scott King famously remarked, "Freedom is never really won. You earn it and win it in every generation."[42]

Individual action is one of the three pillars of black solidarity that serves as a model for national solidarity. Just as black Americans have used superlative citizenship to make the Promise real, all Americans must do the same to bring about a national solidarity toward the same ends.

But personal behavior is insufficient. Solidarity also requires group action. And groups subjected to discrimination are most successful in obtaining government recognition and protection of their rights and liberties when they can show that their objectives are aligned to the national interest.

CHAPTER 4

Inclusion Trickles Down

Any attempt to compel the United States to take action on racism requires showing not only how the national identity is challenged by a failure to address it but also how the country's best interests can be achieved by promoting a more inclusive conception of America. This can happen in the strangest and most unexpected of places, even in a patch of land just a stone's throw south of the Mason-Dixon Line.

A rural highway in northeast Maryland is where the lights of the world stage once illuminated an American tragedy. Route 40 was the Main Street of America, a highway that by 1926 allowed road warriors to cross the country from San Francisco to Atlantic City's tourist traps flowing with illegal alcohol. In the 1960s, about 120 miles southwest of the infamous boardwalk and nightclubs, the Bonnie Brae diner sat in a quiet stretch of road between Baltimore and the inlet where the Susquehanna River pours itself into the Chesapeake Bay. Heading south in Edgewood, Maryland, one was hard-pressed to miss the large letters spelling "DINER" falling vertically down an L-shaped, arrowed sign, pointing to what looked like a white farmhouse with a wraparound porch and a rustic bare-wood corner entrance. On June 26, 1961, it caught the attention of Adam Malick Sow, the new ambassador from the African nation of

Chad, on his way to Washington, D.C. Sow was battling a splitting headache and decided a cup of coffee would take the edge off. His driver pulled the car into Bonnie Brae's lot, Sow stepped into the diner, and what unfolded would come to be known as the Route 40 Incident.

Ambassador Sow was part of a new class of African diplomats who arrived in the United States following the continent's decolonization. Between 1957 and 1961, just over twenty sub-Saharan nations gained their independence. These newly liberated nations needed to establish a presence in the United Nations and develop relationships with the U.S. government, requiring frequent travel between New York City and Washington, D.C. The Cold War between the United States and the Soviet Union was in full swing, and Africa quickly became an arena where the two superpowers jabbed at each other to gain the upper hand. It was in the American interest to ensure that the new African ambassadors felt welcomed and respected in order to curry favor with their nations and counter the Soviet Union's overtures, thereby furthering our strategic approach to winning the Cold War. On that day, Sow asked the diner's owner, Mrs. Leroy Merritt, for coffee; her peremptory refusal to serve a black person was not just an unfortunate indignity but became a crisis of American foreign policy.

Ambassador Sow's request for coffee was met with anger. "We don't serve niggers here," shot Merritt.[1] After a small row ensued as Sow tried to understand what was happening through his French-English translator, he was kicked out of the Bonnie Brae. Though this incident would garner international attention, it was just one in a series of such encounters in northern Maryland. Dr. William Fitzjohn, chargé d'affaires of Sierra Leone, was booted from the restaurant in a Howard Johnson hotel. Ambassador Issoufou Saidou-Djermakoye of Niger was refused service at multiple Route 40 diners, once with his driver and another time with his wife and son in tow.[2] Diplomats from Congo, Cameroon, Togo, and a number of other nations reported to the State Department that they had also faced the same discrimination. When questioned about their actions and told they were harming American interests, the diners' owners were unrepentant. Racial segregation was the way of life in these rolling hills at the base of Maryland's Piedmont; black people from Africa were treated just like black Americans. Besides, as Merritt so eloquently described her encounter with Ambassador Sow to a *Life* magazine reporter, "He looked just like an ordinary run of the mill nigger to me. I couldn't tell he was an ambassador."[3]

The Kennedy administration soon got wind of these slights and felt the pressure to act. The African ambassadors, not looking to embarrass the United States on the world stage, kept their complaints confined to their State Department contacts. Recognizing that U.S. interests were at risk, officials encouraged Ambassador Sow to detail the incident at the Bonnie Brae in his White House meeting with Kennedy. Upon hearing of Sow's experience, the president recognized that this treatment represented a vulnerability on which other nations could capitalize. The African diplomats understood this, too. One advised U.S. policymakers that racial discrimination was "the one and biggest obstacle to America being considered as the foremost nation of the world."[4] Sow remarked that "these humiliations are bad—everyone can exploit them."[5] Not wanting to lose influence in Africa to the Soviet Union because of white diner owners who refused to serve meals and coffee to black ambassadors, Kennedy directed his administration to work with Maryland state government leaders and legislatures, to personally visit restaurants that refused to serve black ambassadors, and to draft letters on his behalf expressing his concerns to Maryland's governor.[6]

All this outreach was met with resistance, especially from the restaurant proprietors. Clarence Rosier, the owner of the Cottage Inn Restaurant, said that he was a patriotic American, but he'd rather move to Russia than have the State Department dictate who he had to serve in his restaurant.[7] Others were more pragmatic, noting they were open to serving black people, but that their primarily white, truck-driving customers would be opposed and would only patronize the establishments that remained segregated. Earl Kammerer summed up the issue facing those wrestling with competing moral and economic motives: "It hurts me not to serve those people. It hurts me here [putting hand to heart]. But if I did serve them, it would hurt more here [slapping his wallet]."[8] The Kennedy administration was able to get state lawmakers onboard with enforcing racial desegregation along Route 40, but the diners' refusal to comply led to more federal lobbying and a series of protests by black activists from the civil rights organization Congress of Racial Equality. A White House assistant told the owners that "the eyes of the world are focused on the restaurants right here on Route 40."[9]

Desegregation finally arrived on Route 40 through compromise. The actions of the federal government, state lawmakers, the media, and black activists broke the impasse, and a few dozen Route 40 restaurants agreed to serve black African diplomats in support of the national interest. All did not go smoothly. There were several instances of diners locking doors and turning off the lights when ambassadors and their staffs arrived, demanding to see credentials before proffering meal service, and apologizing loudly to white customers who had to endure eating alongside black diplomats. Even with these slights, the incomplete victory on Route 40 was sufficient to meet the United States' diplomatic objectives.

However, when word got out that some of these diners desegregated, local black citizens attempted to eat at them and were turned away. The diner owners had only agreed to serve African diplomats to help the national interest; black Americans were still unwelcome. Dining privileges and exclusion from racial discrimination were extended to black people from Africa but denied to black people from America. Black Americans' rights extended only as far as the national interest required, and in this instance, there was no interest in further disrupting public life in rural Maryland by demanding racial integration beyond African diplomats.

Three black American newspaper reporters, resolute on demonstrating the ridiculous behavior of the white diner owners, dressed up as African diplomats from the fake country of Goban and visited restaurants that had turned away black Americans.[10] Though they could not get service as black Americans, as diplomats they were served at nearly every restaurant and were even asked for autographs and escorted to private dining areas. Rights and privileges of citizenship managed to find their way to fake Africans—again satisfying the national interest. Several years passed along with threats of large-scale protests before black Americans were treated almost as well as the costumed diplomats from the fictional country of Goban.

THE BLACK AMERICAN EXPERIENCE has long been described as a textbook example of second-class citizenship. In democracies, second-class citizens are those people whose membership in society is generally accepted but whose access to the full rights and opportunities of citizenship are restricted simply because they belong to a specific group. This lower classification can refer to the legal abridgment of rights or the experience of unequal treatment by socioeconomic and political systems and institutions. Thus, sometimes this status is explicit and enforceable by law, and sometimes it is implicit in how society views and treats specific citizens. Black America has tasted both.

People excluded from full citizenship status often believe that attaining it would lead to social and economic equality. But political theorist Iris Marion Young found that a strict adherence to the principle of equal treatment tends to perpetuate preexisting group hierarchies: the better-positioned group emerging from an unequal society usually maintains its status when the playing field is suddenly declared fair.[11] So while the United States has unquestionably become a more inclusive country and adopted a more expansive conception of who can be a member of the citizenry, the equality it promises remains aspirational if the legacy of hierarchy is not directly confronted.

The notion of second-class citizenship is troublesome to the American myth's suggestion that all citizenship is first-class and, moreover, that no other class exists. We know in practice, however, that this is simply not the case. In response, we did what people usually do when they must navigate the valley between their ideals and their reality: we divined a myth—in our case, the myth of the melting pot. The visual of our differences being melted away in a fired cauldron seemed particularly suited to countering the idea that we are inherently and unjustly different and unequal.

We tend to define *myth* as a well-traveled story or idea that is commonly held but largely or entirely untrue, such as that of a young George Washington declaring that he could not tell a lie about cutting down his father's cherry tree. We know such stories are false, but we are willing to overlook this in favor of the valuable lesson or virtue they communicate. In a sense, we see such myths as gentle lies with honorable intentions.

But when myths are used as a political tool to appease the public, the intent is no longer honorable. Plato labels this sort of story a "noble lie" in his classic allegorical text *Republic*. In the realm of politics and governance, a noble lie is a story told by people in power to maintain control while providing the public with a sense of purpose and unity. Plato explains the concept using a parable usually called the "myth of metals." The *Republic*'s perfectly just country has three types of people: rulers who are made of gold, guardians and auxiliaries of silver, and the common man of brass or iron. The myth says people are created in one of these three elements, and they cannot change their metal or place in society. Daring to do so would place the nation and all its citizens in danger. People of different metals cannot marry, and children usually inherit the metallic makeup of their parents. In those rare instances when a child is born differently, he or she must be removed from the parents and dwell with metallic kin.

In a critical element of the myth, all citizens are told they are related, since metals come from the same earth. The objective of this noble lie is to create national loyalty by weaving one's value into the well-being of the state and to maintain social harmony by convincing citizens that their rank in society is ordained by the heavens. To betray the caste would not only betray the country and one's family but would also be immoral and an affront to the divine order. Though none of this is true, citizens are told this lie to keep the country peaceful, functioning, and unified. A lie, as it were, under the guise of noble intentions.

The United States has, at times, resembled this metallic state. Black people's enslavement was justified as being the divine and natural order of things. The diaries of slaveholders describe the necessity that an enslaved black person must "understand that bondage was their natural status" and "feel that African ancestry tainted them, that their color was a badge of degradation." Further, slaveholders believed it important to "create in [enslaved black people] a habit of perfect dependence," demanding loyalty through the "principle of fear" and convincing them that slavery was in their best interest.[12] During Jim Crow, an order of tiered metals still existed, in which the nation declared that white Americans were more precious than their fellow black countrymen. Despite our myth, which suggests that the Creator made us all equal no matter the condition of our birth, in practice our nation demonstrated a deep conviction in the noble lie that second-class citizenship is essential to its well-being.

In this light, the melting-pot motif takes on additional meaning. E pluribus unum—"out of many, one"—seems newly applicable to the manifestation of a unified and harmonious nation that the melting-pot concept conveys.[13] The implication is that there are no longer any gold, silver, brass, or iron levels of citizenship; they have all been melted into a uniquely American alloy. This concept has taken heat because of its implication of wholesale assimilation that would melt away the cultural diversity of its different groups. But the powerful argument that America was founded on an idea provides a common bond for kinship to be created among dissimilar groups, a notion fully in step with the melting pot. The American alloy that pours from the crucible fills a new mold with a new metal. E pluribus unum.

But another view of the melting pot myth is revealed after asking who is doing the pouring, who is melted, and who is doing the melting.[14] The American myth suggests that the Creator is the metallurgist, but U.S. history demonstrates that those who hold political and economic power are the actual blacksmiths. The inalienable rights that are supposed to be dispensed equally from the melting pot are really just specific rights that the nation-state and those who govern it allow to flow to the different segments of the public. And they also judge the resulting American ingots and sort them according to an arbitrary standard of quality and value. This process is constructed for the sole purpose of ensuring their hold on power and control of resources remains intact.

This is trickle-down citizenship. The course of our national history has shown that the progress of black Americans from enslavement to Jim Crow's second-class citizens to our present state is what happens when rights and protections immediately granted to some Americans at the United States' founding slowly trickle down to those initially excluded from them completely. Only after centuries and war and many lost souls did the precious American alloy of democratic inclusion finally begin to reach its black citizens.

The truth is that black Americans have always experienced trickle-down citizenship. They gradually gained access to more of the rights, privileges, and benefits of citizenship that others have long enjoyed. But this trickling was not the result of happenstance. It was not bound to happen, the inevitable effect of the immutable forces, like time or gravity. It was not the outcome of sporadic, divine deluges of moral epiphanies about human dignity and the equality of enslaved or legally oppressed black people. Instead, the rights that black Americans enjoy more fully today than at any point in American history have trickled down from the actions the nation has taken when pursuing its interests elsewhere, like in Africa through the courting of newly appointed ambassadors traveling along Route 40 in rural Maryland.

The expansion of the American idea to be more inclusive of its black citizens has been the byproduct of the United States protecting or advancing its interests, not the result of a compelling need to adhere finally to the self-evident truths in its founding documents. Whether it employs myths or noble lies to justify itself, a nation is governed solely by its interests. Moreover, trickle-down citizenship is not only predicated on the pursuit of a deeply important national interest; it requires that those seeking equality bundle their objective with that interest as well as the moral heft of the American myth.

The extension of rights to black citizens requires the stars to align. The moral high ground is rarely sufficient to win political arguments, expand access to citizenship, and alter the course of a nation. So trickle-down citizenship must be opportunistic. And patient.

PATIENCE AND OPPORTUNISM—these are concepts that families of black America know well. At my mother's family gathering in 1999, when five of Daddy Joe's six daughters told us of our enslaved African ancestor Kincey, one of the Sisters spotlighted under Georgia's sweltering sun was Orrie Bell, my energetic, quick-witted grandmother. During long childhood summers exploring rural life on my grandparents' farm, she filled me with homemade fig preserve and biscuits at breakfast, blackberry doobie after dinner, and a deep appreciation for the faith and strength of the elders. The censuses from the early twentieth century show quite a few people in Georgia named Orrie who were born in her year of 1915—white and black, boys and girls. But in the syrupy patois of those wise old black folk who weathered the worst of times, *She is the onliest one I have ever known*, and *It is well with my soul*.

My grandmother loomed large in the hearts and minds of the family. She was into her late sixties by the time my memories of her kick in: of riding in the back of her tan Oldsmobile down dusty roads to church, of watching her walk across the yard to the small family country store where passersby stopped for relief from the summer heat, of her standing in a housedress smiling through glasses and loose bangs as we spilled out from our cars' long sojourn south to her corner of the earth. She was a daughter of the segregated South who hoped to bear witness to America's racial progress.

In 1936, at the age of twenty-one, Orrie Bell Humphrey married Bobby Lee, a young man who had grown up a few houses down from her childhood home along the country road guarded by endless rows of puffed cotton bolls and the swaying plumes of corn stalks. He was tall and sinewy and quite the dancer in his day. But once my summer visits began some forty-five years later, he was the quiet, hardworking patriarch who woke with the roosters but settled with his coffee and pipe by the time the sun decided to rise and shine. He made it to the seventh grade before the fields called him to hew a living negotiating Georgia's red clay, as so many had done before him. Orrie was educated at the segregated Early County Training School and developed a lifelong love of reading. My grandparents' house was filled with books of all sorts, and I would come in from playing, drenched in sweat and caked in dirt, to find my grandmother Orrie Bell sitting quietly with her legs crossed and her eyes dancing with the words of some paperback. She would tell me one day in her southwest Georgian drawl fingerprinted with a smile, "I may be an old woman in Blakely, but with a book, I can go anywhere in the world."

The 1950s were a bustling time for my grandparents in Early County, Georgia. Its population was around eighteen thousand—one of its highest levels in history and twice its current size. My grandparents entered the decade as sharecroppers and exited it as landowners with a house and the promise of better schooling for their children. When the Supreme Court determined that racial segregation and the "separate but equal" doctrine were unconstitutional in 1954's landmark case *Brown v. Board of Education*, Bobby and Orrie had six children who had known only segregated living and schooling. The following year, they finally convinced a white loan officer to approve a mortgage for just over one hundred acres of land by flashing every single dollar they owned in his face.

On this land, they built the house where many of their children and grandchildren would grow, including my mother, Sandra Jo—her middle name coming from Daddy Joe and his casual confidence, displayed in the American-flagged photo on the wall. Orrie and Bobby's progress could have been hijacked by those who claimed that charges of racism were overblown, offering the couple as proof that the Promise could touch rural black citizens who adhered to the gospel of hard work, natural cleverness, and a proactive Christian faith. But by the end of the decade, now with a total of eight children, my grandparents were still indigent, the schools still segregated, and economic and political rights still forbidden from trickling down to black people.

My grandparents' oldest daughter, Gwen, was something of a local track phenom in high school in the mid-1950s. Upon graduation from the segregated high school, she was invited to Tennessee State University's summer training program to be part of the legendary Tigerbelles, the women's track team coached by Olympic Hall of Famer Ed Temple. That summer in Nashville, she roomed with Wilma Rudolph, who would go on to win multiple Olympic gold medals and the title of "fastest woman in the world." When the summer was up, Coach Temple told my aunt Gwen that he had an athletic scholarship for her, but my grandparents would need to pay the remaining costs not covered by the scholarship. It was $100, and my grandparents did not have it and could not get it. That may seem like a paltry sum, but $100 then was the equivalent of about $1,000 today. And only two in five Americans today have enough cash on hand to cover a $1,000 emergency.[15] So in 1950s Jim Crow Georgia, where credit cards and personal loans and community wealth were nonexistent, $100 was more than a sufficient roadblock to keep Gwen out of Tennessee State, an already underfunded historically black university despite its world-famous reputation. And segregation ensured her athletic talent was forbidden from the tracks of the flagship state universities. Structural racism is not just some unfortunate shortcoming in our national myth; it is a killer of dreams and potential and opportunity.

When my mother, Sandra—the fifth of the eight children—arrived in high school, she dove into her schoolwork with a passion that had long flowed in the blood of black children who had been instructed about the saving grace of education. Her older siblings, including Gwen, had all left Georgia, moving to the Northeast along with many other black citizens in search of economic opportunity and to escape the racial violence that haunted life in the Deep South. She spent the summers between school years living with family in Newark, New Jersey, and working to make money, experiences that broadened her worldview in a way that further inspired her academic diligence. College would be her way out. When my mother graduated in 1970, she was the valedictorian of her still-segregated high school, named after Booker T. Washington, and she received a full scholarship to Shaw University, a private, historically black liberal arts school in North Carolina founded before the Civil War ended. Though she began elementary school three years after *Brown v. Board*, all her primary and secondary education occurred in still-segregated schools. As my mother left her home for college, the constitutional right to a desegregated education still had not trickled down.

The fall following her graduation from high school, the stars aligned, and the black students in Blakely, Georgia, were permitted to attend the better-resourced high school with their white peers. Desegregation finally descended on the patient and opportunistic black citizens working in the Georgian kiln, where red clay baked and men and women of iron wills persisted, even if the reach of the Constitution arrived a bit too late for five of Bobby and Orrie Bell's eight children.

NOT SURPRISINGLY, given the myths, the expression *trickle-down* has its roots in metal. The late nineteenth-century politician William Jennings Bryan gave voice to this concept in his famous 1896 oration that has come to be called the "Cross of Gold" speech. In it, Bryan criticized the gold standard as the basis for the value of a dollar and, instead, promoted bimetallism, which would allow silver to be used along with gold. It was a hotly contested political issue during this period because the abundant supply of silver would help indebted citizens more easily pay off their creditors, but it would also cause massive inflation that could have terrible effects on the national economy. Bryan, a populist agitator who delivered the address at the Democratic National Convention on his way to the party's nomination, sought to cast the issue of bimetallism as a question about whether government was meant to serve the people or economic elites. "There are two ideas of government," Bryan reasoned. "There are those who believe that if you just legislate to make the well-to-do prosperous, that their prosperity will leak through on those below. The Democratic idea has been that if you legislate to make the masses prosperous their prosperity will find its way up and through every class that rests upon it."[16]

Trickle-down became a go-to description for economic policy in which the most well-to-do in society are treated favorably by the government under the premise that their wealth will find its way down to those with little to none. Actor and satirist Will Rogers is credited with popularizing the actual phrase, writing in 1932 that the government's preference was to appropriate money "for the top in hopes that it would trickle down to the needy."[17] Nonetheless, for over a half century now, *trickle-down economics* has been considered a pejorative in most political circles. The idea that government should be oriented to assist economic elites instead of making the common people its primary focus feels antithetical to America's democratic ideals. Our Declaration of Independence says that government derives its power from the consent of the governed, the free and equal people endowed with unalienable rights. Trickle-down economics conveys a tiered, hierarchical view of a society in which those made of brass or iron realize only residual benefits in a system that is supposed to work specifically for their benefit.

The trickle-down concept applies equally well when the commodity is the rights and privileges of citizenship instead of economic policy. The democratic inclusion that black Americans enjoy today has been widely available to other citizens for much longer. Rights, like the origins of many private citizens' wealth, flow from the government, which has poured them on some citizens in full and then allowed them to trickle down to those below when it was in the nation's interest to do so.

Certainly, all our rights as citizens necessarily originate with the nation-state; that is true no matter our race. But the extension of fuller citizen status to black Americans managed to trickle down only when the United States was obsessed with what it deemed to be more important, and unrelated, international and domestic policy pursuits elsewhere. Black America's progress has often been the byproduct of the nation chasing an interest that requires progress on civil rights to occur for the desired objective to be realized. Black citizenship has never been a focus of the national interest—it has only been a coincidentally favorable derivative of a solution to some other problem.

For a nation that treasures equality and liberty, treating those principles as game pieces to be maneuvered in service of secular goals undercuts the high-mindedness and sanctity we attribute to our ideals. Using them in this way, however, does not detract from the power they hold. Indeed, it is due to their pedestaling that principled appeals resonate and can be acted on when savvy actors align moral interests with a national interest. In this way, trickle-down citizenship, like superlative citizenship, can be used as a political strategy for racial equality. It allows the layering of a moral claim onto a national objective and pairs that claim with the all-important task of protecting the national identity. Put another way, it is co-optive—it employs a strategy that convinces the nation that taking a moral action is the only way it can achieve a specific material interest.

That nations have interests, not morals, can grate on one's patriotic sensibilities. Because a nation is said to have character and identity, it would seem to follow that such an entity must also possess morality. But morality requires a distinction between relatively static notions of right and wrong, and for a nation, what is right for it is what sustains it; what is wrong is what harms it. Neither are fixed—what is wrong today can be right tomorrow. For example, the United States is a nation founded on democratic and liberal principles in which our character and identity are enshrined. And yet the history of black America is a series of battles with antidemocratic, illiberal policies and practices, from slavery and violent terrorism to the lack of enforcement of constitutional rights and protections. We, as Americans today, can agree that slavery and Jim Crow were immoral, and yet those institutions were sanctioned by the government for centuries. We agree that genocide is immoral, but the United States rarely engages to stop genocide when it occurs. This is not because the United States is immoral—it is because the nation, like any geopolitical entity, is amoral.

This is not new thinking. In 1891, the Scottish philosopher W.R. Sorley argued that nations are subject to morality only in the sense that they are composed of people with a moral sense. Nations are rarely sanctioned if they fall short of the people's moral sense as long as they succeed in the primary duty of providing security and purpose, which are central to self-preservation and self-development. Further, according to Sorley, when nations interact, they are driven by their self-interests, not by an internationally accepted sense of morality. And without a global agreement on morality and a sanctioning power to ensure adherence to it, nations' self-interests must assume primacy if they are to survive and thrive on the world stage.[18] World history is essentially a littered collection of stories about polities pursuing interests. It is why the renowned military theorist Carl von Clausewitz famously remarked, "War is the continuation of politics by other means"—because it is a contest of competing interests. If nations were instead governed by morality, perhaps Clausewitz would have opined that war is a transcendental religious exercise rather than a political one.

Nations, however, and the economic and political elites that hold the most sway over them, recognize the power of moral claims. It is why the American myth has been so instrumental in all the racial progress the United States has witnessed since its inception. And it also why our leaders routinely use language that entangles the national interest with their sense of the responsibilities of American morality.

Presidents' uses of moral claims are often at odds with each other and the broader public will. In Donald Trump's 2016 presidential campaign, he made the case that reforming healthcare and reducing the number of uninsured, undocumented immigrants receiving such care were in the nation's economic interest. Further, Trump added, "It is the moral responsibility of a nation's government to do what is best for the people and what is in the interest of securing the future of the nation."[19] When Barack Obama accepted the Nobel Peace Prize in 2009, he proclaimed that the United States had engaged in twentieth-century wars "out of enlightened self-interest."[20] Obama argued that the moral cause of ensuring that more people could touch freedom and prosperity also motivated the pursuit of the nation's interest through violent conflicts. John Kennedy said the White House is the center of both political leadership and moral leadership because "only the President represents the national interest. And upon him alone converge all the needs and aspirations of all parts of the country, all departments of the government, all nations of the world."[21]

At his first inauguration, Ronald Reagan assured the nation and the world that "when action is required to preserve our national security, we will act." But he went on to say that "no arsenal or no weapon in the arsenals of the world is so formidable as the will and moral courage of free men and women"—a weapon, he believed, that was in our possession but that our adversaries lacked.[22] More than a century ago, during his historic speech in Osawatomie, Kansas, Teddy Roosevelt told a rapt audience that "no wisdom of legislation or administration really means anything" without morality. But, he cautioned, securing social and economic interests must be the prime objective, because morality, on its own, is an insufficient and unreliable motive for action.[23]

Collapsing morality and national interest may make for beautiful rhetoric that compels the public, but in practice, interest prevails. Consider the simple issue of national apologies. Americans agree that slavery was immoral, inhumane, and inconsistent with our national values. But when people are asked whether the United States should issue a formal apology for enslaving black people, common ground is hard to find. Only two in five Americans think the government should apologize for slavery, and there are clear racial and partisan cleavages—half of Democrats and two out of three black Americans believe the nation should apologize, compared with 28 percent of Republicans and 38 percent of white Americans.[24] Given that racism in the United States is often presented as an interpersonal matter between white citizens and people of color, these differences in opinion should be of little surprise. Why our government would engage in a civil war and pass constitutional amendments to abolish slavery but not offer a formal apology for engaging in it in the first place is a resonant question. The answer is quite straightforward: it was in the interest of the nation to keep slavery in the late eighteenth century, and it was in the nation's interest to abolish it in the 1860s. But it has never been in the interest of the nation today to apologize for it, because national apologies are not moral gestures—they are political ones.

When a state issues a formal apology, it accepts culpability for what occurred and acknowledges its responsibility to make it right. This is not a small matter. Apologies affect the balance of power between entities, with the one doing the apologizing surrendering some measure of status to the one receiving it. And nations tend to be wholly uninterested in conceding power and influence unless its goals are advanced by doing so. Not only do apologies require states to expend resources, but the return on those expenditures is often in moral currency rather than political capital. And, again, states have little use for moral purity that does not advance a national interest. International relations scholars are devoting more attention to ontological security, or the protection of the nation-state's self-identity, and they have noted that formal state apologies expand responsibility, change the state's identity, and disrupt its narrative and mythology, the creation and maintenance of which is one of the most political acts it undertakes.[25] Nations draw power from safeguarding their resources and protecting their identities—apologies put those things at risk and offer little to no material reward.

This helps explain the U.S. approach thus far when it comes to a slavery apology. Rather than a formal state or presidential apology for slavery and Jim Crow, the rhetoric instead tends to acknowledge the evils of slavery and concede only regret that it occurred. In 2008, however, the House of Representatives issued a resolution apologizing to "African-Americans on behalf of the U.S. people for wrongs committed against them and their ancestors."[26] The following year, the U.S. Senate passed a similar measure, adding a small provision that changed everything: "Nothing in this resolution authorizes, supports, or serves as a settlement of any claim against the United States."[27] The resolutions admitted an injustice had occurred, but they accepted no blame, and thus no responsibility, and the Senate version explicitly exempted the United States from culpability. While the resolutions are notable instances of morality in and of themselves, they had no impact on the national interest. This is the only reason they passed—because it cost the state nothing. And it still took more than 140 years after the abolition of slavery to happen. In this way, when considering only the politics of the matter and not the morality of the symbolic gestures, the resolutions held as much policy weight as the congressional resolutions that congratulate winning Super Bowl teams.

Because of the differing language in the two resolutions, no joint congressional statement resulted that could be endorsed by the president. If that had occurred, complete with a ceremonial signing in the East Room of the White House, it would have had all the trappings of a formal state apology. Instead, in the end, the interest of the state won out over the moral imperative, just as Theodore Roosevelt said would always happen.

Trickle-down citizenship is a concept that accounts for the alchemy that mixes morality, national interest, democratic principles, "real Americans," excluded groups, and heavenly ordinations of our republic into an elixir that helps those with power see the political advantages to be gained by extending rights and inclusion to those historically excluded. It is a recognition that acquiring rights is a fundamentally political endeavor, even if the case made for why those rights should be extended is couched in moral terms. But this does not suggest that the American idea is solely a transactional concept with no foundation in higher truths. Rather, the United States' slow inclusion of previously excluded groups is a testament to the power of the values, principles, and Promise on which it was founded to move the nation forward.

The preamble of the Constitution refers to the goal of the American people being the formation of "a more perfect Union." Wrapped up in this well-traveled and deeply respected vision of America is a recognition that we live in an exceptional nation that has yet to live up to its Promise, as well as an understanding of the moral distance that must be traveled to get from who we are to who we profess to be. And because we are people organized into a nation-state, politics is the vehicle that moves us along the path. There is little shame in using political means to achieve a moral end. Trickle-down citizenship is both a resolute declaration that America falls short and evidence that people united in a common cause can inch it toward becoming more perfect, more united, more American.

THE TRICKLE-DOWN CITIZENSHIP that has characterized the black American experience exposes America's primary shortfall: we are a nation of tiered citizenship that believes in equality. This resilient belief is what powers an ever-expanding notion of who can be truly American. But the fact that our ideas about who qualifies as a full citizen are in continuous need of expansion proves that equality remains elusive. The same pride we have in the country's racial progress since its founding must be matched by the stark realization that one's race affects one's life chances. This is a truth we must embrace if we are to find the common ground and bonds of kinship necessary to create a national solidarity across racial lines.

There are two important and competing realities to contend with to fully understand the trickling down of democratic inclusion. First, the history of black America could be viewed as confirmation that the American mythos is actually a modern version of the Socratic noble lie. The abridgement of black citizens' rights, and the evolution of tactics employed to keep full citizenship beyond their grasp, certainly appears to resemble the lesser existence of citizens described by the myth of metals. Meanwhile, the national narrative

of equality, liberty, and opportunity is trafficked in massive quanti-
ties to placate the populace and suggest each individual's station
in life was either the work of the Creator or the result of personal
weakness and defect. Trickle-down citizenship at a given moment
in time could be spun into a logic that suggests our founding principles were used only to inspire people of the Revolutionary Era to
support independence and never intended to be fully realized for
all Americans—then, later, or now.

But this view ignores the temporal quality of trickle-down. A
longitudinal consideration of black Americans' rights shows the
steady progress from being totally devoid of all rights to achieving
a citizen status that is far less disparate than it has ever been. In
this way, the American mythos may indeed be an idealized narrative scrubbed of the inconvenient facts, but it is durable and flex-
ible enough to envelope Jefferson's arguments for independence,
Lincoln's rhetoric on emancipation, and King's call for civil rights.
Trickle-down accords with our mythos because it implies forward
motion. The progress it embodies is proof that, with the right incentives, we can inch ever closer to a nation of equality. If, as King
suggested in his adaption of a quote from the American Transcen-
dentalist Theodore Parker, "the arc of the moral universe is long, but
it bends towards justice," then second-class citizenship is a point on
that arc[28]—trickle-down citizenship is the bend.

Trickle-down citizenship also demonstrates the formula for
creating the national solidarity needed to overcome racism. It
shows that coupling a moral imperative with a national interest can
effect change if it is couched in terms that align with our mythos.
Attempts to confront racism by appealing exclusively to the public's sense of morality will fail, just as they failed Bobby and Orrie
Bell's children and the segregated education they received despite
its unconstitutionality. However, if the national interest alone is
leveraged to dismantle the results of structural racism in our society,
it, too, will fail. Massive federal stimulus bills to rescue the national

economy—like those signed by Presidents Bush in 2008, Obama in 2009, and Trump in 2020—that increased racial disparities in small-business assistance, home ownership, and household wealth are proof. And if both these pieces are in place but unanchored in the American mythos, the economic and political elites that command outsize influence of our nation will not have the tools to influence and inspire the public to accept a changed course. Trickle-down citizenship is a reminder that the extension of rights to previously excluded groups is a matter of cold political calculus, not of warm, fuzzy feelings about our exceptionalism.

Black America has leveraged the trickle-down strategy to push racial progress in the United States. When the Cold War was raging, civil rights leaders pointed to the national security harm being done by racial discrimination at home. When presidential campaigns were running the risk of losing elections—like Truman in 1948 and Kennedy in 1960—they reached out to black constituents through symbolic and material civil rights policy gestures to mobilize black voters. Everything from desegregating the military and passing Great Society legislation to issuing a national apology for the Tuskegee experiment and making Martin Luther King's birthday a national holiday is the result of political calculations by parties and presidents, not by a national dawning of moral clarity on the race question. Trickle-down citizenship recognizes elites' political and electoral interests and piggybacks policies for racial equality onto them.

Superlative citizenship and the concept of rights trickling down to those previously excluded are two of the three pillars of black America's strivings that can be emulated nationally to establish a multiracial solidarity. Whereas superlative citizenship is an individual action, trickle-down citizenship is a group pursuit focused on leveraging the national interest to attain its own goals. By fulfilling our obligations to the state—even when that commitment is not completely reciprocated—and by capitalizing on the moral, national, and narrative forces that bend the state toward truer equality, we can create a country that staves off the destructive effects of racism. Moreover, we can make our contribution to constructing the nation of our myths. Yet, while we would like to think that passing better laws and implementing policies of equality will solve the issue, the project is such an enormous undertaking that even the instruments of democracy alone cannot get us there—only solidarity will do. And the practice of black solidarity is the third and final pillar of the model for a national version; it is also the most critical. It shows that true solidarity requires us to be obligated to one another for a moral cause.

CHAPTER 5

Black Solidarity

Theodore Roosevelt Johnson, my grandfather, was born in 1918, three months before the "war to end all wars" ended. His parents, Will and Annie, branded him with visions of a more racially equitable America via his name. But for whatever hopes that name carried, Theo's reality soon aligned to the unjust and unequal life of a black citizen in segregated South Carolina. By the time he was eleven years old, he was plucked from the classroom and planted in the rows of farmland where the blood, sweat, and tears of black Americans were sowed alongside their dreams for liberty and equality.

When he was nineteen, Theo married Louisa, the only child of Celia Richardson. Though the 1940 census suggests otherwise, my family knows Celia was born in Trinidad. My father still recalls how she spoke and that her words never lost the distinct seasoning of the island's creole. Family lore has it that she made her way to the United States sometime around 1920, arriving in South Carolina already pregnant with Louisa. Celia married a preacher some years later, but the identity of my grandmother Louisa's biological father in Trinidad went to the grave with her mother.[1] Theo and Louisa immediately began a family and soon moved in with Celia and her husband, subsisting on his $500-a-year salary as a wash boy and the $350 Celia brought home as a hotel maid. My grandparents eventually had eleven children who survived into adulthood. Life in Marlboro County consisted of the same things it always had—farming, exploitive economic arrangements, and racial inequality. Amid all the injustice, Theo received the call to ministry.

By the time he was in his forties, Reverend Theo Johnson had all the markings of a local boy made good. He and Louisa owned land in Marlboro County and grew brightleaf tobacco with plenty of help from their children, boys and girls alike. My father, aunts, and uncles recall the Reverend proudly walking around his farm calling out orders, clad in a suit and bootblacked oxfords. They say he always kept a new car and moved through the town with a peacocked swagger that was his daring declaration of dignity and importance—Jim Crow be damned. But my father and his siblings aimed to be much less conspicuous while laboring between the towering rows of tobacco. At the height of the season, they would often miss school to work in the fields harvesting the crop, kneeling down between the plants to hide from the school bus filled with their friends as it passed by. But every morning, their eagle-eyed classmates spotted them among the wide green leaves and yelled from the windows, between laughs and pointed fingers cutting through the air, "We see y'all up in there!"

Despite the salience of agricultural work, Theo and Louisa recognized the importance of education. As my father tells it, the Reverend was especially adamant that his daughters had options other than being a washerwoman or domestic in a white person's home. Black women working in white households not only experienced labor and wage exploitation, but also were subject to sexual and physical violence. Undoubtedly, their lives would be marred by an intimate form of constant degradation, since black women were cast as immoral and promiscuous. As one Southern white woman wrote in 1904: black women "are the greatest menace possible to the moral life of any community where they live . . . I cannot imagine such a creation as a virtuous black woman."[2] Theo and Louisa were having none of that for their girls. They wanted each of their five daughters to go to college and escape Jim Crow's economic and social traps, the first generation of the Johnson family to do so. And though Theo and Louisa did not live to see it, their dream came true. All my father's sisters went to college, and today one is a minister and two hold doctoral degrees.

My father, Theodore Roosevelt Johnson, Jr., was born in 1950, the fifth of six boys. For reasons not immediately clear, the Reverend waited until this fifth son to pass on his name. Theo took a different approach to his sons and demanded they earn their keep by tending the soil, and that is work none of the boys wanted to spend the rest of his life doing. So my father—known by the Southern-fried pronunciation of his name, *Thehdoe*—left home as a teenager to find opportunities elsewhere. After a meandering path of work and secondary education landed him in Dallas, Texas, he returned home when his mother fell ill in 1971. The last words she spoke to him were "Thehdoe, please go back to school."

On August 17, 1971, Louisa Johnson died, and the next day my father enrolled at a community college in Rock Hill, South Carolina.

A couple of years later, now going by the name Ted, he was off to Shaw University. The college was established in December 1865 as a Bible class taught to newly freed black Americans under the shade of large Carolina pine trees and in paltry cabins devoid of comforts but filled with intellectual curiosity. When he arrived on campus in the fall of 1973, it was situated in the heart of the capital city, due south of the capitol itself, etched with concrete walkways connecting the buildings, and interspersed with large grass plots adorned with the colorful bricks and Greek letters of the university's vibrant fraternities and sororities. Shaw was where my parents—Sandra Lee from the red clay of Early County, Georgia, and Theodore Roosevelt Johnson, Jr., from the tobacco fields of Marlboro County, South

Carolina—met, and Raleigh is where they would raise a family. They both were reared in segregated communities, attended segregated schools, worshipped in segregated churches, and went to a predominantly black university. Like generations of black Americans before them, they learned the importance of racial solidarity while confined to segregated spaces. They knew that family, faith, and education were instrumental in managing racial discrimination, but the marrow in their bones carried a wisdom scored by the crack of the overseer's whip, the biting grip of the policeman's canine, and the searing heat of racial violence. That wisdom showed them that solidarity was the only means to survive racism and the best means of making inroads against the destruction it fuels.

The winter before my father left for Shaw University, Reverend Theo Johnson was giving a eulogy for one of his parishioners. Standing tall in the pulpit, he engaged in the preaching tradition that black ministers have honed through the decades, adorning his words of celebratory remembrance with melodies, etymologies, divine parables, and crescendo closings that intersperse passion with pregnant pauses. The congregation worked to a fever pitch, Theo concluded by thrusting his hand to the heavens and exclaiming, "I'll see you on the other side!" He then took his seat as the church filled with shouts, wails, and tears. In the pastor's chair he sat, head bowed and hand on his heart, looking to be deep in a somber prayer. Once the church stood for the benediction, however, it became clear what had really happened. He had died right there, at just fifty-five years old, in his own bully pulpit.

Two years, two graduations, and a day-after-Christmas wedding later, Ted and Sandra Johnson welcomed their first child into the world. My father gave me the name that his now-deceased father had given him, which had blossomed from the dreams sowed by two black sharecroppers inspired by a White House dinner: Theodore Roosevelt Johnson, III. I was born on August 17, 1975, four years to the day after my father said goodbye to his mother, Louisa.

*　*　*

JUST OVER 400 YEARS AGO, the African captives who made the *black American* conceivable arrived on the shores of Point Comfort at the southeastern tip of the Virginia Peninsula. Some 350 years later, the passage of the Civil Rights Act of 1964 ended the constitutionally flimsy "separate but equal" doctrine that ensured social and civic distance between black and white Americans. These two occurrences bookend the long story of lawful racial segregation in America. Altogether, more than 85 percent of black peoples' presence in the United States has been characterized by compulsory exclusion from equality and full citizenship, and the remaining time ticks with persistent racial inequality and segregated housing, schools, and social institutions. Bearing the brunt of such discrimination for so long and being effectively ostracized from the larger society required the creation and evolution of group survival tactics.

The first waves of transatlantic black arrivals in the American colonies were from different places in Africa, shared different ancestors, spoke different languages and dialects, practiced different customs, held different religious beliefs, and were different from their fellow captives in any number of other ways. They shared one thing: black skin. Once in the American clime, this one immutable feature of birth fused dissimilar people into a singular group for no reason other than their race and for no purpose other than their free labor. Subjected to racial violence, e pluribus unum, many peoples became a people. This nascent group—the African Americans—found solidarity in a shared experience of enslavement and a shared desire for liberty. Black solidarity is neither the product of some tribal genetic tendency nor baked into DNA like the texture of hair or the melanin in skin; it is not a biological impulse that cannot be resisted. Instead, black solidarity emerged as a deliberate, necessary, and targeted political tactic in response to injustice and human suffering.

Black solidarity can mean different things to different people. For some, it suggests a social bond and identity reflected in each member's adherence to a set of cultural norms and behaviors. Another interpretation contains qualities of nationalism wherein segregation is not necessarily an evil—in fact, some separatists deem it desirable—as long as it is accompanied by true black freedom and liberty. But while these versions may have some utility in countering the devaluation and negative stereotypes of black people, they do not advance the American project.

The most beneficial form of black solidarity to both black Americans and the American idea is a political activity necessitated by racism's vise-grip and concentrated on making the Promise more inclusive. In *We Who Are Dark*, Harvard professor Tommie Shelby defines this sort of solidarity as one based in a pragmatic nationalism wherein black citizens are called to do two primary things. The first is to "acknowledge the negative historical impact and current existence of antiblack racism in America" that presents a "common oppression." The second is to "act collectively to end [these racial injustices] or at least to reduce their impact on [black Americans'] lives."[3] This form of solidarity is not policy-specific, and it does not set priorities among the range of ills that plague black America. Group members are free to differ on how to ameliorate racial inequality or what policy demands to champion. Instead, Shelby argues, this solidarity is a narrowly tailored political unity that aims to overcome the effects of racism and serves as the basis for concerted black activity to realize equality. "Not because [black Americans] should limit their political activity to matters of racial justice," Shelby says, "but because this is as much as they can reasonably expect from black unity in the post-civil rights era."[4] The broad goal of combating racism in order to expand democratic inclusion permits an enduring unity without sacrificing group heterogeneity. It preserves individualism while marshaling political solidarity.

When black solidarity is framed in terms of political unity, it can be construed by some as primarily concerned with voting, both in terms of access to the polls and choices made at the polls. But group solidarity speaks to a broader construction of politics and maintains concerns that extend beyond the question of which politicians get elected. Its central organizing principle is to challenge those systems and institutions that perpetuate racial inequality. Writ large, politics is the interaction between entities negotiating the roles and activities of governance. Solidarity is a means to increase a given group's ability to influence the process and outcome of politics. Of course, in a democratic republic, elections are a means to accomplish this. But so are protest movements, media and issue framing for the public, transformative leaders, cultural appeals, and a host of other methods of exerting political pressure. The political solidarity found within black America organizes all the tools at its disposal toward one main objective: the realization of a racially equal and just society—to make the United States more American.

Black solidarity, then, is neither a strategy to unite black Americans against white fellow citizens nor a means to exclude others who are deeply interested in ensuring that the nation lives up to the Promise. The Civil Rights Movement of the mid-twentieth century is a model example of black solidarity; Americans of all races and ethnicities participated in that quest to make the United States a more perfect union. Also within that extensive movement were a variety of competing visions and strategies to effect change and reform. Because solidarity is exercised by people, there will be attendant moral sensibilities, cultural markers, and a social character. But homogeneity and exclusivity are not prerequisites for black solidarity, except as they pertain to a shared commitment to the primary objective of disassembling structural racism and a willingness to make personal sacrifices toward that end. The most productive form of black solidarity is not anti-white, and it is certainly not anti-American.

But black solidarity is necessarily black. The shared history of violence and deprivation, and shared set of experiences, provides the staying power for black solidarity. Thus, the group solidarity oriented to bring about racial equality that has proved elusive for centuries will be inevitably black-centric. In its demand for self-determination and individual liberty, it is also inevitably and inextricably American.

For all its political applications, black solidarity was fundamentally the product of the most basic human instinct: survival. The first black people in the United States quickly came to understand that binding together with others who were similarly situated was the only way to endure racial oppression and make it to another day. Among them, just as among black citizens today, there were disagreements on the best approaches to removing the boot of racism from the neck of black America—indeed, from the neck of all America. Some like Denmark Vesey and Nat Turner turned to violent assertions of black dignity and liberty. Others like Frederick Douglass, Sojourner Truth, and W.E.B. DuBois focused their talents on moral and political appeals fashioned to highlight the hypocrisy of racial inequality in America. Ida B. Wells employed journalism as the medium for her fearless civil rights activism, Booker T. Washington believed economic self-sufficiency was the appropriate course for equality, and Martin Luther King, Jr., famously adopted a strategy of nonviolence to compel black inclusion in the Promise. But the survival and liberation of black Americans were the driving forces behind all their actions, even if they had to be a martyr to the cause. Though they differed in philosophy and method, they were united—across time, distance, and ideology—in a common cause.

In a liberal democracy, a group's well-being is ultimately a question of politics. This is why a program of survival evolved into political unity—the latter is an offspring of the former. Along the way, an identity was constructed and grounded in the racial inequality and injustice presenting an existential threat to black citizens. To be black in America is to have a group of people immediately and intimately familiar with the racial discrimination—historical and contemporary—that has plagued you and those like you. Emanating from these experiences and the solidarity they create are cultures, traditions, and customs that characterize what it means to be a black American. The racism that shapes these experiences is the target of black America's political solidarity. In this way, black solidarity encompasses aspects of group politics, group identity, group interests, and group behavior. And yet it does not require differences within the group to be resolved; it accounts for them while prioritizing the common objective of each—survival and liberty. The result is a politics replete with a diversity of views and preferences that still benefits from a unifying sense of identity and existential purpose. Racial identity becomes predominant and political.

Black solidarity has two primary competing effects on members of the group. Theories of social identity suggest that members of a minority group that holds less power than the majority group simultaneously magnify similarities with their group and seek to differentiate themselves from within the group.[5] They do the former because aligning themselves with other group members provides a measure of empowerment against the more populous, better-resourced whole group. They do the latter because of an innate human need to be distinguished from all others in the group. Black Americans recognize the necessity of standing in solidarity, but they also have a human desire to be distinct and unique. Racism attacks both. It exacerbates the need for unity while also reducing black people to a throng of carbon copies—it makes solidarity an existential imperative and mutes the individualism of each group member. The consequence is a group seen as homogenous by those on the outside looking in and as heterogeneous by those on the inside peering out, creating a destructive incongruence between how black citizens are viewed and how they view themselves.[6] There is no more tension within the group than there is in the

American idea that rugged individualism is the prized feature of a united people. Rather, the strain occurs when the group's diversity is disregarded and each member is painted with the same shade of apathy. For this unfortunate outcome, political unity is the best solvent.

Solidarity among black Americans is the most powerful and enduring force for racial progress to ever be unleashed in the United States. The goal-oriented perseverance it fuels has sustained generations of black Americans through slavery, violent oppression, and various methods of civic and socioeconomic exclusion. In the process, not only did it slowly make the country more inclusive; it pushed the nation closer to its professed ideals. But solidarity is not easy; it is not without cost. It produces stressors on its practitioners, who simply want to be seen as fully American without having to disavow or subjugate racial and cultural pride. To cope with these effects, black Americans have created havens where they can shed "the mask" and "the veil" and exist in a more liberated state, just as the Spirit of '76 would encourage.[7]

These are the spaces in which my parents were reared and where black Americans like Karen Mills still seek refuge, affirmation, and empowerment.

AFTER SPENDING A COUPLE of enlightening but disheartening years at the elite Bronx High School of Science, Karen Mills knew that the next step in her personal and educational journey would be taken at a historically black college or university (HBCU). The racial and cultural diversity of her high school opened her eyes to a bigger, more beautiful world, but it also exposed her to more of its ugly bits. During her years there, returning from summer vacation meant returning to special messages scrawled across the doors for her and all of her black classmates: "Niggers go home."[8] Hearing about instances of racial discrimination playing out in the school's hallways also meant hearing about the black student who stumbled into the school's hallways covered in blood and bruises after being beaten by a mob of white teens. And adjusting to the rigors of an academically demanding institution meant adjusting to white school counselors who doubted her abilities and suggested she slink back to her predominantly black and Hispanic neighborhood school.

When Karen graduated high school, she sought a brief reprieve from the ugliness of racism, deciding to attend Hampton University, an HBCU just a short, brisk walk from Point Comfort, where the first black captives arrived in the American colonies in 1619. "I wanted to be surrounded by smart, professional black people who were like-minded," she says matter-of-factly. But a deeper impulse stirred her longing for an HBCU education. "I didn't want everyone who was supposed to be my role model or everyone who was instructing me and guiding me—I didn't want them all to be white. I wanted them to look like me. I didn't want to have to think about whether their guidance or advice was based on negative perceptions of black people."

Karen was raised in the Parkchester community of the Bronx, built in the early 1940s as a whites-only community. Racial minorities were forbidden from living there until 1968, so Karen's early childhood in the 1970s was accompanied by white families fleeing and black and Hispanic residents arriving. Her grandfather was from Jackson, North Carolina, where the rampant racial discrimination of Jim Crow fostered a lifelong distrust of white people. He left in search of a better life and more opportunity, like 6 million other black Southerners during the Great Migration, landing in New York City, where he found his wife and a new beginning. He was a presence in Karen's life and helped her make sense of the racial dynamics occurring just outside her window. The rapidly diversifying community was also rapidly segregating. The black, Hispanic, and remaining white families lived in abutting sections of town but went to different schools, with the black and Hispanic students attending the public school and the white students attending the parochial school across the street. "I never didn't know that there was a race issue in our country," Karen said. "It was unavoidable and always a topic of conversation in our house."

Karen's intelligence, personality, looks, and infectious laugh have always made her a force of nature. Growing up, she was routinely the smartest student in class and often the most outspoken. She was also attractive, her light complexion and hair texture entering longstanding debates within black America about beauty and colorism. From its earliest days, black America has housed complexions that ranged the full spectrum of skin tones. Colorism is a form of intraracial discrimination and social stratification that pits lighter-skinned group members against darker-skinned members.[9] And it is not confined to black America—it exists among people around the world, from the sands of Arabia, the tropical climes of South Asia, the Far East countries whose shores taste the Pacific, the tightly packed and expansive states in Europe and Africa, and the many societies adjacent and in between. But historically, in the United States, skin-color hierarchies were a product of broader societal racism and have had particular effects on black women's prospects, outcomes, and life chances.[10]

Karen, like most black Americans, was acutely aware of colorism and racial groupings in a community that was black, brown, and white, but her complexion was never grounds for questioning group belonging. "I never struggled with racial identity, no matter what I looked like, no matter what my hair looked like." She then quipped, "In my mind, I was always the blackest one in the bunch!" Again, she, like most black Americans, knew that black community, unity, and solidarity often mute differences—including socially significant physical ones like skin color—when survival, security, and well-being are the predominant questions that govern the American experience for black people across the color spectrum.

Hampton University is where she went to take a breath from the Bronx's racial tensions. The college's waterfront campus is tucked into a pocket of Virginian land just as a sliver of the Hampton River bends into Jones Creek. The university grounds used to be the site of illegal gatherings under a large Southern live oak tree where black Americans who had escaped slavery secretly learned to read and write. The college was founded in 1868 by a Christian abolitionist group to educate newly freed black Americans, and that old tree still welcomes visitors to campus today. It is known as the Emancipation Oak—one of the Ten Great Trees of the World—because it is where the Emancipation Proclamation was first read to the local black population during the Civil War. Like the more than one hundred other HBCUs in the United States, Hampton offered a different kind of freedom for Karen and the scores of black students who have converged on its shores for a taste of black solidarity and an education for life: freedom from the daily slights and injustices of racial discrimination.

Today, Karen Mills is an attorney. The same impulse that led her out of the Bronx also took her to Georgia. Following her time at Hampton, she worked in New York City and could not escape the incidents of racial violence and discrimination happening around her: the racist attacks at Howard Beach in Queens, the killing of black teenager Yusuf Hawkins in Brooklyn by baseball-bat-wielding white kids, and the infamous Central Park jogger case, in which five black teens were falsely accused of raping Trisha Meili, one of Karen's coworkers. During a trip to Atlanta to visit an old friend and black classmate from Bronx Science, she saw black professionals and families filling neighborhoods with stately homes and driving expensive cars at every turn. "It was *shocking* to me! Black people were down here doing the damn thing, and I knew right then that this is where I needed to be. This is where I belong." She packed her bags and never looked back, except for a short stint just outside New York City for law school, where her memories of racial discrimination were greeted by fresh accusations of her being little more than an affirmative-action charity case. In all her years in Atlanta, she has never been called *nigger* to her face—that has happened to her only in New York. In adulthood, her teenage wish to be "surrounded by professional black people who are like-minded" finally became reality.

DESPITE BLACK SOLIDARITY being a much more expansive concept than how the group votes, the truth is that the electoral unity it spurs is one of the most notable features in American politics. Black citizens have voted with historic partisan uniformity for nearly six decades. Since the passage of the Civil Rights Act of 1964, Democratic nominees for president have averaged more than 88 percent of the black vote, peaking at 96 percent in 2008 for Barack Obama's historic candidacy.[11] For midterm congressional elections, Democratic candidates have averaged nearly 90 percent for three decades.[12] Black voters' perceived loyalty to the Democratic Party is perhaps the most well-traveled trope in contemporary American politics. For this reason, impressions of black solidarity are often reduced to the phenomenon of uniform voting behavior, often translated as the simplistic observation that "all black people vote Democratic." In this way, solidarity is cast as little more than an affirmation of the myth of the black monolith.

What exactly is the black monolith? It is a term that suggests black America behaves like an undifferentiated political herd in which each member shares the same political ideology, the same policy preferences, the same political character, and the same stingy adherence to every tenet within the Democratic Party's platform. It asserts that black Americans have little desire for much else except blind allegiance to a political party willing to make unprincipled concessions in exchange for votes. Those Americans on the outside looking in do not see any diversity of opinion or the variety of issue positions within black America—they see only the monolith. It plays into the worst stereotypes of black Americans created over the course of the nation's history to justify racial discrimination and explain racial disparities. However, in this formulation, the black monolith is myth.

Great political diversity exists within black America. Though black voters demonstrate near uniform electoral support of Democratic candidates, only 59 percent identify as Democrat—37 percent consider themselves Independent or refuse party affiliations altogether. On the ideological spectrum, just 26 percent of black Americans characterize themselves as liberal, while 27 percent identify as conservatives and 44 percent as moderates.[13] Even among black Democrats, 68 percent identify their political views as moderate or conservative, while only 29 percent say they are liberal, a number that has barely budged in the last two decades.[14]

In fact, how black Americans define terms like *liberal, conservative,* and *moderate* is different from how other Americans do. White voters tend to sort themselves into the party that corresponds most closely to their political ideologies—white conservatives are overwhelmingly Republicans and white liberals are overwhelmingly Democrats. Black conservatives, however, mostly still lean Democrat, though they hold some values and prefer some policies that align more closely to the Republican Party's platform. The reason for this is because black Americans tend to define their politics based on attitudes toward social welfare and religious mores, with less emphasis on moral absolutisms and the role and size of government.[15]

The political diversity of black America exists within a commitment to political unity typically expressed through partisan support, and it is more tangible when assessing specific issues. For example, black Americans are split 56 percent to 39 percent in favor of legalizing marijuana.[16] Nearly 60 percent of black Americans prefer school-choice options to traditional public schooling.[17] Black Americans are almost evenly divided on whether U.S. immigration policies should be more restrictive.[18] When a political science professor examined fifty-one state referendums, black voters split on average at a rate of

64 percent to 36 percent between liberal-leaning and conservative-leaning voters.[19] In other words, when party is removed from the equation and black voters are able to vote on specific policy issues, they generally demonstrate a 60–40 split, which is quite comparable to Americans of all races and ethnicities.

But the reality remains that black voters do indeed cast 90 percent of their ballots for the Democratic candidate in every presidential and congressional election. The reason is that for black voters, every presidential and congressional election—and even the vast majority of gubernatorial and senatorial elections—is a single-issue contest. Next to civil rights, other issues pale in comparison. If racial inequality and injustice are permitted to dictate the American experience of black citizens, then policy debates about immigration, healthcare, tax policy, the environment, and any other political hot potato are little more than discussions about how black people will be excluded. History has taught that the civil rights objectives that work toward establishing equality and full citizenship must be the primary aim of black America if it is ever to realize security, liberty, and prosperity. Black political solidarity is trained on that target, and black voting behavior acts on it.

Because U.S. politics operates in a two-party system, the electoral choices of all Americans are determined by being able to distinguish between the Republican and Democratic Parties' policy positions and the social affect associated with the parties' reputations. The Democratic Party underwent a transformation regarding civil rights in the mid-twentieth century that led to it claiming the mantle of racial progress. Support for the Civil Rights Act became a litmus test for black Americans, and when the 1964 Republican presidential nominee, Barry Goldwater, came out against it, while the Democratic president Lyndon Johnson voiced his ardent support, black voters had seen enough. Ninety-six percent of black voters supported Johnson in that election, a lopsided total that would not occur again until the first black president ran in 2008.

In the intervening years, the Republican Party cast its lot with conservative white voters who were less receptive to civil rights reforms and advancements. Thus, the two-party system presents a caricatured choice between a pro–civil rights Democratic Party and a racial revanchist Republican Party. And when candidates do little to dispel these depictions, there is only one rational party choice for the civil rights single-issue voter.

Though support for the party deemed to be more progressive on civil rights is a prudent and logical endeavor, black solidarity provides the guardrails to ensure members of the group are on the same page and follow through electorally. Solidarity requires action, commitment, and sacrifice, so the expectations of each member must be communicated and policed. For black voting behavior, this occurs in three predominant forces that shape the choices group members make at the polls: linked fate, everyday talk, and social pressure.

Linked fate is the colloquial term given to a phenomenon called the "black utility heuristic." It was introduced by University of Chicago professor Michael Dawson in his 1994 book *Behind the Mule*, the title derived from a quote by Mississippi Delta guitarist Booker T. Washington White, who noted that the blues originated in the shared miserable experience of "walking behind the mule way back in slavery time."[20] Linked fate "suggests that as long as race remains dominant in determining the lives of individual blacks, it is 'rational' for African Americans to follow group cues in interpreting and acting in the political world."[21] In other words, "it explicitly links perceptions of self-interest to perceptions of racial group interests."[22] The political needs of the group must be met if each member is to have a legitimate shot at exercising individual liberty.

Because history has taught black Americans that they will be treated as a group, and not as individuals, it became clear that each member's well-being was inextricably tied to the group's well-being. If black people on the whole were doing poorly—as in slavery and during Jim Crow—then chances are that each black person would suffer the same fate. Free black people did exist in portions of the United States during slavery, and some black people escaped most of the violence and oppression of Jim Crow. But those exceptions were extremely rare and largely by dint of luck. For virtually every black person in the United States over most of the nation's history, his or her individual fate was tied to the fate of the group. If the rates of unemployment, poverty, incarceration, and poor health outcomes are disproportionately high for black Americans today, then each black individual is more likely to suffer those same fates. The most efficient way, then, to improve one's life chances is to improve the group's chances.

For all these reasons, linked fate often causes black Americans to prioritize the interests of the group over their own. Solidarity turns that prioritization into political action, most easily observed in voting behavior. The fact that nearly nine in ten black voters have supported national Democratic candidates for more than five decades is the result of individuals acting uniformly in what is understood to be the group's best interest. Though there are just as many black conservatives as there are black liberals, they both largely vote for Democratic candidates for the sake of the group.

Black Americans discover what is in the group's best interests via the channels of "everyday talk." The theory of everyday talk, articulated by political scientist Melissa Harris-Perry (then Harris-Lacewell) and detailed in her book *Barbershops, Bibles, and BET*, states that "although none of the individuals engaging in conversation will be instantly convinced by the arguments of others ... each person who has shared in this interaction will adjust his or her political attitudes to the extent that he or she is convinced by the various arguments being made."[23] In black America, these discussions occur in places that scholars call "counterpublics," areas where marginalized communities formulate their own worldviews outside of the larger public eye. Black barbershops and beauty salons, churches, colleges, fraternal and sororal organizations, traditional and social media outlets, and wherever predominantly black audiences congregate are considered black counterpublics. Here, beyond the view of the general public, black Americans engage in wide-ranging discussions that work together to hone the group interest. Black Americans do not blindly take cues from political elites; instead, they formulate their views through an infinitely complex network of local interactions that percolate upward to leaders and elites.[24] The product is not only the formulation of the group interest but also the communication and affirmation of it.

With a general agreement on the group's political interest and its prioritization over self-interest, the third constraining element of black voting behavior is social pressure and accountability. Because solidarity requires individuals to conform to group interests and norms, those who choose to do otherwise risk social penalties. Political scientists Ismail White and Chryl Laird have termed this phenomenon "racialized social constraint," which they argue is "a process of enforcing norms of black political behavior" out of an expectation that conformity increases social standing in the group and that defection harms one's standing.[25] Threats of ostracization, the fear of being shamed, or the desire to avoid damage to one's reputation exert pressure on individuals to remain in solidarity with the group.

One of the most common methods of achieving this is by labeling group defectors with intraracial pejoratives, such as *Uncle Tom*, *coon*, or *sellout*. A quick search of these terms on any social media outlet reveals black Americans chastising other members for taking positions or actions perceived to be detrimental to the group. White and Laird, along with political scientist Troy Allen, found that "there are widely held and historically entrenched expectations within the [black] community about how group members are to behave politically," and these are highly intense and crystallized.[26] They found that black political solidarity could sometimes be undone by appeals to an individual's self-interest, but the social penalties exacted for doing so served as an effective method for policing behavior and keeping members aligned with the group. This is an effective enforcement arm of black political solidarity.

Simplifying black voting behavior as little more than an exercise in loyal partisanship to the Democratic Party misses the critical role black political solidarity plays in pushing the United States to be more racially inclusive and more representative of its professed ideals. This sort of solidarity is not anchored in a political party—black voters supported Republicans in lopsided fashion for several decades before helping elect Democrats. As Representative Bill Clay of Missouri said upon the founding of the Congressional Black Caucus in 1971, "Black people have no permanent friends, no permanent enemies . . . just permanent interests."[27] Those permanent interests center the most basic American rights: equality, full citizenship, and the opportunity to succeed. Black political solidarity has doggedly propelled the nation closer to this goal, a benefit that advantages all Americans.

MANUFACTURING STURDY BONDS of unity within an exceptionally large group of people is not an easy accomplishment and not easily replicated. Black solidarity is the product of an inhumane catastrophe and is continually fueled by the presence of inequality. In the face of oppression, solidarity became a survival tactic for black Americans. And the quest for security and well-being that brought it about also manifested a new culture from the multitude of transatlantic captives and their descendants. In a sense, black solidarity is a concrete rose, an unlikely thing of beauty arising from inhospitable conditions.

The black solidarity that pushes America to be truer to its ideals does not seek to accomplish this through consensus and organized calls for specific policy demands, like reparations or affirmative action or federal programs explicitly targeting material racial disparities. The tremendous diversity within black America—the assortment of political views, varying levels of socioeconomic status, regional distinctions and subcultures, and even the range of skin tones— creates different and distinct experiences that are masked by the veil of collective action. So instead of demanding unanimity in policy preferences, black solidarity tells us that until the nation recognizes the inherent value and equality of black Americans such that racial injustice is deemed unacceptable and rooted out, no amount of constitutional amendments, Supreme Court holdings, or legislative programs will deliver the American Promise in full to any citizen, no matter race or class.

For these reasons, these attributes of black solidarity are what make it a model for the sort of multiracial solidarity the nation needs to prevent racism from threatening its existence. Though it will not map perfectly onto a national solidarity, the primary parts are in place. National solidarity must recognize that racial injustice and inequality are not an inconvenience of negligible importance or the product of insufficient personal effort. It has to view racism as fundamentally at odds with the core of the American idea and the well-being of the United States. It then requires each citizen to refuse to accept systemic inequalities that disproportionately impact racial groups and to exert pressure on the state to address them. Because black American solidarity is a purely American creation, it can be replicated nationally if we agree that racism is an existential threat to America and the government is on the hook to rectify it. It is a guide for how we can create a version of civic and political solidarity that crosses lines of race and class. Expanding this sort of solidarity to be available to, and practiced by, a cross section of Americans is how we can protect the Promise for future generations.

Black group solidarity is more readily achievable because of a shared history, a relatively common set of experiences, and similar obstacles to realizing life chances encountered by its members. National solidarity, too, needs a shared system of beliefs, narratives, and customs that will facilitate its emergence among the American citizenry across lines of race, ethnicity, and class. Whereas the Promise gives national solidarity its goal, and advancing the cause of equality by diminishing racism provides its purpose, an inclusive national culture and a shared American identity are required to foster social and psychological bonds between solidary group members. The glue for national solidarity is the American civil religion.

PART III

A Framework for National Solidarity

*Citizens of America expect more. They deserve and they want
more than a recital of problems. We are a people in a quandary
about the present. We are a people in search of our future. We
are a people in search of a national community. We are a people
trying not only to solve the problems of the present: unemployment, inflation . . . but we are attempting on a larger scale to
fulfill the promise of America.*

*We are attempting to fulfill our national purpose, to create
and sustain a society in which all of us are equal.*

. . .

*Are we to be one people bound together by common spirit
sharing in a common endeavor or will we become a divided
nation? For all of its uncertainty, we cannot flee the future. We
must not become the new Puritans and reject our society. We
must address and master the future together. It can be done if
we restore the belief that we share a sense of national community, that we share a common national endeavor. It can be
done.*

*There is no executive order; there is no law that can require the
American people to form a national community. This we must
do as individuals and if we do it as individuals, there is no
President of the United States who can veto that decision.*

*—Barbara Jordan, "Who, Then, Will Speak for the Common
Good?," keynote address to the 1976 Democratic National
Convention*

CHAPTER 6

Finding Civil Religion

The long quest for civil rights is what created and has sustained black American solidarity. It is a product of the same deep-seated desire to access the Promise that fueled the nation's founding, sustained it through catastrophe and injustice, and allowed it to become more inclusive over the centuries. Material gains from public policy battles are not the things that compel group members to fight, to sacrifice, or to obligate themselves to one another. Things do not inspire individuals to stand in thick solidarity with one another—beliefs do; values do. And demonstrable acts of group commitment reify those bonds.

Similarly, national solidarity needs a value system, one rooted in America's civic traditions that can serve as a bridge for citizens across the color line. And that value system needs a set of practices to build affinity among the citizenry. Even a baseline understanding of the harm racism causes in our society is not enough to cause citizens across racial lines to feel bonds of kinship. Americans will not be moved to establish solidarity based solely on the promise of the fruits of full citizenship being available to all. Understanding alone will not do. Rather, a common set of beliefs and practices that meld individuals into a collective is required. They constitute the scaffolding necessary for the assembly and stability of national solidarity. Just as black solidarity gathered its strength from a belief in the divine license to dignity and a moral quest for civil rights, national solidarity must arise from adherence to a particular system of civic faith and moral decency.

In 1967, Robert N. Bellah, a professor of sociology, proposed that such a system exists and is observable in a theological dimension to the American way of life, one shared and practiced by the overwhelming majority of us. He called it the American civil religion and defined it as the set of beliefs, symbols, and rituals that vitalize the religious aspect of American public life.[1] The concept is not entirely new—Bellah adapted it from the eighteen-century philosopher Jean-Jacques Rousseau, who introduced the idea in his cornerstone text, *The Social Contract*. For Rousseau, the dogmas of civil religion consisted of belief in a beneficent deity and Providence, a life to aspire to, a desire for justice and punishment for evil, the sanctity of the social contract and laws, and the rejection of religious intolerance.[2] The civil profession of faith, in Rousseau's construction, is an adherence to social sentiments that makes one a good citizen and demonstrates a commitment to the nation and the citizenry. While the United States is often thought of as a Christian nation, Bellah makes the case that America's civil religious tenets are free of specific Christian creed and canon. Instead, he suggests, our civil religion is unitive, central to the national identity, and best suited to the task of helping ensure the continued march toward the Promise.

The concept seems simple enough, but it, like many conversations that include the word *religion*, is fraught with pitfalls. What, after all, is meant by *religion*? Is civil religion compatible with the belief systems of those from different faiths, or even people who are atheist or spiritually agnostic? How exactly is a nation that prides itself on the separation of church and state supposed to strengthen itself by aligning itself more closely to a religion? The purpose of religion can be said to provide meaning when none is to be found elsewhere, acceptance when rejection surrounds us, and life when confronted by the risk of death.[3] Religion is essentially a system of beliefs and accompanying practices. It connects us to metaphysical and supernatural realms that give our existence a higher purpose than just survival and ascribes meaning to our daily lives and actions. Nations have this need, too—to be able to answer existential questions about their purpose and assign significance to their deeds; this is where they find national identity, and this is where citizens find what connects them to one another. Civil religion does this work for nations in much the same way traditional organized religions have done this work for their believers. Civil religion is the "theological glue that binds a nation together" by giving a nation and its people meaning, purpose, and affinity.[4] It does not replace organized religion, nor does it hope to inspire sharp-elbowed nationalism or worship of the state. Rather, it provides raison d'être.

Still, questions about and interpretations of civil religion persist. Even the conceptions of the idea from Bellah and Rousseau are not quite the same. One of Bellah's former students, Yale University professor Philip Gorski, outlined three key differences between eighteenth-century civil religion and the contemporary American version. The latter is voluntary and not compulsory, more scriptural than ritual in that it provides a framework for thinking about the nation and not a prescriptive liturgy for glorifying it, and comfortably exists alongside organized religion without any desire to replace it.[5] Others have suggested civil religion is a "nonsectarian faith that has as its sacred symbols those of the polity and national history" or the sacralization of parts of civic life through public rituals and ceremonies.[6]

The truth is that civil religion is only religious in the sense that it employs an idea that is meant to compel us to think beyond ourselves and about the greater good, gives us a means to bond and demonstrate our commitment to that idea and each other, and establishes a kinship among its practitioners based on the view that there is something sacred about the idea and our role in effecting it. Civil religion's deity is not Christian, Islamic, Hindu, or the province of any such religions. Rather, the divinity in the American civil religion is its founding idea, a concept about value and belongingness that acts as the ethereal, higher calling each citizen must acknowledge to establish a well-ordered society. If, as the Declaration of Independence states, governments derive their power from the consent of the governed, then the belief and faith of "We the People" are the source of the nation's existence and legitimacy. There is no communion or call to prayer in civil religion, but there are public activities and exercises that signal a commitment to the American project and its professed principles. There are no prophets or gospels, but there are messengers and documents that we revere in near-sacred terms. So, civil religion is religious only in the sense that it has many of the characteristics of one. More accurately, it is a quasi-religion that unites societies through a critical national allegiance and elements of religious practice.[7]

The potential of civil religion to serve as the basis for national unity is well acknowledged. The sentiment periodically dominates magazine essays and newspaper editorials when some event or holiday spurs reflection on what unites Americans. Sociologist Rhys Williams sums up civil religion and its potential as understandings and practices that recognize the sacred dimensions of the citizenry; a set of beliefs and rituals that provide a transcendent national identity; and an idea especially capable of managing social diversity.[8] When analyzing the American civil religion, Williams suggests it "shift[s] the gaze away from sectarian differences and [gives] a common point of allegiance." This is clearly what Bellah observed when analyzing the sweep of American history and noting the religious rhetoric and iconography that have populated American history and framed the principles at the heart of the national identity. Americans from George Washington and Lyndon Johnson to Frederick Douglass and the trailblazing black feminist activist and author Anna Julia Cooper made national appeals that were obviously grounded in a civil religious view of what it means to be American and how to best realize the Promise.

The power of civil religion to foster national solidarity is evident in four basic elements that Gorski describes as canon, pantheon, narrative, and archive. The canon is made up of the widely read and revered texts that sit at the center of public thinking and debate: the Declaration of Independence, the U.S. Constitution, the orations of the first generation of Americans who cast the nation as a product of Providence, and certain writings from those challenging the nation to live up to its principles. The canon tells us there are self-evident truths about our equality and our rights to life, liberty, and the pursuit of happiness that are unalienable. It tells us government derives its power from the citizenry, and its job is our safety and well-being. It tells us that the blessings of liberty are ours to secure today and for posterity. It is a measuring stick that displays the distance between who we are and who we say we want to be. The canon includes presidential rhetoric like George Washington's first inaugural address upon assuming the office of the presidency. In it, Washington often referred to an unnamed deity—an Almighty Being, the Invisible Hand, the Great Author—to whom he attributed the United States' "token of providential agency," "future blessings which the past seems to presage," and "sacred fire of liberty" with which it was entrusted.[9] It includes King's "Letter from a Birmingham Jail," in which he shared his hope that "the dark clouds of racial prejudice will soon pass away and the deep fog of misunderstanding will be lifted from our fear-drenched communities" so that "the radiant stars of love and brotherhood will shine over our great nation with all their scintillating beauty."[10] The canon not only deifies an idea and provides the divine blueprint for how a civil society should be organized, but it consecrates the endeavor.

Gorski defines the pantheon as those heroes, martyrs, and saints of American civic life who serve as a cast of paragons modeling civic excellence and virtue. He places Washington, Abraham Lincoln, and King at the apogee, which is rounded out by principled and exemplary Americans who inched the nation closer to the Promise. Members of this pantheon need not have been perfect Americans; they need only to have imbued the nation with civic virtue by their example in a singular act or the scope of their lives. It is equally the domain of Benjamin Franklin and John F. Kennedy as it is of Sojourner Truth and Rosa Parks. As Ronald Reagan said upon signing the statute that made King's birthday a national holiday, "America is a more democratic nation, a more just nation, a more peaceful nation because Martin Luther King, Jr., became its preeminent nonviolent commander."[11] When civil rights icon and congressional member John Lewis passed away in July 2020, Barack Obama eulogized him declaring, "He as much as anyone in our history brought this country a little bit closer to our highest ideals. And someday, when we do finish that long journey toward freedom . . . John Lewis will be a founding father of that fuller, fairer, better America."[12] The pantheon shows that the values outlined in the canon are tangible, possible, and transformational when actioned. It yanks high-minded principles from the ether and gives them human form as a testament to their viability and potential.

The civil religious narrative is the story of the past that provides a vision for the future. This element usually focuses on a people's journey or pilgrimage, a feature common to many religions. The traveling is symbolic of transformation, from a place of persecution and frailty to one of enlightenment, strength, and well-orderedness, usually coming at some significant cost in terms of time, resources, or life itself. Bellah points out that the American civil religion has often borrowed from biblical archetypes, such as the Exodus, promised land, chosen people, blood sacrifices, and rebirth. The most powerful orations in American history contain these themes—Lincoln at Gettysburg honoring the fallen soldiers who sanctified the land with their blood and "gave their lives that the nation might live";[13] King in his last speech the night before his assassination declaring that

he had been to the mountaintop and "that we, as a people, will get
to the promised land";[14] Kennedy in his inaugural address casting us
as the chosen people, saying, "In the long history of the world, only
a few generations have been granted the role of defending freedom
in its hour of maximum danger . . . Let us go forth to lead the land
we love, asking His blessing and His help, but knowing that here on
earth God's work must truly be our own."[15] The civil religious story
does not belong solely to such moments, though; it permeates the
ideas of many people across our society, such as Anna Julia Cooper,
who offered this wisdom in September 1902: "A nation's greatness
is not dependent upon the things it makes and uses . . . America can
boast her expanse of territory, her gilded domes . . . but the question
of deepest moment in this nation today is its span of the circle of
brotherhood, the moral stature of its men and its women, the elevation at which it receives its 'vision' into the firmament of eternal
truth."[16] This civic narrative describes the task at hand—preservation
of the nation and progress toward the Promise—and encapsulates it
in a mythological quest. It brandishes the power of story to inspire
and orient the citizenry.

The remaining element is archive, which Gorski describes as
the people, texts, and legends that fill the American vessel awaiting
their turn to join the narrative. Much of the contemporary American narrative was once archival—Washington knew little of King's
promised land, and the authors of the Declaration and the Constitution did not know that Lincoln would rely on ideas they contained
to justify escorting the nation into civil war, updating the American
canon, pantheon, and narrative in the process. In this way, the archive
contains the stories whose civic utility have yet to be discovered or
employed. They are not just any stories; they are often monomyths.
This type of story, more frequently referred to as the "hero's journey,"
was described by literary scholar Joseph Campbell as a narrative that
tells of a protagonist leaving home on an adventure of some sort,
acquiring useful knowledge and skills while on the quest, emerging

victorious over an enemy or seemingly insurmountable challenge, and returning home victorious with new talents that enlighten and improve everyone.[17] This template is evident in a range of stories, from religious figures like Moses, Muhammad, and Jesus to the main characters in popular movies like *Star Wars* and *The Lion King*. Lives of contemporary American figures, like Barack Obama or the late senator John McCain, are lined with marks of the hero's journey. In civil religion, sometimes the hero is a singular figure and sometimes a collective people who serve as the personification of the nation. Perhaps the story will find the moment, or the person will find the story, but there is no shortage of them in the American collective memory for use when the civic need arises. Transformative figures are usually the means by which an archival item is adopted into the national narrative.

Americans exercise civil religion and all its elements in the same way they do other religions: through professions, rituals, observances, and reverence for symbols. In Christianity, believers profess their faith; partake in various rituals such as baptism or communion; recognize the meaning of symbols like the cross, the dove, and the holy text of the Bible; and celebrate the birth of Christ at Christmas and the resurrection at Easter. In Islam, the *shahada* is the declaration of faith; *salat* is the ritualistic prayer performed five times a day; the *hajj* is the journey to the sacred city of Mecca; a star inside a crescent moon has come to be a recognized symbol of Islam; and Ramadan is a month of commemorating when the religion's sacred book, the Quran, was first revealed to the prophet Muhammad. In Judaism, *shema* is a declaration of the faith; rituals include ceremonies such as bar and bat mitzvahs, circumcision, and seder; the Star of David and the Torah are sacred symbols and text; and observances include Yom Kippur, Rosh Hashanah, and Hanukkah. Similar religious rites and liturgical occurrences exist in Buddhism, Hinduism, and the range of religions practiced by peoples around the world.

The American civil religion has its way of life, too. We have our professions of faith—there is the Pledge of Allegiance we learn as children and the oaths we take to the Constitution, as jurors in carrying out justice, as members of the military, or even as new citizens. We have our rituals, like moments of silence on September 11, the playing of the national anthem before nearly every major public event, and wreath-layings at Arlington National Cemetery. We have sacred texts in the Declaration of Independence and the Constitution. And we have plenty of civil religious observances—Veterans Day, Memorial Day, Independence Day, and even Presidents' Day and Martin Luther King Day. Bellah further notes that "the inauguration of a president is an important ceremonial event in this religion" because "it reaffirms, among other things, the religious legitimation of the lightest political authority."[18] As Ronald Reagan said in his first inaugural address, "We are a nation under God, and I believe God intended us to be free. It would be fitting and good, I think, if on each Inaugural Day in future years it should be declared a day of prayer."[19] We certainly have no shortage of symbols for our civil religion—the flag, the Statue of Liberty, the bald eagle. And memorials to monumental conflicts and the great messengers of the American civil religion—the pantheon—are every few paces along the National Mall in Washington, D.C., and scattered across the landscape of an adoring and reverential nation.

Civil religion is the belief system that makes national solidarity possible. Certainly, Lincolnesque speeches and fireworks filling a July night sky with spidery illuminations will not make civic friends out of democratic strangers any more than the Sermon on the Mount and Christmas make all Christians treat one another with love and compassion. But our civil religion is the most appropriate and best-suited means to awaken national solidarity in America and enable it to accomplish its mission of weakening racism in the United States.

Because the United States is not an ethnically homogenous nation, connections between citizens must be forged on some basis other than ethnic origin and histories. The American civil religion provides this. There is no personified supreme being enthroned on high observing and assessing our actions; there is only the Promise, the principal object of our faith that asserts we are all inherently equal, that each of us will respect and defend the rights and liberty of others, and that the state will not deny our equality or unduly constrain our exercise of liberty or access to opportunity. Parishioners of the American civil religion all believe in this Promise—it is the cornerstone of the nation and the source of civic kinship. Inevitably, some citizens will recognize certain things as unjust, such as complicating the ability of some Americans to vote or doling out heavy-handed prison sentences for relatively minor infractions, and yet still be unmoved to take action. Similarly, there are those who will want to take action against specific injustices, but whose outrage is not attended by compassion for the people being harmed by it. But for those who believe in the Promise— that is, those who believe in the inclusive America inferred in the opening lines of our sacred texts and not in an exclusive United States hoarded for an arbitrarily chosen few—the duty to stand in solidarity against injustice is more readily received and durable.

We do not have to guess about this—following the killing of George Floyd on Memorial Day 2020, we witnessed citizens in every state in the country and of every race, ethnicity, gender, age, and religion engaged in sustained and focused protests. The tragic event was like others that have occurred throughout American history and like the very public deaths of other unarmed black men killed by police. But the demonstrations following Floyd's death channeled a widespread moral outrage and directly responded to a painfully clear injustice, facilitating a multiracial solidarity where older white Republican conservatives chanted "black lives matter" alongside younger black democratic socialists. For some period of time and to some appreciable extent, principle muted the things that divide us most—politics, race, region. These protests became civil religious rituals evangelizing the values of equality and liberty that fill our sacred texts. And though racism did not disappear and injustice continues, they were undoubtedly dealt a blow by a united citizenry. The protests provided a glimpse of the power of principle and ritual to bind us one to another in a just cause.

Americans may not have a common heritage, but we have a shared story that our civil religion outlines. Within that shared story, of course, our experiences are quite dissimilar—the story of women gaining the right to vote and access to political agency is not the story of black people emerging from slavery and enduring Jim Crow, and neither of these is the full story of black women who have had to brave both of those troubled waters. The story of working-class white families is not the story of the white economic elites who descended from the earliest landed gentry. Native Americans' stories are different from all others—even from each other—and are unique in their origins, temporality, and journeys. The immigrant story in America looks very different depending on the country of origin, race, and time period of arrival for those seeking opportunity, citizenship, and inclusion.

But these stories intertwine to form a national narrative that is collectively ours. The American story is one of shortcomings and progress, together. It is one of principled stances and stifling hypocrisy, together. It is a new tale of power vested in the people and an old tale of people with power running roughshod over those without it, together. The American narrative that belongs to all of us and is a defining feature of the national identity is a story of forward lurches interspersed with backward stumbles. It is a centuries-long journey of transformation that inches the nation closer to the Promise, even if that goal remains elusive and may be, as Gorski has intimated, the "ultimately uncompletable project of a truly United States."[20]

That we may never fully realize the Promise should not be disheartening; the American narrative is structured more on the content of the journey than on resting at the destination. As with most religions, the point in guiding our way of life is to inspire and encourage the transformation that occurs during the traveling even if we do not live to see the destination. Indeed, in many religions the destination—heaven, for example—is achievable only after life has ended; living a life worthy of entrance to the province of reward is the point of life altogether. The story is in the living. This is why the Constitution refers to a "more perfect Union" instead of a perfect one—"more perfect" suggests that there is always more ground to cover before it is fully realized. It is why King punctuated his speech about the promised land, delivered the night before his death, with the haunting line, "I may not get there with you." The journey is where relationships solidify and where commitment and resolve are tested. For this reason, the "going there" matters far more to our lives than the "getting there." The civil destination you arrive at is where a new story begins. Our civil religious narrative is the story of our journey together, of our growing together. And it is equally each of ours.

Evidence of one's pride in the United States and the desire for inclusion in America is typically demonstrated in civil religious terms. As has been shown, the nation's most prominent historical figures used such language to laud or chastise the nation whenever it succeeded or failed to live up to its principles. But as with any religion, symbols and rituals are a public declaration of devotion. Participating in celebratory or ceremonial events—reciting the Pledge of Allegiance, observing moments of silence to commemorate national tragedies and those who have died in the nation's defense, or applauding healthcare workers daily on their way to begin a hospital shift during the 2020 coronavirus pandemic—are gestures that communicate the desire for American belongingness. The reason most national politicians wear the American flag on their lapels and conclude major speeches with "God bless America" is to signal to the public their civic piety. The ritual of standing up, removing hats, and placing a hand over one's heart during the national anthem is a matter of civil religiosity.

Civil religious observances are so palpable and revered that they have muted national law in some instances. For example, it is law in the United States that the actual flag should never be worn as apparel; never be used for advertising purposes for any reason whatsoever; never be used on any sort of box, basket, or carrying receptacle; and never be used as a costume or athletic uniform. Punishment for violating the Flag Code can be a fine and up to a year imprisonment. This law, however, is never enforced. For the actions deemed as disrespectful—like affixing symbols to the flag or burning it in protest—the Supreme Court has determined that such acts are protected by the Constitution's freedom of speech provisions. And for those violations done as a sign of national pride—like wearing the flag as a cape at a sporting event or a political rally—the law turns the other way because it dares not demonize expressions of national pride or criminalize a loving embrace of the flag.[21] It is an article of faith in American society that displaying symbols of national pride is an unmitigated good.

National solidarity can only emerge from the morass of identities, experiences, and histories that exist within the citizenry if the doctrine of the American civil religion becomes the set of values and practices that bind us together. The country cannot expect to tackle an injustice as entrenched as racial inequality if citizens cannot summon the will to obligate themselves to one another. The civic friendships required to spawn national solidarity need us to believe in the Promise, need us to agree on the defining principles and ideals in our canon, and need us to *do* American by demonstrating our commitment through participation in or acknowledgement of the nation's rituals and cultural practices. And solidarity itself is the surest way to ensure America endures. This is a realization that the nation's first citizens recognized, even if they, too, fell terribly short—a realization captured in the civil religious proclamation that closes the document establishing our independence: "And for the support of this Declaration, with a firm reliance on the protection of Divine Providence, we mutually pledge to each other our Lives, our Fortunes, and our sacred Honor."

ON A MILD AUGUST EVENING in 2016, a steady breeze carried the scent of the nearby salt marshes across Santa Clara, California, mixing with the aroma of hot dogs and pyrotechnics in a stadium near the southern end of the largest estuary on the Pacific face of the Americas. The home team's football fans had gathered there to watch the San Francisco 49ers in their first preseason game of the season. As the stadium rose to its feet with the playing of the national anthem, the crowd paid just as little mind to the briny scent wafting through the air as it did to the black man in street clothes sitting on the sideline bench for the song's duration.

Colin Kaepernick, the quarterback who had led the team to the playoffs and a Super Bowl just a couple of years earlier, was recovering from a shoulder injury and looking forward to earning his spot in the team's starting lineup. His decision to remain seated during the national anthem was not a result of a star player feeling despondent about his place on the team; it was the result of a black man feeling despondent about his place in America. With racial tensions growing in the United States as summer clashes between black communities and law enforcement filled cable news' evening time slots, Kaepernick was fed up with racism throwing salt in the game.

The next week, the 49ers visited Denver for another tune-up game, and Kaepernick, still injured and in street clothes on the sideline, again sat during the playing of the national anthem. No one seemed to notice, and if they did, no one seemed to care.[22] The following game, back in Santa Clara with Kaepernick now in uniform, however, was a different story entirely. Pictures from the pregame ceremonies show the black quarterback sitting on the bench during the anthem, and he was asked about it by a reporter following the game. Kaepernick responded that this was a form of protest intended to be a statement against the racial injustice and inequality present in the United States. He was crystal clear in his reasoning: "I am not going to stand up to show pride in a flag for a country that oppresses black people and people of color."[23]

The national uproar was immediate and intense. Many fans and Americans in general were appalled that a player would dare not stand for the national anthem. Pundits accused Kaepernick of being selfish, ungrateful, unpatriotic, inappropriate, and a range of other indictments intended to exact a social penalty for violating an American norm. The National Football League issued a statement saying that players are encouraged, but not required, to stand during the national anthem. But the core of the problem people had with Kaepernick's gesture was summed up by New Orleans Saints' quarterback Drew Brees: "He can speak out about a very important issue. But there's plenty of other ways that you can do that in a peaceful manner that doesn't involve being disrespectful to the American flag."[24] This was the crux of the issue—people were incensed by Kaepernick's willingness to dishonor the nation's most prominent symbol. The crime he committed, if the U.S. Flag Code were actually an enforceable law, was no more serious than the crime Americans commit when they drape a flag over their lawn chairs at a picnic or leave a weathered, tattered flag twisting on a rod affixed to their house. But the rebuke of Kaepernick was not about violating the code; he had done something much worse in the eyes of a number of Americans—he had sinned.

The backlash was not unexpected. Protests, whether the Boston Tea Party in 1773 or the Montgomery bus boycott more than 180 years later, are intended to rankle. Effective forms of protest almost always attract negative attention as critics clamor to express their sympathy with the right to free speech but pepper such declarations with the predictable inquiry, "Isn't there a better way?" This question is really asking if the protest can be done quietly—that is, in a manner that is not disruptive to people's lives or offensive to their beliefs. Kaepernick knew his actions would be upsetting to many and that there would be repercussions. He told the press, "If they take football away, my endorsements from me, I know that I stood up for what is right."

What Kaepernick did not anticipate, however, was that he would be accused of hating America and hating the U.S. military. Once again, another quarterback chimed in with comments that captured the essence of the outrage, saying, "I find it completely disrespectful, not only to the military, but to the men and women who wear the blue uniform and protect our cities every day."[25] Realizing how his protest was being perceived and recast as anti-military, Kaepernick asked to meet with Nate Boyer, an Army veteran who played for a short stint in the NFL, to get a better understanding of the criticism. Boyer suggested that Kaepernick kneel during the anthem instead of sitting in order to signal respect for those in the military who gave their lives that the nation might live while also maintaining his protest. As Boyer explained it, "Kneeling's never been in our history really seen as a disrespectful act. I mean, people kneel when they get knighted. You kneel to propose to your wife, and you take a knee to pray. And soldiers often take a knee in front of a fallen brother's grave to pay respects."[26] And this is exactly what Kaepernick did the next week and every week afterward. Other football players across the league joined him, as well as a diverse group of professional players in other sports and amateur athletes in college and high school. The national debate and controversy did not subside, and the issue—the method of protest, not the cause of it—was hijacked in dramatic fashion by politicians and pundits alike, ultimately turning the whole episode into an efficient means of dividing the citizenry instead of using it as a moment to wrestle with the downward spiral of the nation's race relations.

The reason Kaepernick's protest became a national focal point boils down to one simple thing: a distorted interpretation of civil religion. His protest defied the norms around America's most prominent symbol and ritual, an action received by many citizens as sacrilegious and blasphemous. It signaled a rejection of the nation's principles, mythologies, and pantheon. Even when he attempted to modulate his protest by kneeling, a gesture specifically intended as a show of respect for tenets of the American civil religion, it remained inconsistent with accepted practice and did little to stem the tide of accusations that he was the civic version of a heathen.

Anthropologists and theorists have long noted the connection between myths and rituals, and the role they play in unifying people, ordering societies, and providing existential meaning to their believers and practitioners.[27] Refusal to participate is one thing, but participating in a way perceived as disrespectful invites a deeper sort of scrutiny. Nonconformant participation in these rituals can be interpreted not simply as a desire for exclusion, but also as an explicit attempt to disassemble the unity, order, and meaning they provide. In this regard, Kaepernick's chosen form of protest irritated even the most casual observers of the norms associated with the American civil religion. The passions and fervor of zealots who often assert personal ownership of the nation's symbols ran especially hot as they interpreted his actions as an attack on their identity and culture—to them, it was as if Kaepernick had symbolically set the flag aflame and then salted the earth where it burned. Meanwhile, the reaction to Kaepernick's freedom-of-speech demonstration provoked the ire of those who agreed with his critique of the United States and were deemed unpatriotic for daring to denounce national practices that fall short of the Promise. The method of protest was both brilliant in drawing attention to how the United States falls short of the Promise and ripe to be commandeered by those whose motives were more political than principled.

That a minor scrum cost Kaepernick his playing career and became the subject of national debate—even influencing presidential politics—tells us two very important things about civil religion: it is meaningful, powerful, and consequential; and, in the wrong hands, it can be commandeered to divide the people it could otherwise unite.

THE PROBLEMS WITH CIVIL RELIGION become obvious rather quickly. It can begin to smell like an oppressive nationalism that denigrates all who are not blessed enough to be included in the collective, membership in which is usually based on an arbitrary standard. It also immediately brings to mind the violence and oppression that has been carried out in the name of religion. After all, chattel slavery and racial segregation were often pitched as the divine plan of a Christian God. The Ku Klux Klan buried its racism in a disfigured version of Christian morality, and prominent nineteenth-century South Carolina politician James Henry Hammond justified enslavement on the floor of the U.S. Senate by asserting, "Our slaves are black, of another and inferior race. The status in which we have placed them is an elevation. They are elevated from the condition in which God first created them, by being made our slaves."[28] Terrorists using the Islamic religion as a justification for violence have become a central focus for twenty-first-century national security and foreign policy strategies. History is littered with examples of people using religious beliefs and practices to destroy, oppress, or control others. And religion has also been used to establish divisive societies in which believers are virtuous and all others are inferior and unworthy. If civil religion is just another axis on which a people orient their denigration of others, then not only is it wholly inappropriate and ill-suited for national solidarity; it condones nations exercising their worst impulses and excuses any negative effects that result.

Concerns about civil religion are warranted. We have seen its negative potential in action. In those moments when the security of the United States is threatened, adherence to the tenets of civil religions spikes. In the last century alone, the bombing of Pearl Harbor, the threat of nuclear conflict during the Cold War, major wars waged in far-flung corners of the globe, the September 11 terrorist attacks, and, to some extent, the coronavirus pandemic of 2020 all elicited a national pride akin to religious zeal that swept over the country. In the face of grave danger and challenges to the national narrative and identity, Americans united and found solidarity. This civil religious zeal continued in the wake and aftermath of these dire threats, lending purpose to all the sacrifices—in terms of not only lives disrupted but also lives lost—of citizen exemplars proffered in exchange for the nation's life and well-being. It, as religions often do, helped people make sense of the inexplicable while also adding another chapter on virtue and bravery to the national narrative and identity.

However, in each of those moments of civil religious devotion, oppression of those labeled as less American continued apace. Japanese Americans were interned by order of President Franklin Roosevelt, and the action was upheld by the Supreme Court. Americans, including civil rights leaders, were accused, excoriated, and ostracized for purportedly supporting communism during the Cold War without any proof. Muslim Americans—even people whom others mistook for Muslims—were assaulted and their mosques vandalized in the immediate aftermath of the September 11 attacks, a form of religious and racial discrimination that still persists in the United States. During the coronavirus pandemic, Asian Americans were harassed and assaulted, with one family of three repeatedly hacked with a dagger in a Texas Walmart. The pandemic even became politicized with heated, often partisan conflicts between citizens who wore masks and those who did not. The storming of the Capitol on January 6, 2021, was the product of parishioners of a bastardized civil religion—rioters who simultaneously claimed to be perfected American patriots while clothed in symbols of racist, anti-American violence. And each time destruction and persecutions occurred, the rationale was based on a religious-like adherence to a love of America or its principles that compelled some to behave as self-appointed soldiers of the divine and protectors of the realm. That is, they rooted their discrimination of others in patriotic zealotry, frequently centered on a white group identity.

Theorists and practitioners are quite aware of the power of civil religion, and, as a result, its propensity to be hijacked for nefarious purposes. Sociologist Marcela Cristi warns that because many are dazzled by civil religion's ability to unify otherwise dissimilar citizens, not enough attention is paid to the "ideological, manipulative intent (or potential) of civil religion." The role that the state and political elites have in shaping civil religion is often discounted, and civil religion's advocates often do not fully consider that it "may help legitimize the domination of the most powerful cultural or social group in society."[29] Many political leaders in the United States have used citizens' reverence for and emotional connections to American symbols, rituals, and sacred texts for political gain and in a manner that proves more divisive than unifying. Civil religion is sometimes used as a weapon to eviscerate political opponents rather than as an instrument to encourage social harmony and orchestrate political accord.

The primary rivals of civil religion—those concepts that superficially resemble it but are distinct and achieve vastly different detrimental outcomes—are religious nationalism and radical secularism. Cristi describes religious nationalism as the sacralization of the nation itself—not its values or ideals—and notes that conservative Protestantism in the United States employs civil religious discourse to articulate its political demands in religious and nationalistic terms.[30] Gorski defines it more ominously as a "toxic blend of apocalyptic religion and imperial zeal that envisions the United States as a righteous nation charged with a divine commission to rid the world of evil" that is little more that national self-worship and "political idolatry dressed up as religious orthodoxy."[31] In effect, this virulent strain makes a "blood and soil" argument for the United States, declaring that the nation's territory and identity are bound up in Christianity and the white race. It mires our national narratives, symbols, and canon in an ethnocentric view of the United States and encourages the suppression of all people and things disruptive to that notion, even if they are civil religious figures. The birther claims around Barack Obama are evidence of this philosophy at work: the false accusations that the nation's first black president was not born in the United States and thus not a citizen or real American, that he was Muslim, and that he ascribed to socialism all were ethnoreligious nationalist appeals that reacted to the disruption of the national order they perceived from a black man with a foreign parent and a Muslim name in the White House.

Religious nationalism views the United States as an arm of Christianity, suggesting that there is a bloodline that flows from that religion through the nation-state and into its chosen people— men of the white race who authored the founding documents and brought the miraculous vision of an independent democratic nation into reality. It commandeers the nation's flag, anthem, sacred memorials, and notions of patriotism and ordains them such that any perceived infringement requires a response of righteous indignation. As a result, it believes the shedding of blood becomes a means of sacrifice that purges threats from the nation and acts as a means of purification of the bloodline.

Dylan Roof, the self-avowed white supremacist who gunned down nine black church members on June 17, 2015, during a Wednesday-night Bible study in Charleston, South Carolina, was animated by this perverted and violent ethnonationalism. Challenges to the religious-nationalism worldview are viewed as apocalyptic battles between good and evil, like those described in the Bible as fights "against the leaders and the powers and the spirits of darkness in this world" and against evil in "heavenly places," like the United States.[32] Altogether, it is an extraordinarily dangerous worldview because it demonizes others, marking them as evil and unworthy of compassion or compromise; it casts conflicts and hardships as divinely designed tests of faith that people are helpless to avoid or resolve; and it suggests that violence and the spilling of blood are the only way enemies can be annihilated. It not only discourages unity—it turns citizens into mortal enemies and excuses discrimination as God's will for a pure nation.

The other primary competitor of civil religion is what Gorski calls radical secularism, which sits at the pole opposite religious nationalism. He defines it as a "noxious blend of cultural elitism and militant atheism that envisions the United States as part of an Enlightenment project threatened by the ignorant rubes who still cling to traditional religions."[33] If religious nationalism views the United States as a divinely ordained Christian project, radical secularism asserts there is no place at all for religious elements. It suggests that communalism and technocratic governance are sufficient values in and of themselves for a well-ordered republic—no religious appeals are necessary. And while this approach may avoid some of the pitfalls religion introduces to societies, it provides no higher calling or belief system that organizes and mobilizes the public. It is clinical and philosophical, not emotional or spiritual.

Imagine the words of the Declaration of Independence, the soaring rhetoric of Abraham Lincoln, the moral appeals of Martin Luther King, Jr., and the Promise itself—a covenant in its own right—without any religious framing or iconography. The Gettysburg Address would not exist, and presidential inauguration speeches would be reduced to dry readings of the party platforms—useful, perhaps, but too reasoned for emotional appeals. Radical secularism is ill-equipped to foster the bonds of kinship required to establish national solidarity.

Establishing civil religion as a means to create civic friendships among democratic strangers is hampered by religious nationalism and radical secularism. Even in their modulated forms, the disunity and dispassion they produce are apparent in the partisan polarization and social isolation plaguing the nation's current civic landscape. The far right leverages religious nationalism in an attempt to create the America that exists in its nostalgia, and the far left's radically secular appeals lack the unifying messaging required to move the public. But the employ of each of these civil religion rivals proves to be politically expedient and advantageous, delivering political defeats to other members in the citizenry instead of bringing people together under a set of shared beliefs and common practices and incentivizing continued adherence to them despite their negative effects on the nation.

Part of the trouble with establishing a civil religion is bound up in Americans' general retreat from religiosity. Today, more than three in four of us believe religion is losing its influence on American life, and the number of us who never attend church has doubled in the last thirty years. We have lost faith in the church—more than one in four of us has little or no confidence in organized religion, a 250 percent increase from the early 1970s. In 1948, nearly 70 percent of Americans identified their religious preference as Protestant and only 2 percent indicated they had no preference at all, levels that held steady for decades. But by 2018, only 35 percent identified as Protestant and 20 percent—a staggering tenfold increase—had no religious preference.[34] Meanwhile, the number of us who identify as Catholic, Jewish, or Mormon has remained steady for the last seventy years. Because the American civil religion borrows much of its rhetorical and liturgical elements from Protestantism, the drop-off in the latter's standing and following previews the resistance that awaits civil religion advocates.

On the other hand, the decrease in Americans who see themselves as both religious and spiritual has been matched by a corresponding increase in those who identify as spiritual but not religious. This increase is happening at similar rates among men and women, across race and ethnicity, in both the Democratic and Republican

Parties, in all under-sixty-five age groups and at all levels of education.[35] Being spiritual but not religious typically signals a belief in a higher power or sacred force that is accompanied by a rejection of religious depictions of enthroned deities and the institutions built around them—"believing without belonging," as British sociologist Grace Davie puts it.[36] Despite some perceptions that it is a thin belief system most appealing to loners interested in escaping the discipline and public commitment that accompanies religious institutions, scholars have found that individuals identifying in this way are especially communal and find meaning in a range of activities that require dedication and devotion, from the arts and physical-fitness cliques to book clubs and parent-centric groups.[37] Moreover, their sense of belonging and a social connectedness matches that of those with high levels of religiosity and who attend religious services regularly. They have larger core networks of people with whom they engage in discussions and have more close ties than practitioners of organized religion do.[38] In the American way of life, there is still a deep clamoring for meaning and connection that historically led to membership in religious institutions and is now increasingly expressed through secular social and civic connections.

One of the primary benefits of a national solidarity undergirded by an American civil religion is that it counters and weakens the bastardized versions—religious nationalism and radical secularism—that only divide the country. Further, it does not drag in all the negative aspects of religion that cause followers to believe the subjugation of others is evidence of the sanctity of their faith. All these hazards show not only that a civil religion–based national solidarity is necessary, but also that the impulses that create the divisive versions are the very things that solidarity neutralizes. In theory, this is fairly clear. But as political scientist Andrew Murphy puts it, "The important challenge going forward, I think, is to find a way to bridge the theoretical analysis of American civil religion and the concrete details of American politics and society."[39] This is the task that lies before us as Americans.

My upbringing was what one might expect for a child of college-educated parents who made decent salaries as corporate profession-als in the 1980s. For as long as I can remember, we lived in quiet neighborhoods with green lawns, nearby parks, two-car garages, and lots of white people. From Maryland to upstate New York and finally to central North Carolina, and the city where my parents met, I was used to being one of the few black children—and often, the only one—in the neighborhood, in the classroom, or on the athletic team. By the time I had entered middle school, I was the oldest of four siblings—two girls bookended by two boys; ten years separated my brother and me, six years between my sisters. By virtue of our upbringing, we not only knew how to comport ourselves among white people but were comfortable doing so.

But we were black children in a black home first. The church we attended multiple times a week for youth nights, choir rehearsals, and marathon Sunday services that stretched deep into the afternoon were filled with black people. My parents' social circle of friends, college classmates, sorority sisters in crimson and cream, and frater-nity brothers with the Greek letter Ω burned into their arms were all black. The food we ate, the places where we cut and styled our hair, the family we met for holidays and summertime reunions in humid climes, and our customs and practices all screamed African American. Though I spent the bulk of my daily social and school time among white neighbors and classmates, I never questioned my race, whether or not I belonged, or the authenticity of my blackness in those voluntarily segregated places and times. It sounds odd to say something so obvious so expressly, but I have always known I was black.

As one would expect, however, the peaceful coexistence of these two worlds—life in white suburbia and life in the black counterpublic—were destined to collide, just as they had that autumn morning when an eleven-year-old called me the n-word. The most consequential collision occurred in the middle school gym, laid with scuffed maple planks and enveloped by the throng of preadolescents huddled in wooden retractable bleachers waiting for school to begin. The color line was explicit—the gym was filled with white students sitting together and interspersed with an occasional dash of color, except for one section where students bused in from the predominantly black side of town congregated after arriving together. I typically sat with my white friends from the neighborhood, but one particular morning, I felt an urge to sit in the black section for the first time. So I spotted a friend there, sidled up beside him, and immediately felt insecure being in this space where I had never been. The fleeting glances and elbowed giggles from the kids around me were hard to ignore, each of them wondering why the black guy who sat with, dressed like, and used the same slang as white teens was suddenly in their section. Awkward and introverted, I just wanted the damn bell to ring.

The bell rang, but it did not save me. I stood up and slung my backpack over a shoulder, feeling someone's glare. It was Dre, one of those affable souls whose gregarious nature meant he could find a friend anywhere—black or white. But he could go from joking to deadly serious in a flash, and it was not clear which version was eyeing me. When I turned to meet his gaze, he did not even blink when he asked me one simple, disruptive question: "When did you start acting black?"

Acting black.

I had never considered that there was a way to be black—and that having mostly white friends was reason enough to question my group allegiance. The clarity and understanding dawned quickly. The question felt like a social penalty for not acknowledging plainly

enough connections to other black students. When it comes to confronting racism, realizing civil rights protections, and feeling group
belongingness, it is not enough to just be black—you must *do* black,
demonstrating a desire for inclusion, a commitment to the people,
and a belief system of similar orientation.

FOUR YEARS LATER, and not until the news crew showed up did
I start to second-guess the decision to ditch school and march. A
reporter positioned herself between us and the cameraman, and I
immediately drowned in visions of my parents catching me in a
political protest on the local news, their vision blanked out by flashes
of shock and anger. In May 1992, I was supposed to be inside the
high school holding my own with the smartest teens in the state at
the North Carolina School of Science and Math, not out in front of
it holding a picket sign and harmonizing my way into "No justice,
no peace" chants.

As an insecure adolescent, I found my years in middle school
felt like a series of choices about racial identity. I simply was not
skilled enough, charismatic enough, or athletic enough to straddle
the two worlds. In the span of just over a year, my friend circle
went from mostly white to almost exclusively black. By the time I
entered high school, my Billabong jackets and Quiksilver tops gave
way to leather medallions featuring red, black, and green stacked
in a silhouette of the African continent and T-shirts emblazoned
with the proclamation "It's a Black Thing!" followed by one pitying,
punctuating sentence: "You Wouldn't Understand."

When motorist Rodney King was videotaped being beaten into
the asphalt by a group of Los Angeles police officers during my
sophomore year of high school, it presented another choice that
revolved around race. Americans were immediately divided over
the incident, as is often the case when conflict across the color line
becomes a proxy for the tensions that trail the nation's unresolved

issue with racism. The country held its breath for a year while the justice system deliberated. When the verdict came in the next year, acquitting all four officers of assault, riots of racial outrage played out on television screens across the country, and the black students at my high school three thousand miles away were also glowing white-hot.

We, like many other Americans, saw the outcome of the case as a miscarriage of justice. And we took the acquittal personally because it communicated to us—hopeful teenagers whose presence at this exclusive school was the receipt proving our families had bought lock, stock, and barrel into the liberating power of education—that black Americans were less valued, less deserving of compassion and dignity, less worthy of the Promise. We decided to walk out of school the following day and stage a public protest. My decision to participate was not an attempt to prove my racial authenticity; it was not "acting black" through a superficial performance. It was a display of solidarity through a ritualistic demonstration of a commitment to a shared higher principle.

Our protest was inspired by similar ones happening across the nation. But because of the spotlight on our school, a residential public institution that was the pride of the state, ours drew the attention of local newspaper and television reporters. We stood at the edge of campus near a busy intersection and let the passersby know that America had fallen short. When the news camera started rolling, the glint of fear and anxiety that made me blink in the face of solidarity quickly gave way to pride and resolve. The sight of my classmates taking a moral stance that could have resulted in serious material loss to each of us—a loss that some of our families would not have easily absorbed—emboldened me. Shrinking away from the camera would have meant shrinking away from them, from our shared experiences, and from the systems of belief that connected us, something I was not willing to do. It would have meant supplanting bravery and obligation with cowardice and selfishness. Solidarity required sacrifice, a religious sort of commitment, a willingness to risk our place.

The school's administration set aside a day to allow the faculty and student body to talk openly about race relations in America. At the schoolwide assembly, one by one, students set their inhibitions aside and voiced their experiences for all those gathered. Black students talked about unfairness in the criminal justice system, experiences with discrimination on campus, and life in the neighborhoods they grew up in before landing in this environment of resources, access, and privilege. Native American students talked of how their culture and customs were co-opted for entertainment and mocked out of ignorance and unappreciation. Asian and Indian American students talked about battling stereotypes and small slights that can have a large impact on one's formative years, like assuming mathematical or musical talents or encountering people's unwillingness to learn how to pronounce names correctly. White students talked of how unfair it was to be held personally responsible for the historical experiences of other people, of not being aware of the words and actions that others interpreted as offensive, and facing their own brand of discrimination when they were labeled as a racist or a redneck because of the part of the state they called home.

One of the last people to speak at the assembly was a stocky white male student with long brown hair and sandals. He had listened intently to what everyone had to say and was especially moved by the black students' accounts of the different ways racism impacted their experience of America. He talked about his upbringing in a part of North Carolina where he did not have the opportunity to meet, talk to, or befriend people who did not look like him. The day had been quite a shock to his system to hear about the lives of the black students who were now in his classes, in his dorm, and at his lunch table. And, with tears welling up in his eyes, his words laced with passion, frustration, and sadness, he simply said, "I didn't know!"

What I recall most, however, was the deep and pervasive sense that everyone in the gym that day just wanted to get it right. By talking to one another across the color line, it became apparent that each student there wanted more community and a realer sense of connection to one another. I could not shake how much of the issue centered on simply not understanding each other and how much we adhered to the same set of core beliefs about what America should be.

This entire episode showed me that most people just want to be acknowledged, heard, understood, and not prejudged, especially on the question of race in America. This desire seems to be a prelude to resolution and progress toward the Promise. But because we rarely talk to each other, listen to each other, or understand each other, we do not form strong bonds of kinship with each other. Instead, we blink, waver, and second-guess any decision to sacrifice for those who are unlike us. If we are going to be vulnerable across the color line, it will require that we subscribe to the same faith in the Promise.

THAT SAME YEAR of high school, my grandfather died. Bobby Lee was the only grandfather I had ever known. Theodore Roosevelt Johnson, my father's father and the man whose name I carry, died two years before I was born. His wife and my paternal grandmother, Louisa Brown Johnson, died on my birthday four years before it became my birthday. Bobby and Orrie Bell Lee, my mother's parents, were the wise and sturdy pair from the red clay of southwest Georgia who kneaded the distinct love that grandparents have an especial talent for giving. And now he was gone. He was buried in a church cemetery at the end of a short road of dust and gravel presided over by a small white house of worship with dark wooden floors that had rested there for over a century. Standing in the church surrounded by family, I for the first time saw a body without a spirit in it. The body without its animating force is only a shell of life—when the spirit is gone, what remains behind pales to what once was and what could have been.

My grandmother Orrie Bell—the granddaughter of an enslaved man and proud daughter of Daddy Joe—was alone after nearly sixty years of marriage and poured herself anew into her children and grandchildren. On her first birthday following the passing of her husband, she wrote me a letter. For a variety of reasons, I was struggling in high school, and she let her pen fly across multiple pages of notebook paper to encourage me, challenge me, and remind me that she believed in the purpose God had given my life. Later that year, she spent a week at my family's house, and each day around noon she and I dined together—just the two of us—talking on whatever topic emerged as I devoured the cream cheese and crushed pineapple sandwiches she had prepared.

In the defining years of my life, as I wrestled with identity, society's expectations of me given my race and class, and finding my place in America, Orrie Bell saw only the best in me. She deeply believed in all the generations of sons and daughters she had given life to, even when we did not believe in ourselves. Despite her upbringing filled with experiences of being devalued and disenfranchised because of her race, she maintained a religious conviction in the resilience of a faithful people, the forward march toward racial equality, and the power of prayer. She convinced her children and their children through the love and confidence she poured into us that we belonged and had a special purpose, no matter what the world may say. In doing so, she provided the blueprint for my belief today that the nation must do the same—allow the spirit of America to be the animating force for the United States and maintain a religious level of faith in the Promise until it is so.

PERHAPS THE GREATEST PERFORMANCE of the national anthem came at the 1991 Super Bowl, when renowned songstress Whitney Houston, clad in a flag-inspired tracksuit, belted out a rapturous rendition of the song just ten days into the Persian Gulf War. It was so moving and so appropriately captured the nation's spirit in the moment that the recording became a bestseller, with royalties going to charities supporting military personnel and their families. Houston descended from people who weathered the same segregated corner of Georgia where Bobby and Orrie Bell raised a family. And she brought her big, melodic, gospel-sized voice, saturated with the joys and pains of black America, to the national anthem and consecrated the Promise in the most prominent civil-religious hymn we have. In just two minutes—with military salutes and flyovers, flag-waving fans with hands on hearts, fireworks, and national pride swelling as the Gulf War raged thousands of miles away—America was enraptured. It demonstrated not only that the Promise is indeed big enough for us all, but that lamps containing the purest form of civil religion remained trimmed and burning in the pews of the black church.[40] And, when permitted, those lamps can be a light that makes the city on a hill shine.

Caution, however, must be taken. Blind adherence to the demands of civil religion's evangelists—or, worse, extremists practicing religious nationalism or radical secularism—does not foster an inclusive solidarity. The rituals of civil religion must account for the uneven history in which they were forged. For instance, the concluding line of "The Star-Spangled Banner," written in 1814, refers to the United States as the "land of the free and home of the brave" at a time when slavery was a sanctioned institution, when Native American populations were forcibly evacuated from their land, and when a significant portion of the population was denied the full rights of citizenship. And in the years since, social, political, and economic inequality along lines of race, ethnicity, and gender has persisted in a way that contravenes notions of a free and courageous nation. Yet the country's shortfalls have also been accompanied by incredible bounds of progress on race, equality, and the provision of means to address harms when they occur. There can be no dispute that the people of the United States are more free today because of the bravery of its denizens. And as the Kaepernick episode evinces, the national anthem can be spun to pit those with legitimate critiques of the United States against those who believe displays of respect and loyalty to the nation should prevail without exception.

Civil religion for national solidarity is malleable enough that it needs to neither demand blind professions of faith nor embrace outright rejection of rituals—it simply requires civic liturgies that account for our history and our potential. For example, when the national anthem is played at sporting events or graduations, it can be preceded with a short meditative tribute that accounts for the nation's faults while also extolling its virtues. And instead of the usual introductory words, "Please remove your hats and stand for the singing of the national anthem," a more solidary call should be made; perhaps along the lines of "Though the work toward the Promise of America continues, let us come together—each of us in our own way—for the playing of the national anthem." As Kaepernick clearly showed, it is possible to participate in civil religious rituals *and* exercise freedom of speech. Kneeling or bowing one's head while locking arms with one's compatriots is still a form of observance, even if it grates on those who value ritual more than rights. Reckoning with the nation's past and centering the principles that unite us can produce new wrinkles to our practice of civil religion that build solidarity while acknowledging the disparate experiences—past and present—of Americans.

With civil religion in its truest form, national solidarity becomes possible. It unifies Americans across lines of race, class, and region and provides a belief system that establishes the basis for the bonds and obligations required to overcome the effects of racism. It recognizes and welcomes with open arms the contributions that each of us, no matter our race or ethnicity, can make to the nation's advancement. It is well chronicled that should a multiracial, across-class solidarity ever rear its head, the immediate response from those who hold power will be to pull racial threads in hopes the whole cloth unravels. Civil religion motivates us to cling to one another in those times and prevents the national fabric from being rent. It is not coincidence that slavery and racism are often cast not as criminal acts but as the nation's original *sin*.

But even a people standing in national solidarity and bound by a common faith in the Promise need to know the instrument of the injustice they have formed to defeat. The civic component of national solidarity compels us to resist the temptation to blame each other and to refocus our efforts against the one entity that can permit racism to endure or weaken it and its effects—the nation-state.

CHAPTER 7

Racism Is a Crime of the State

Racism is a bit of a charlatan, attempting to trick people into thinking it is mostly an interpersonal matter and wholly incapable of infecting systems, structures, and processes. The polarization that occurs whenever racial identity is mentioned—the racial tensions and animus that are kicked up like dust on our dried-up political landscape—is framed as little more than the work of a few shameful bigots and identity-politics opportunists playing victim for attention and material gain. Racism works to convince us that its domain is in the hearts of men and that racism itself plays no role in whatever political and socioeconomic disparities exist between the different racial and ethnic groups in the United States. It is a master of misdirection and disguise, parading around as a scapegoat instead of its true self. When racial conflicts surface among us and ascend into the sky to blot out the Promise, racism is the shoulder devil whispering to some that the issue is much ado about nothing and goading others into believing that hateful individuals alone are responsible for the mess; the racial inequality resulting from the nation's economic, political, and social systems and processes, it suggests, is more a function of insufficient ingenuity and grit than it is of bias clinging to structural factors. This is the lie that racism tells us: that it is a moral failing to be driven from the souls of individuals, not a systemic flaw that takes proactive public policy to dismantle.

National solidarity has a different message. It recognizes that the form of racism complicating access to the Promise is not the kind in the hearts of men but the sort in the structures of society. It knows that there are prejudiced people in the country who dislike others for no other reason than their race, but it is far more concerned that one's ability to exercise the inalienable rights to life, liberty, and the pursuit of happiness is not hampered by race or ethnicity. Whereas racism looks to pit citizens against one another, national solidarity encourages affective bonds to mitigate the effects of racism and build a better, more resilient nation for today and for posterity. It understands that racism is not the creation of present-day Americans, but it knows the only way to realize the Promise is if we are willing to practice solidarity across racial lines. Most importantly, it makes the clear case for *what* is to blame for the damage done to the country: national solidarity says racism is a crime of the state, and we, the people, must hold the state to account.

This reframing of the issue may feel a little soft on first touch, but it is critical to the whole of the American project and its continued evolution that racism is no longer viewed as a Hatfield and McCoy feud between white and black people. At its core, racism is a force for division in order to establish and foster inequality. One of its most effective tactics in keeping the public divided is labeling one side as victims and the other side as perpetrators. If we can identify the people who were harmed and the people who caused the harm, we know who to blame. When we know who to blame, we know whose job it is to fix the thing that is broken. And when we disagree on who or what to blame and who is truly being victimized, the ensuing argument about who is right or wrong becomes the focus of attention instead of the pursuit for equality and greater cohesion across the color line.

In the United States, debates about racism are typically—and inaccurately—reduced to arguments about one simple statement: white Americans use violence and the law to victimize all other racial and ethnic groups of Americans. When painted with this broad brush, racism becomes a thing that white people do to black people, for example, and, as a result, it is then incumbent on white Americans to make it all better. But once the list of harms is published in the public sphere—among them the gap in wealth, income, and employment between the races; the disparity in school resources and education outcomes; persistent housing segregation that leaves majority-black American communities underserviced and undervalued; discrimination in healthcare access and treatments that reduces the quality of life and accounts for lower life-expectancy rates—individual white Americans look around incredulously and wonder why they are personally to blame for these ills and why it is their job alone to cure them. Meanwhile, black Americans survey the nation and wonder why there is such resistance to ameliorating the un-American conditions that continue to plague the parts of society where they live, work, and play.

One side points to all the progress and reform and suggests that individualism and self-determination are the keys to overcoming the historical effects of racism. The other side, struggling under the weight of racial inequality, wonders why their fellow citizens chalk the troubles up to their personal deficiencies and failings instead of acknowledging the system-wide set of circumstances that unfairly stacks the deck against its success. The finger-pointing begins and dueling ensues as each side feels its honor and integrity have been insulted. While we are busy shooting each other down, racism rides off into the sunset, emboldened, to live another day. The problem remains unresolved, and each successive generation returns to the same old dusty locale for its turn in the showdown.

The truth is, when citizens argue about racism, we let the government off the hook and handicap our ability to rid the nation of the racial inequality that ultimately harms us all. Our arguments often result from squabbling over two different conceptions of racism—one interpersonal, the other structural—and thereby cloud the discussion about the proper remedies and the entity charged with addressing them. Studies show that when people of color discuss racism, they are usually referring to systemic or institutional practices that complicate every aspect of American life for them. But when white Americans hear the term *racism*, they usually associate it with a racism of the heart in the form of interpersonal prejudices. That is, one group tends to see racism as a set of barriers to equal treatment and opportunity, and the other group views it as the explicit things that people say and do.

Suddenly, a discussion about the racial wealth gap created by centuries of discriminatory policies turns into a heated exchange about "bones"—white Americans make the point that they do not have a racist bone in their body, while black Americans refute the notion that racial disparities are the result of their lazy bones. These dissimilar points of origin make it incredibly difficult to find common ground or agreement on what is to be done. And because our social circles are becoming more segregated even as our society has become more integrated, we are not talking to one another with the frequency or depth needed to recognize that we are not talking about the same thing. We turn our ire and fire on one another instead of directing it at the nation-state.

Racism is the system of beliefs and practices that maintain or exacerbate inequality of opportunity among ethnoracial groups, asserting the superiority of one over another. Scholars believe it occurs at three conceptual levels: internalized racism is when individuals hold worldviews that justify racial inequality; interpersonal racism occurs when contact with others affirms racial inequality; and systemic or institutional racism is when the structures in society reinforce and perpetuate inequality.[1] The racism that threatens to dissolve America is not the sort that pumps in the bodies of certain people but the version that orders society into a racial hierarchy. Certainly, if the majority of a nation's population hates a racial minority group, it is likely the norms and laws that arise in that society will establish and entrench a racial caste system. More commonly, however, the devaluation of a racial minority group is the product of a system of radical racial inequality and provides the justification for the continued subjugation of that group. More to the point, practices and policies of racial inequality often lead to individual prejudices, not the other way around.

Structural racism is the thing poisoning America's well. It is the institutional version in its superlative form. Institutional racism consists of established laws, customs, and practices that systematically reflect and produce racial inequalities in society, whether or not the individuals maintaining these practices have racist intentions.[2] Structural racism in the United States complicates the ability of people of color to access resources, opportunities, and mobility in society as a means to secure or maintain power.[3] In sum, the form of racism that most directly threatens America and the Promise is the type that corrodes our social, political, and economic structures such that people who are not white are not viewed, treated, or accepted as fully American. This sort of racism is hard to pinpoint—it neither jumps out like the racist who screams insults in anger while committing hate crimes nor becomes unmistakably clear when looking at housing or education data absent broader context. Instead, it is most detectable once the veil is lifted and socioeconomic phenomena, historical social and policy analysis, and rhetoric from elites and the public make the issue plain.

To see America's problem with racism at work, consider what happens when economists point out that the median white household's wealth is more than twelve times as high as that of the median black household's—a disparity largely driven by differences in housing equity, where two-thirds of American household wealth is found.[4] When a civil rights advocate argues that the housing market is a perfect example of racism in the United States, a reasonable response would be to ask, "What is racist about the process of buying a house?" While the nation in the past permitted overt regulatory and statutory racial discrimination in who could buy homes and where, contemporary laws and policies have forbidden such practices for decades now. Thus, a black American family who wants to buy a home should be able to do so without being hampered by bigots proclaiming a neighborhood is "whites only" or banks refusing to finance the purchase because of the applicant's race. Following this line of thinking, black Americans can buy a home wherever they like and can file a civil suit against any discrimination that occurs. With the playing field now leveled and our society now equal, to continue along this line of logic, the only reason black families have not been capable of building wealth through housing equity must be a function of personal choices. Going further with the thought, racism is not to blame for making poor financial decisions, lacking the discipline to save the down payment for a first or better home, having a low credit score that complicates mortgage approvals or an inadequate income to afford a home, or being unable to afford the higher cost of homes in desirable areas that are most likely to help build wealth. Culture is the culprit, the argument goes, not racism. Indeed, some black people live in gorgeous homes whose value has increased substantially—would a racist system have permitted this?

But looking at the issue structurally, the racism in the systems is clear. When examinations of mortgage applications and approvals are undertaken, the evidence shows that black families with the same income and credit qualifications as white families are turned down at disproportionately high rates.[5] In fact, when income and credit scores are assessed, black Americans are paid less than their white colleagues for doing the same work and are awarded lower credit scores than white peers who are similarly situated.[6] Because of historical policies that locked black families out of the housing market and pension plans, black families today cannot access the capital long available to white families to buy their first homes. Nearly three in four Americans get help on the down payment for their house from the sale of a previous home, a monetary gift or loan from family or friends, income from investments or stocks, and accessing retirement savings.[7]

Aside from these structural barriers, sociological studies have shown that internalized and interpersonal racism also complicates home buying for black families, from prospective buyers' devaluing of homes occupied by black families to realtors steering black families away from the most desirable available properties.[8] Taken together, buying a home is never simply buying a home for most black families: it is an obstacle course of inequalities that they have to navigate in a way that white families do not simply because of the racial group to which they belong. That is structural racism at work; it makes the Promise more difficult for black Americans and tells the curious onlookers that the spectacle unfolding in front of them is the product of personal deficiencies that just so happen to be clustered among black people. The citizenry then takes to arguing about the latter assertion while leaving the former reality in place.

Clearly, then, improving each citizen's view of race one heart at a time is not how structural racism is dismantled. A black family does not get a mortgage approved every time a white person ceases to scream racial epithets. Instead, if we believe Americans should have equal access to the Promise and opportunity, unbridled by the color of their skin, then all the customs, laws, practices, resources, opportunities, and mobility available to help white citizens prosper and remain protected should also be available to black ones. And when they are not, it is the state's responsibility to make it so, or at least to protect its citizens when access to those rights and privileges of citizenship is hampered or denied. Thus, the only way to manage structural racism is to compel the state to take action.

*   *   *

LIKE RACISM, the state is a concept that is often hard to pin down—even scholars do not agree on how to define it. In the United States, we tend to use the terms *nation*, *state*, and *government* somewhat interchangeably, though in the strictest sense, these are quite distinct. At its core, a state is simply a formally organized government that has jurisdiction over a population and given territory with the capacity to make and enforce rules through legal procedures and the use of force.[9] Renowned sociologist Max Weber focused on this latter attribute of the state, arguing it holds a monopoly on the legitimate use of physical force. A state's legitimacy is a function of its ability to exercise power and the acceptance of this ability by its people and other states. States tell us who can be citizens and who cannot. They tell us which behaviors are legal and which are not. They establish systems of government that provide the bounds for the societies over which they exert authority. Even concepts like liberty and security are constructed by the state, as it determines which parts of our lives are subject to scrutiny and which are protected from it. It is an inherently political entity and the most efficient means to influence an entire society at once.

A state is a geopolitical entity governed by its interests—that is, it is consumed by self-preservation, pursuing those things that are advantageous and avoiding or eliminating those things that are threatening. In this sense, a state is amoral. It is willing to permit or carry out actions without consideration of whether they are right or wrong, and more concerned with whether such actions are good or bad for it. And yet, states are run by people with a sense of morality. How is it that a moral people can hold the reins of a state that does not adhere to its society's sense of morality? Are we to believe that all Americans thought slavery was morally correct? Are we to believe that all Americans believed dropping two nuclear bombs on Japan was a moral act? Are we to believe that all Americans are okay standing idly by when genocide unfolds in other nations? And yet in each instance, it is inarguable that the thing that was in the state's material interest—the nation's creation and economic security gained by maintaining chattel slavery, the rapid end to war with Japan, and an unwillingness to risk American lives by intervening in atrocities taking place elsewhere—was not ultimately the morally correct thing to do. Yes, people made these decisions, but they were compelled to do so by the system of government that bound the actions of its leaders. Certainly, some brave and principled souls attempted to steer the state away from its interests and toward principle, but it is a massive beast to break, saddle, and bridle. Those who resist it risk being trampled by it and its monopoly on violence, as many brave Americans have learned throughout history. As a result, too many state leaders and citizens tend to remain quiet when it comes time to do the hard things, an entirely rational act of self-preservation. And the state's pursuit of its interests often prevails over taking the moral action.

Structural racism is immoral, and the overwhelming majority of Americans believe that we should not be judged by the color of our skin. More often than not, however, the state sees very little gain in disrupting the social order, especially since those who would feel the most sense of loss with the eradication of racial hierarchy are also overrepresented in the systems of government that collectively man the helm. Thus, the presence and persistence of structural racism is permitted by the state. Not only can it not be undone by individuals alone, but the monumental effort it will take to address racism in the United States is not a national priority. The state permits structural racism, resulting in a breach of its end of the social contract as it leaves some of its citizens less protected and less able to access the rights and privileges available to others. This is not a mere inconvenience or unfortunate set of circumstances; it is a crime—a crime of the state.

The concept of state crime is not as straightforward as it may seem. A crime is a violation of criminal law, and states determine what those laws are in their territories and exact punishments on those who break them. A conundrum arises if a state violates one of its own criminal laws, assuming such a thing is even possible: it must hold itself accountable, since one of its primary duties is the enforcement of its laws. Criminal laws are often written to govern individual behavior and are ill-suited to state action. For example, when one person kills another, he or she can be charged with murder or manslaughter and be punished for that action. But when the state kills someone, such as when a state or the federal government carries out the death penalty, that is clearly not a criminal act according to U.S. law. International law is helpful here. There is little question that genocide can be a state crime, but that is because almost every nation on earth ratified or acceded to the United Nations' Genocide Convention in 1948. But criminologists contend that such strict constructions of crime as a solely legal concept do not fully capture the harms that states can cause. Thinking of crime as a broader phenomenon than what is explicitly captured in a statute is helpful in understanding how states can become criminal actors.

Definitions abound, but a comprehensive characterization of state crime has five primary features: it harms people or property, results from a state's action or inaction, is a breach of a trust or duty it has to the citizenry, is committed by an agent of the state, and is carried out by the state itself or the elite groups controlling it.[10] Questions, however, remain. For example, who gets to determine what constitutes a harm, when has trust been violated, when is someone acting as an agent of the state, and who qualifies as such? The varying interpretations of these terms can allow this definition to be contorted in such a way that either everything or nothing can be a state crime. To narrow the conception of state crime a bit so that it applies to the questions of racism, it can be defined as a state action that violates a widely understood human rights rule and risks sanction as a result.[11] In this rendering, racism is a clear violation of the human rights rules aligned to principles in the Declaration of Independence and the American civil religion, and the Constitution and democratic processes are the mechanism by which the citizenry—the source of our government's legitimacy—can penalize the state.

Structural racism is not a crime in the traditional legal sense, but it is certainly a violation of the people's trust in the state: a human and civil rights infringement that causes harm, contravenes our shared moral beliefs, and has been permitted to endure in the interest of the state and the elites who control it. As such, it is a state crime, and not only is the state responsible for addressing the resulting harms, but it is the only entity capable of doing so. But it will not do so on its own because it is not compelled by a sense of morality; neither the state nor the political and economic elites who benefit most from its present course see it as in their interest to disrupt the nation and insist on a proactive implementation of programs to disentangle racism from our structures.

In his explanation of the American civil religion in 1967, Robert Bellah expressed his belief that the United States and Americans were facing a time of trial, an existential question the nation had to answer correctly to ensure the Promise could form and endure. It is, in his estimation, our third such trial. The first time of trial dealt with the question of independence and spawned the sacred text and ideals in the opening paragraphs of the Declaration that gave us the Promise, the national North Star. The second time of trial concerned the institution of slavery and the question of whether black people could be Americans, resulting in the religious iconography of Civil War bloodshed and the assassination of a president to cleanse the nation of its original sin. The third time of trial, still upon us now, is whether the United States will meet the "responsibility and the significance our republican experiment has for the whole world."[12] We have the opportunity to demonstrate to the world, adorn the historical record, and mark our contribution to posterity by establishing a multiracial representative democracy that is truly egalitarian. National solidarity among the citizens is required if we are to emerge victorious from this time of trial—an outcome that's possible only if we hold the state accountable for its role in enabling structural racism—and guard the Promise until the next generation assumes the watch.

The only way success will be realized is if we accept two inconvenient truths that run counter to how we think of our roles in the nation's problem with racism: we, the people, hold the power to move the state, and we all, including white Americans, suffer from racism's deleterious effects. Finding solidarity with one another is the only way to successfully hold the state accountable for the role it has played—both actively and passively—in the crime of structural racism.

THE EARLY YEARS of adulthood compress a multitude of experiences into small pockets of time. In less than a year, my first venture into self-sufficiency removed me from an immersion in one form of solidarity and submerged me in another—from a bastion of group solidarity at a historically black university to a citadel of American solidarity in the U.S. armed forces. I was prepared for this significant transition by a tricky childhood managing my black and American identities in segregated spaces, learning to seamlessly code-switch between the two at a moment's notice. Experiencing both forms of solidarity at institutions seen as pillars of black and national solidarity was an education in the two Americas that raised me. I learned more about what it meant to be black in college, and I learned more about what it meant to be an American in the military. I also learned more about my obligation as an American to reduce racial inequality while being black in the military and my duty as a black citizen to ensure a strong and viable nation that can deliver on the Promise while an American at an HBCU. There were, naturally, deep differences and of course deep similarities between the two. The common thread that stitches the two together, though, is that real solidarity does not exist for its own sake—it needs a cause, an aim; and its power is found far more in connections to people than in associations with the institutions.

The road to this realization began a few weeks after my high school graduation when my family bundled itself into a long sedan and headed up U.S. Route 1 out of Raleigh, North Carolina, turning a sharp right just a few miles after crossing into the Commonwealth of Virginia. The destination that muggy morning was its Tidewater region, where the first documented black men and women arrived in the colonies as captives, where wealthy colonist Nathaniel Bacon's multiracial coalition took shape in 1676 to challenge the monarchy's injustices, and where the Emancipation Oak has stood for at least three hundred years. To get there, we passed through the land where Nat Turner, an enslaved black preacher, led a rebellion in 1831 against slaveholders that incurred an even more violent retaliation once it was put down. We covered the same dirt path, since paved over with asphalt and the dreams of the thousands of students who had sojourned there over the years, that Booker T. Washington trod on the final leg of his five-hundred-mile trek to get an education. Our car sailed to the same place he and those students docked to make a future for themselves: the waterfront campus of the historically black Hampton University.

After a lifetime of being the only black student in my classes, or one of a very few, it was both a culture shock and a shot of joy to suddenly be in a school with nothing but classmates who looked like me. No longer was I the token black kid who served as the window into one of the nation's curious exoticisms whenever questions about rap music, black habits and customs, or hairstyles and care came up in conversation. And adorned with high-flattop faded hair with an auburn-dyed step and part under a Los Angeles Kings hat that had a Malcolm X pinback button affixed to it, I certainly looked the part of black pop culture spokesman. I was, however, quite far from qualified to be such a thing. Instead, at Hampton in a class full of black students, I could focus on differential equations and French verb conjugations without the haunting realization that a wrong answer might confirm a classmate's stereotypical view of black people's intelligence. While race did not disappear as a factor in the lives of the students at Hampton, it was muted in a way that allowed us to taste an ounce more of liberty and freedom than we could in most of America.

The black college initiation is an introduction to how racial solidarity is learned, exercised, and showcased. At Hampton, like students in other black schools, we took a mandatory course titled University 101 that is geared to ensure "current and future students embrace Hampton's rich heritage and perpetuate its legacy."[13] In other words, we learned the mythologies of the university and the people who sent their children there. We were taught the university hymn—"O Hampton, a thought sent from heaven above, to be a great soul's inspiration"—and sung the black national anthem "Lift Ev'ry Voice and Sing." We partook in the rituals—from walking around, and not through, the circular plot of grass outside the university's historic Ogden Hall, to racing across the waterfront to beat freshman curfew, to screaming a baritone "SHAKE DEEZ" during drum-lined cheerleading interludes at football and basketball games. An entire culture around the black college experience builds bonds of kinship among those who attend.

These acts are not simple examples of school tradition and spirit—they are part of the lessons black colleges impart to each student about his or her obligation to contribute to the improvement of black America's plight, to practice the self-discipline and patience needed to compete and advance in the face of racial discrimination, and to develop a sense of pride in and commitment to black America. In nearly all of our classes, no matter the subject, the contributions of black Americans to the United States were part of the everyday curriculum, not sequestered in a Black History Month listicle. During election season, civil rights activists like Jesse Jackson came to campus and led voter registration marches to stress the importance of the franchise. Political views on racial issues were debated and worldviews shaped in moderated educational forums as well as in late-night dorm arguments between bites of cheap pizza and budget packs of ramen cooked over illicit hot plates. The historic phrase "Lifting as we climb" permeated everything—it was in the air, in the words and the way we spoke, and framed in the barbershops and salons just off campus. It signaled that we were in college not just to better ourselves, but for the betterment of all black Americans. The solidarity we learned was geared to dismantle the systems of racial inequality, interrupt the base and vile caricatures of black America, and push the nation closer to the Promise and the equality it assures.

After finishing up at Hampton, my system received another shock, courtesy of four U.S. Marine Corps drill instructors—hulking men of different races who were each clad in camouflage uniforms, black boots polished by the gods, and campaign covers that hid their eyes from us young aspirants hoping to become naval officers. Two days into the ordeal known as the U.S. Navy's Officer Candidate School, these men laid siege to our lives and sensibilities: kicking open doors to our rooms, banging trash cans lids, barking commands through bulging eyes and throbbing veins along their foreheads, and rushing us into a line along the painted cinder block passageways that often saw levels of humidity from human exertion and sweat that rivaled the clime of Pensacola, Florida, where the spectacle took place. They tested our resolve with gruff yelling and rapid-fire commands to carry out exercises in pits thick with sand. All along the way, they indoctrinated us into forms of kinship and solidarity. Through our grunts and moans and screams, they would say things like, "Bullets and push-ups do not care who you are! They don't care what color you are! The only thing that matters are your brothers and sisters beside you and accomplishing the mission. Do you understand?!" And from push-up position, breathless and pitiful, the response from our class filled the halls: "Yes, sir!"

I did not grow up in a military family. Becoming a naval officer was not a lifelong dream; no soul-stirring visions of military service guided my professional aspirations. Instead, feeling directionless in college without a clear vision of my goals or purpose, wanting a guaranteed job after graduation, and hoping to travel the world a bit until I figured out who and what I wanted to be, I found the Navy's pitch too attractive to pass up. And perhaps most importantly, I viewed it as a necessary rite of passage into manhood, finally declaring my own independence. Being black and American were titles stapled to me—I suppose choosing to attend a historically black university and volunteering to serve in the military were, on some level, attempts to earn and embody both designations.

In training, the military's mythologies, rituals, and symbols defined much of our everyday life. We learned about Navy history, its weapons and vessels, its historic battles, the heroism to be found at every rank, and the march song "Anchors Aweigh." Whenever the national anthem played, we immediately stopped what we were doing—cars stopped as well—and faced the American flag and the direction of the music, rendering crisp salutes until it was complete. Anchors, ships, eagles, and gold bars, stripes, and leaf-shaped embellishments are the symbols we structured our lives around. The Navy has an otherworldly reverence for flags: the nation's flag, the Union Jack—even our most junior officers are designated ensigns and our most senior officers are called flag officers because they fly their own over the people and things they command. This is branded onto the core of our being. The uniform, historically worn so that combatants can distinguish their compatriots from the enemy, and the rank on it became central to our identity and manner of relating to one another.

Our graduation day was a series of rituals completed only when we performed the first salute ritual and passed silver dollars to the Marines and sailors who had trained us, finally wearing the gold bars on our uniforms that served as a gleaming marker of our commission as Navy officers. This ragtag bunch of Americans from across the country was now a well-ordered collection of men and women draped in all-white dress uniforms, making for a powerful visual between the blaring sun overhead and the trodden greenery of the parade field underfoot. While our race and ethnicity were still apparent, they were muted by the uniform and our uniformity. And the solidarity we now felt with those who had served before us and with those who were by our sides now was oriented toward the preservation of American ideals and the protection of the nation from adversaries that want to see its demise. The type of solidarity we experienced was not the thin sort that sometimes arises among people who join the same club or cheer the same team, but rather one that required high levels of sacrifice for a higher-order cause bigger than all of us—the well-being of our loved ones, the general safety of the public from foreign interference, and the Promise of the nation.

Whether black solidarity at Hampton or American solidarity in the Navy, I subscribed to and performed a set of beliefs and actions in order to signal my acceptance of the obligation to those fighting for racial equality and the American way of life. Of course, an education in these solidarities is not limited to the venues I have described. We learn how to do black solidarity in many places, including family settings, barbershops and salons, and community and church gatherings, as well as through media that caters to black audiences. We learn about national solidarity in national rituals and holidays; through the nation's mythologies, revered political texts, and rhetoric; and by the actions of brave Americans challenging national shortfalls. But the black college and the military are exemplars of the places where we learn how to practice and demonstrate certain types of solidarity.

National solidarity not only requires shared objectives and beliefs, an obligation to members of the group, and a set of practices and customs to build esprit de corps and signal commitment to others; it also requires a recognition that its most important elements are the bonds between members of the group—not uncritical fealty to institutions. In other words, the state should foster solidarity—not discord—among its citizens. And when it fails to do so, falling short of its professed principles in the process, national solidarity does not ask the citizens to bow before the state in acceptance but demands that the people stand and hold the nation to account.

Bo Obama PROVIDES A GLIMPSE into the insidious effects of structural racism and the harm it causes every American, no matter one's race or ethnicity. Bo, of course, was the Obama family's pet, a black-and-white Portuguese water dog. A recent nationally representative survey of a thousand Americans used the dog to demonstrate how Americans' racial attitudes spill over into our assessments of everything we encounter. People were shown a picture of Bo and asked how favorable they felt toward him. But half the people were told the dog belonged to Obama, and the other half were told it was the pet of the recently deceased Democratic senator Ted Kennedy, who also happened to own a Portuguese water dog. The respondents were also asked whether they agreed that black Americans could overcome prejudice like Irish, Italian, and Jewish immigrants have done if they just tried harder and did not rely on special favors from the government.

The results, which controlled for political views and personal opinions of Barack Obama, were shocking. Those who viewed black Americans less favorably or believed that black Americans just need to try harder to overcome racism had a lower opinion of Bo when they were told it was Obama's dog and a higher opinion when told it was Kennedy's.[14] In other words, people's views of black Americans —views not necessarily couched in personal prejudice but rather influenced by the caricatures and stereotypes of black culture that structural racism entrenches in our worldview—impacted their views of things associated with black people. Exposure to racism casts a fog over us and hinders our ability to see issues clearly and examine them objectively, to the detriment of nearly everyone in the social hierarchy.

The Bo Obama example is not immaterial. There are real consequences when structural racism spills over into our judgments. Political scientist Michael Tesler, who conducted the study linking racial attitudes to Obama's pet, also looked at how racial resentment influenced Americans' views of the Affordable Care Act, more commonly referred to as Obamacare. Two years after it was enacted, those who harbored higher levels of racial resentment—a sociological measure of racial attitudes based on survey responses—looked more unfavorably on the Obama administration's healthcare proposals. Compared with partisanship and political ideology, Tesler discovered, "racial attitudes became more important in white Americans' beliefs about healthcare."[15] In fact, when asked about support specifically for Obamacare, only 37 percent of Americans in 2013 said they liked the law. But when asked about specific provisions contained in the law, 70 percent of Americans favored them.[16] Though the majority of Americans liked what Obama's healthcare reforms put in place, they no longer viewed it favorably once they learned Obama was the architect. The retreat from an otherwise desirable set of healthcare policies was led by those with higher levels of racial resentment. The lessons in this quick case study are illustrative of how structural racism can cause us to disapprove of things that we actually want and that may improve our quality of life. It causes us to harm ourselves.

The inconvenient truth for white Americans is that structural racism is not just costly and detrimental to them; it is exploitive and increasingly lethal. In his book *Dying of Whiteness*, social psychiatrist Jonathan Metzl chronicles the middle- and low-income white Americans he met across the country whose racial resentment led them to support policy positions that directly harmed them and their families. He talked to a forty-one-year-old white cab driver in Tennessee named Trevor who was sick with hepatitis C and needed a walker to get around. But Trevor said that he would rather die than receive health insurance through Obamacare. "No way I want my tax dollars paying for Mexicans or welfare queens," he replied.[17]

Trevor was true to his word—he died, proud of his state legislature for blocking Obamacare provisions that would have enabled him to receive treatment and live. In describing Trevor's approach to the issue, Metzl echoes arguments about the damage racism does to Americans and the social contract.

Structural racism can cause some of those at the upper end of the racial hierarchy to prioritize their place in the social order over the material benefits of a responsive state and beneficial policies that would improve their quality of life. It causes them to internalize views of black Americans steeped in racial resentment such that any measure framed as helpful to that group suddenly feels antithetical to their political ideologies and their conception of the American way of life. It can convince some white Americans to choose maintaining the social status quo instead of improving their own socioeconomic status or that of their fellow citizens of other races.

Racism is a crime of the state not simply because it has hampered and at times outright denied equality and justice to black Americans, but because it harms the whole of society, including white Americans. It persuades too many of the latter that their well-being is at risk from more nonwhite leaders holding the reins of government and more nonwhite people residing in the United States demanding the same fullness of citizenship. It places the blame for all that troubles white America—challenges in their healthcare, economic status, and communities, for example—at the feet of Americans of color and casts the latter as unworthy and ungrateful. It shifts responsibilities for the state's shortcomings and unresponsiveness to resource-greedy people of color who are depicted as shiftless, lacking in personal character, and unwilling to behave as responsible citizens.

Racism's sleight of hand convinces too many white Americans that they cannot coexist with people of other races in an egalitarian society where power is shared instead of cornered. It presents white Americans with a Faustian bargain that pits their happiness and access to opportunity against an inclusive society where the state is responsive to all people irrespective of race. It cloaks material theft from white America in emotional appeals that portray Americans of color as threats to society, the social order, and American culture. It slyly and deceptively communicates that the United States can either work for them or it can pursue a program of racial equality, but it cannot do both.

Consider social welfare programs. Though they include all sorts of government assistance, including Medicaid, workers' compensation, and unemployment aid, the average American usually associates welfare with the Supplemental Nutrition Assistance Program (SNAP)—formerly referred to as food stamps. In 2018, more than 41.5 million Americans participated in SNAP, and about 36 percent of those recipients were white, the highest percentage of any race or ethnicity in the country.[18] Stereotypes of the welfare recipients, however, cast them in some people's minds as conniving black women with lots of fatherless children and little ambition. Politicians and activists who have favored cutting welfare spending often utilize the "welfare queen" trope to racialize the issue and depict it as a handout for undeserving black people. This play on caricatures and prejudices affects public support for welfare spending. In the past, studies have demonstrated that when white Americans associate the welfare queen and lazy black stereotypes with welfare, they were more likely to support shrinking the programs, a result partially due to the disproportionate number of media portrayals of poor people as black.[19]

More recently, studies have shown that white Americans' opposition to welfare programs increased when they perceived threats to their majority status or economic advantage over other races and only when those programs were portrayed as primarily helping minorities.[20] Related effects can also be seen on black Americans. The well-traveled stereotypes of listless black people preferring to live off free government aid has so stigmatized federal assistance that black support for redistributive programs like welfare has decreased over the last few decades, too.[21] Political and economic elites routinely attempt to justify cutting some of the $68 billion the government spends annually on SNAP to use the savings for their benefit alone by convincing Americans that welfare spending supports the lazy habits of black people.

Though it is true that the SNAP enrollment rates of people of color are higher—a reality connected to broader economic disparities— white Americans make up the largest absolute number of recipients. As such, more white families will be hurt than black families if welfare is cut. For example, if funding cuts remove 3 million SNAP recipient households, the plurality—more than a million—will be households headed by white Americans, more than the number of households with black and Hispanic heads combined.[22] However, if white Americans are consistently harmed equally as much or more than Americans of color, racist appeals would soon lose their punch. Political elites' answer to this quandary is simply more government intervention, the very thing that those who support welfare cuts often say they despise. By providing a few bread crumbs to white Americans, the racial hierarchy is reaffirmed and white Americans' demand for a government safety net is placated.

One way this is accomplished in the SNAP example is through the addition of an employment requirement to eligibility guidelines. Because the black unemployment rate is twice the rate of white unemployment—a fact that has been true for several decades in both booming economies and recessive ones—requiring SNAP recipients to hold jobs means black families are more likely to be expunged from the program. The end result is a policy shell game in which the state justifies cuts to welfare spending by cushioning the cuts with eligibility requirements that have the effect of discriminating against black recipients and advantaging white recipients, subtly reaffirming a racial hierarchy and further entrenching racial economic disparity. The welfare example demonstrates how many white Americans may support a policy that hurts them more in exchange for preserving the social order and a fraction of the benefits they actually want the state to provide. All this does not suggest that these white Americans hate black people—rather, it is evidence of the racist ruse that political and economic elites employ to pull the wool over citizens' eyes while picking the nation's pocket. This is structural racism at work.

The impacts of racial appeals extend beyond healthcare policy or welfare programs. In education, when it is perceived that minority school districts are receiving too much taxpayer money or the black student population increases at a predominantly white school, white Americans are more likely to support cuts to local and state education funding and resist attempts at further integration, with some white communities even going so far as to secede and form new school districts.[23] Unsurprisingly, those cuts tend to be disproportionately administered to the schools filled with children of color, particularly those populated with black and Hispanic students. But when education spending is cut, white students suffer, too, since they compose about half of the approximately 50 million students in publicly funded schools, and per-pupil spending is associated with educational outcomes.[24]

In employment, the perception that jobs and promotions that go to black workers are diversity hires and not based on qualifications leads to white Americans' fierce opposition to affirmative action programs, despite the reality that white women have been these initiatives' primary beneficiaries, particularly in their first few decades, when the Department of Labor estimated 6 million women—the vast majority of whom were white—held jobs made possible by affirmative action.[25] Across nearly every material aspect of our society that requires government expenditures and action, structural racism is used to divert resources away from the citizenry and into the coffers of elites. Again, this is not the result of racial animus harbored by individual white Americans across the nation toward black Americans or other racial and ethnic groups. It is the byproduct of a government that permits inequality to persist and expand simply because it is in the interest of those to whom it is most responsive—political and economic elites. And racism is a readily available ploy to facilitate the grift.

The politics of racial resentment are deeply connected to views that the state is too big and fundamentally untrustworthy. That is, structural racism convinces too many white Americans that an empowered state with a diversifying demography equates to the loss of their social status and puts their place in the United States at risk. In this way, a proactive government begins to feel like a threat because resources, such as government funds and services, that were previously more available to them are being reallocated and expended on nonwhite populations.

This activates what sociologists call group position theory, a concept articulated in the late 1950s to describe how racial attitudes influence the social order of groups. The theory suggests that we hold inherent preferences for members in our group; that we view those outside of our group as intrinsically different; and that the sense of our group's position involves assumptions about our claims to certain rights, resources, statuses, and privileges, as well as the perception that other groups desire a greater share of such rights, resources, statuses, and privileges.[26] When a majority racial group senses a minority racial group seeking access to its claims, it is perceived as a threat. This leads to racial threat, a derivative of group position theory positing that white Americans see the rise in the percentage of people of color as more competition for power and resources.[27] In order to maintain its hold on the claims its members have grown accustomed to accessing, the majority group implements social controls to limit incursions.

These controls are binned into three broad categories: beneficent measures like social welfare programs, coercive actions such as policing and imprisonment, and lethal means including deadly force exacted by mobs or law enforcement.[28] It is clear that social control meant to address the perception of a threat requires the reach of the state to implement at scale. This leads to a desire by the majority group to cut the state's beneficent controls on the minority group—such as government assistance, education, and healthcare—and implement more coercive and lethal controls, which are clearly seen in the Unites States, from slavery and Jim Crow violence to the grossly disproportionate rate of incarcerated black Americans in federal and state jails and prisons today. The state, then, becomes the means by which the majority group benefits and the instrument by which the perceived threat of minority groups is mitigated through social controls.

When the state cuts social programs in a society where explicit racial discrimination is outlawed, every citizen ends up being harmed by the retrenchment, including the majority group, which tends to be the primary beneficiaries of such programs. Yet the majority group prefers an interventionist, law-and-order state to protect the perceived threats to its claims on certain rights, resources, statuses, and privileges. The product of this mix of controls—a decrease in beneficence and an increase in coercion and lethality—is a state comfortable with reducing its material commitments to the citizenry while increasing its oversight and enforcement of the social order of racial groups. Structural racism provides the means to accomplish this because it leverages the racial threat felt by white Americans and justifies the actions it takes that disproportionately harm Americans of color as simply being responsive to the demands of the most empowered parts of the public. It is democracy in doublespeak that appeals to our basest instincts while working behind the scenes to advantage the elites who wield the most influence.

Political scientists have long inquired about which constituencies have the largest impacts on U.S. government policy. Political scientists Martin Gilens and Benjamin Page found that average citizens and public interest groups have little ability to influence policy priorities or outcomes.[29] Instead, economic elites and organized business interests have the most impact on what policies the

U.S. government enacts and when. In fact, the paper revealed that the state was fifteen times more responsive to the policy preferences of economic elites—those in the 90th percentile or higher of income distribution—than it was to the desires of the ordinary American. As another scholar put it, the upper-middle class, which he considers to be those in the 80th percentile or higher, hoard the American Dream by pushing and supporting expensive government policies that help them to the detriment of the rest of the nation, such as mortgage interest deductions, legacy college admissions preferences, complex occupational licensing requirements, reduced tax burdens on investment income, and exclusionary zoning practices, among others.[30] Moreover, organized business interests, colloquially referred to as lobbyists in political rhetoric, are eight times more likely to compel the government to take action than average citizens are and nearly twice as likely as public interest groups. Certainly, there are times when the interests of elites and average citizens align or the desires of public interest groups are similar to those of business. But the reality is quite stark—government may derive its power from the people, but the economic and political elites wield outsize influence on the state's policy agenda and outcomes.

Structural racism—not internal or interpersonal—is at the root of the despair that some white Americans feel about the nation shifting under their feet. And it is killing them. Not only does it lead to the support of policies that ultimately harm them, but it also spawns crises in white America, like the opioid epidemic, rising depression and mental health challenges, and soaring suicide rates. In the last twenty years, the rate of white Americans dying of drug overdoses has more than tripled, far and away the most such drug-related deaths of any racial group in the United States.[31] Suicide rates for white Americans have risen year over year and by a total of 40 percent over the last two decades.[32] Middle-aged white Americans without college degrees living in rural areas—those most harmed by cuts to government assistance usually occasioned by racial appeals—are dying at the highest rates ever.[33] Studies explain exactly why this is happening: cumulative trauma resulting from disruptions in these white Americans' economic, social, and political lives.[34] Because racism permits white Americans to maintain a particular way of life and a certain sense of their group position, when elites exploit racial tensions to govern state action, white Americans' anxieties intensify and result in backlash and self-destruction. Racism is not good for anyone in the hierarchy, black or white or otherwise.

In this tale of control and exploitation, it may be tempting to view the public as pawns duped by those with power and influence. Instead, regarding racism in America, the public is vested with civic agency by the state. Typically, the term *state agent* refers to a government office or those authorized to act on the government's behalf in an official capacity. Tax collectors, police officers, and building inspectors are common types of state agents. And, of course, military members are agents of the state, as my military deployments helped me understand. The public, too, has been empowered and often encouraged by the state to behave in ways that perpetuate racial inequality, even if that is not our intent and we harbor no personal animus toward others based on race or ethnicity. But our society is constructed in a way that makes the gains of one racial group feel as if they are coming at the expense of another. We are not passive participants in this game of group competition. We have agency. In a nation that has shaken off the shackles of past illiberal institutions, racism can succeed in undermining the Promise only if we do not hold the state accountable for the rules it has established that create racial divisions and if we do not contest racial inequality when we encounter it. We have the collective agency to perpetuate racism or to mitigate it.

National solidarity requires us to accept that racism is a crime of the state, and we are empowered to hold the state, and the elites with its reins in their clutches, accountable. But charging racism to the state's ledger will still require white Americans to recognize that in order for America to fulfill its potential, it will need to expand and become more inclusive, just as it has done for the entirety of its history. This will feel uncomfortable; it will require superlative citizenship and sacrifice. Black Americans will need to understand the continued importance of civic forbearance and grace so that the divisiveness of group politics does not undermine the potential for national solidarity. Something will be required of every American if America is to survive this time of trial. We will need to decide what sort of people we really are and what sort of country we really want to have. Most importantly, we need to decide whom we will hold accountable—the state or each other. We can either succumb to the destructive narrative that a multiracial society is not possible because it is impossible for one race to achieve anything unless another is robbed of resources and opportunity, or we can decide to obligate ourselves to one another to complete the unfinished work of dismantling racism and allow future generations to experience a type of security and prosperity the world has yet to witness.

CHAPTER 8

Solidarity Is Not Colorblind

In 1999, a year into my tenure as an officer in the U.S. Navy, the blue waters of the Pacific ushered me and a crew of three hundred sailors across the world stage. The billion-dollar warship that we called home escorted us to ports throughout Asia and the Middle East and waited patiently for days at a time until we returned to her to resume our journey afloat. From the green-capped, vegetative islands that line the entrance to Busan, South Korea, to Bahrain's steamy beige landscape with rising heat waves blurring one's vision, each stop revealed something that became clearer and clearer as the waters, lands, and people ebbed and flowed: one never feels more American than when outside the United States. This is a sensation that only became more acute for me over my two decades in the military, visiting and living abroad.

A particularly memorable instance of this feeling washing over me occurred in 2008 amid a brief encounter with a tall, black-as-night Caribbean soldier in stressed jungle fatigues, a strap slung over his shoulder attached to a machine gun. His eyes immediately set on me when I stepped out of the humidity of Georgetown, Guyana, and into the quaint Immigration and Customs area of its airport. Everyone in sight was black—the armed soldier, the customs agents, the airport staff, and most of the passengers who had just touched down in this nation most Americans associate with the expression "Don't drink the Kool-Aid," following a religious cult's mass suicide there in the late 1970s. The soldier didn't need to encounter me in the international arrivals section to know that I was a visitor in his country and not a son of it. As a black American, I was out of place, and the whole place knew it. There was no mistaking me for anything else—my Americanness could not have been more noticeable if the Stars and Stripes were tattooed across my face. After all, I was an out-of-uniform American naval officer in Guyana as part of a well-publicized military humanitarian-assistance engagement. And three weeks earlier, Barack Obama became the first black president of the United States. American patriotism and black American pride trailed me in a haze thick enough to redden the eyes of any onlooker.

The soldier with the gun made his way toward me, and I instinctively responded with the gesture that many black American men make when encountering each other: the head nod of acknowledgment, an unspoken communiqué of recognition and solidarity—a nonverbal way of saying, "I see you, brother." But there was no response. Instead, he stepped in front of me and, without a hint of the familiarity I am used to when coming across other black people at home in the southern United States, flatly asked for my passport. He flipped it open while looking me square in the face, searching for something I could not quite get a handle on. His eyes dropped to inspect my passport, and the corners of his mouth turned down as he nodded in what seemed like amused approval. I prepared myself for the gentle excoriation that usually follows once black folks learn my full name. As one young lady who had the misfortune of catching my eye in high school said to me over cafeteria french fries: "You got a rich white-boy name."

The soldier's eyes lifted to meet mine, and he said, "You have a very fancy American name, Meesta . . . Tee-uh-door . . . Roze'vet . . . Jun-son . . . da tird," his head slightly bobbing up at the start of each name, his tongue dripping with Guyanese patois. We sort of chuckled to each other, and he handed the passport back to me, a smirk settling into his face as he said, "Welcome to my country, brudda."

Walking to the customs agent, I was suddenly struck by the oddness of the exchange—not due to the indifference in his approach or the unacknowledged customary black American greeting, but what he said. He did not say my name sounded white, but that it sounded American. That he chose the label "American" felt significant to me. The United States is a place where words are racialized. That is, we ascribe race and ethnicity to words that are not inherently so bounded. We do not ask the race of terrorists because, to us, the word itself implies an Arabic person. Immigrants are Hispanic; thugs are black. Americans are white, a perception that endures from the nation's inception wherein only "free White persons of good moral character"[1]—in the words of the founding generation—were permitted to become Americans. So to hear a black person describe my name as "American" struck a chord in me that had never been strummed.

More to the point, that he viewed me—not just my name, but me—as an American first and black second was notable. In the United States, that dynamic is almost entirely absent, making the feeling foreign in multiple respects. For many, the term *black American* is seasoned with more than a pinch of paradox, as if the two things long sold as inherently incompatible still have not managed to find a way to blend. But as a military man who proudly wore the cloth of the nation for years, I was used to being seen as an agent of the state first. Whether I was with shipmates conducting United Nations–sanctioned security patrols to apprehend smugglers of Iraqi oil, aiding Bangladeshis following a pummeling of wind and water from Tropical Cyclone Sidr, or riding astride the cyber cavalry to help Marines in battle emerge from urban warfare unscathed, the uniform told the world I was American and assigned actions of the state to me—its stereotypical depictions of black people taking a back seat to the display of power from the United States. When you are an agent of the state, you are the embodiment of its rights and wrongs, its strengths and weaknesses, its present and history. When it does good in the world, you share in the glory. But when it commits a crime, you are either the criminal or a willing accomplice. And yet, race never disappears entirely—my Americanness can never be colorblind.

The trip to Guyana went off without a hitch. The friendly banter shared with the armed Caribbean brother after an unfamiliar and slightly tense start was a quick taste of how the subtlest notes of black solidarity can be detected across experiences and competing identities. I wore my American identity like a badge of honor because of the humanitarian assistance rendered while there. I traveled to the far reaches of the country by helicopter to see playgrounds built and schools refurbished for rural communities of indigenous Amerindians. We ferried Guyanese citizens to a U.S. Navy ship off the coast of Georgetown for medical treatment, including surgery to open the eyes of a three-year-old girl who was born with the upper and lower lids of each eye almost entirely fused together. While we were overnighting in a hotel before heading home, one of the managers showed us a picture taken in Georgetown a couple of weeks prior. It was of a piece of posted cardboard with words in red marker scratched across it outlining the reduced prices for drinks sold at the establishment. Across the top was the reason for the special occasion: "Obama Victory Celebration."

I was proud to be an agent of a state with our history that could elect a black man to the presidency. Though the experience crystallized the fleeting and rare feeling of being American first and black second, it was also a compelling argument that it is indeed possible to be both, equally and simultaneously and without hierarchy. I do not have to wash away race to be fully American, and I do not have to shed my Americanness to be proudly black. While the United States may have an unhealthy obsession with race, America has never required us to choose. It embraces the spectrum of color in its identity and has no desire to see it blanched into an unembellished canvas of colorblindness.

THE IDEA THAT A COLORBLIND SOCIETY should not be Americans' hope for the nation can be a puzzling proposition. Many Americans were raised to believe that ignoring the color of one's skin is the antithesis of racism and should be the goal of every decent person. Indeed, colorblindness was a clear objective of the Civil Rights Movement when activists were seeking an end to racial segregation and systematic discrimination. The American Dream, popularly defined nearly a century ago as "that dream of a land in which life should be better and richer and fuller for every man, with opportunity for each according to his ability or achievement," is colorblind.[2] The Promise, too, is necessarily colorblind; equality, liberty, and the rights of citizenship should not be contingent on race. It is quite understandable, then, that the rejection of colorblindness is often received as a kick in the shins to the very ideology that gives the American idea its legs.

Colorblindness refers to an idealized state in society in which "skin color is of no consequence for individual life chances or governmental policy."[3] A society that is colorblind is nonracial and, therefore, does not discriminate against people on the basis of race because such a designation is immaterial. Those who describe themselves as colorblind are saying that they ascribe to a belief that race should not be determinant of one's ability to access social, economic, and political liberties.

Creating a colorblind society is arguably the focus of the most transformational acts of race policy in our nation's history: the Fourteenth Amendment to the Constitution granted citizenship in a colorblind fashion; the Fifteenth Amendment explicitly states that voting, one of the most basic and critical signs of democratic inclusion, "shall not be denied or abridged by the United States or by any state on account of race, color, or previous condition of servitude"; and the landmark Civil Rights Act of 1964 outlawed discrimination on the ground of race or color across society, including public accommodation, public education, and employment. The march of racial progress in the United States seems to be cadenced by the same hopeful refrain: our country shall be colorblind. And the echoes of this hope can be heard in the words of presidents from John F. Kennedy to Ronald Reagan, who explicitly articulated the desire for colorblindness in our society and pleaded with Americans to get in step. For all his initial resistance to making King's birthday a national holiday, Reagan said in February 1986, "We want what I think Martin Luther King asked for: We want a colorblind society. The ideal will be when we have achieved the moment when no one—or when nothing—is done to or for anyone because of race, differences, or religion, or ethnic origin; and it's done not because of those things, but in spite of them."[4]

This all sounds quite reasonable. Agreement is ubiquitous on colorblindness's utility in removing barriers of discrimination, particularly in political and legal institutions.[5] A nation determined to escape the trappings of state-sanctioned racial discrimination knows that its institutions cannot consider the race of constituents when delivering services and the protections citizenship affords. This is desirable. There is nothing inherently wrong with, or morally corrupt about, colorblindness as a guiding political principle.

And yet, the colorblind ideology has glaring weaknesses that make it inappropriate for the current moment and for the next stages of the nation. The first weakness is it suggests that the full remedy to racism is the implementation of policy and the passage of laws that eradicate the consideration of race in our democratic systems and processes. It asserts that from some arbitrary point in time—the enactment of a statue or the ruling of a court, for example—the country became free of racial discrimination, declared that race is no longer a determinant in a citizen's American experience, and proclaimed that history has no role in inequality henceforth. But we know the post–Civil War constitutional amendments did not prevent black citizens from being denied the right to vote or extend protections from violence to them in any lasting fashion. We know despite the Supreme Court holding in *Brown v. Board* that racial segregation in educational institutions violates the Constitution; yet the practice continued, and schools today are just as segregated as they were decades ago. We know that despite the passage of laws protecting voting rights, outlawing housing discrimination, and forbidding unequal treatment in employment practices, these things still occur at scale along racial lines. And when black Americans seek relief from these violations, a colorblind society is incapable of fully considering the claim or serving justice because the remedy must necessarily consider race.

Colorblind solutions to harms realized by specific racial groups are ill-suited to the task of creating a fair and just society. They lead to a gymnastics of contemporary logic that declares any race-specific solution is racially discriminatory—as Supreme Court chief justice John Roberts wrote in a 2007 opinion for a case about racial diversity in a school system: "The way to stop discrimination on the basis of race is to stop discriminating on the basis of race."[6] That is, colorblindness does not see the sense in fixing problems of racial inequality by implementing solutions meant to help the racial group being disadvantaged because such help discriminates against those not in receipt of it.

The second issue is that the colorblind ideology provides ready structural and interpersonal excuses to explain away why one racial group does not enjoy the same rights and privileges as another. Since colorblindness is nonracial, the origin of any challenges that arise in a society or are encountered by members of a minority racial group is attributed to any other factor but race. Colorblindness obscures any notion of racial hierarchies, structural racism, or interpersonal racism impacting one's life chances because such things are forbidden by statute. So it implies that the actual reason a racial minority group or an individual member of such a group experiences barriers to liberty and opportunity must be a function of some group or personal behavioral deficiency. Similarly, it suggests that the disproportionate share of power, wealth, and resources that racial majority groups hold is a function of ingenuity and determination instead of structural issues that facilitated their outcomes. Colorblindness accepts theoretical and moral objections to racism while rejecting any real policies, actions, or behaviors that could be effective in overcoming the effects of it.[7] It sees racism as a thing that used to be a problem—and perhaps still exists today in the hearts of indecent people—but that has largely been resolved, as evinced by the incontrovertible racial progress that has occurred over the sweep of the nation's history.

France has attempted to create a colorblind society, and the pitfalls described above have opened up. On its face, it would seem that the French would have an easier time of bringing it about than the United States, since France has only one-fifth of the population and is estimated to have a population that is 85 percent white. Even France's employ of colorblindness makes it quite difficult to know the details of its demographics because it passed a law in 1978 outlawing the collection of its citizens' racial or ethnic identities.

In 2018, France revised its constitution to scrub the word *race* from it, a measure unanimously adopted by its legislature. The rationale for it was to encourage French people to identify primarily as citizens of the country and thereby be less susceptible to the divisions that racial and ethnic identities enable. When France won the World Cup in that same year, South African comedian Trevor Noah joked that Africa had won, since 80 percent of the French players were of African descent. France's ambassador to the United States took issue with Noah's comments, noting that France does not refer to citizens based on racial identities and, unlike in America, "there is no hyphenated identity."[8] In the eyes of the French state, racial categorizations lend themselves to identity politics—referred to as *communautariste*—that undermine national and social cohesion.[9] Whereas in the United States, laws were amended to forbid discrimination on the basis of race, France forbade even the mention of it. In its view, the national motto of "Liberty, Equality, Fraternity" must be colorblind and offer no quarter for racial or ethnic identities.

But while France's constitution may be colorblind, the French way of life is not. Black and Arab French citizens are twenty times more likely to be stopped by police. Areas with high concentrations of poverty are disproportionately filled with black and Arab residents. French people of color are two to three times more likely to be unemployed than white citizens with the same level of education.[10] Arabs in France are estimated to make up 10 percent of the population but account for 60 percent of the nation's inmates.[11] Feelings of racial prejudice and resentment against immigrants of color are widespread, and racist and anti-Semitic incidents have risen sharply over the last few years.[12] The country does have anti-racist laws and programs in place, but it has not proved very capable of preventing housing, employment, or commercial discrimination or punishing it when it occurs.[13] More than four decades after France outlawed the collection of racial data, residents with African- or Arabic-sounding names were less likely to receive a callback when responding to a housing advertisement and significantly more likely to receive a negative response.[14]

When race is not considered an important constitutional or governmental category for protection, it is nearly impossible to use the power of the state to root out racial prejudice in its institutions and processes. Structural racism requires a large and coordinated response that can be implemented and enforced only by the state. And France's centralized policymaking apparatus shuts out minority groups from providing input and does not prioritize the important process of getting public buy-in when it enacts antidiscrimination laws.[15] The end result is a colorblind nation that does not protect its citizens from racism unless it is accompanied by explicit hate speech. And as people of color readily attest, having a government address structural racism's toxic effects on health, education, economic security, physical safety, and general socioeconomic well-being is far more important than its chastisement of individuals who cannot seem to keep racial slurs off their tongue.

Colorblindness in the United States would face even more troubles than it has faced in France because of how central racial identity has been to our nation, filled with more people, diversity, and federalism. Our national mythology—from the shining city on the hill to the melting pot—mandates recognition that our unity is bolstered by our diversity. The United States is constructed from the perseverance of Native Americans, immigrants, and African Americans who have each contributed unique histories, journeys, and experiences that give fullness and vibrancy to the American way of life. Colorblindness washes away the distinctiveness of our varied paths and insists that the only identity that matters is the national one. It is an ideology that stands athwart the color spectrum and yells, "Can't we all just be American?" And by removing race from questions of law, policy, and justice, a government that derives its power from the consent of the governed views its very dissimilar citizens through very a similar lens. The greatest moments of national courage have come when we confront major threats head-on. Colorblindness causes us to see our racial issues through rose-tinted glasses. It sidesteps the main thrust of what threatens us and hopscotches over the hard stuff.

The shortcomings of the colorblind ideology, however, do not suggest that the concept has never had merit. Visions of a colorblind society as the realization of an American utopia once served a critical purpose. After all, one of the primary flaws of the Constitution's early iterations and interpretations is the preoccupation with race that excused chattel slavery and permitted statutory racial segregation—it was color-conscious in that it recognized the full citizenship of certain free white men and accepted that people of other races and ethnicities could not successfully make the same claim. Americans fighting to extend equality without regard to race often assert that the Constitution does not see race, and therefore that race should not be read into it. Supreme Court justice John Harlan declared in 1896, "There is no caste here. Our Constitution is color-blind."[16] Civil rights activists leaned on the colorblind ideology to advance their cause, too, including Thurgood Marshall, who successfully argued in *Brown v. Board* that "separate but equal" racial segregation was unconstitutional by professing, "That the Constitution is color blind is our dedicated belief."[17] A colorblind view of the Constitution was the means to rebut the color-conscious interpretations that gave license to slavery and the separate-but-equal doctrine and constructed a society that explicitly advantaged white citizens.

But once the nation's laws and policies recognized that the exclusion of black Americans from the full rights and protections of citizenship was unconstitutional, the inequalities that resulted from centuries of discriminatory practices required remedies that could not be colorblind. The Promise recognizes that the problems resulting from a history of color-conscious policies need to be addressed with color-conscious solutions. The colorblind ideology helped make the case for ending the most egregious forms of racial segregation and discrimination, but it is not equipped to finish the race toward the Promise. For that, we will need national solidarity, and it cannot be colorblind.

NATIONAL SOLIDARITY BRINGS dissimilar people together for a common cause. Part of the challenge of creating such a thing is that diversity in a solidary group is both a strength and a vulnerability. We know that social connection is harder to create in areas with large populations of diverse peoples. But the American experiment has also taught us that the nation is at its best and strongest when its people unify across lines of race and class to tackle challenges together. Thus, it is possible to overcome the issues that racial differences present within a society by activating the political and civic solidarities that bind us together with shared values and provide us with a common objective. Colorblindness may be a worthy goal for our social interactions, but we cannot afford to blind ourselves to racial difference if we are to find national solidarity. When the whole point is to counter the existential threat that racism poses to America, muting racial diversity defeats the purpose. National solidarity formed to manage the detrimental impacts of racism must embrace our racial diversity; it must be color-conscious.

If colorblindness advocates for not considering a person's race, then color-consciousness is simply the recognition that race is a significant determinant of one's American experience in social, political, and economic spheres. One cannot reverse the havoc racial segregation wreaked on the United States and the American idea by ignoring race. It requires we be aware—conscious—of the role that race played in who could access citizenship and the Promise and who could not. In the quest to beat back the effects of racism on our country, recognizing racial difference is elemental and unavoidable.

This may feel counterintuitive. If racism establishes a racial hierarchy that advantages those at the top and discriminates against those relegated to a lesser status, then pointing out racial differences would seem to only further delineate the order instead of toppling it. A more rational approach, one might think, would be to blanch the whole thing and remove race as a distinction, presuming a racial order could not exist if there is no race. Further, perhaps doing so could encourage the creation of national solidarity by erasing the racial differences that hinder its formation.

The major problem with this tack, however, is that those at the bottom of the order will insist on inclusion in the newly colorblind society, and everything we know about human behavior suggests that once this happens, the demand for equality will become racialized. It will not be lost on anyone in the colorblind nation that those making the most noise for full citizenship look different from those who are mostly satisfied with the state of things. As political scientist Juliet Hooker puts it, "The social ontology of race—the way it works through markers on the body, in a visual register, to demarcate the boundaries of trust and empathy—and the physical and moral distance it establishes between citizens" makes it all but impossible to ignore.[18] When those at the bottom of the order in a suddenly colorblind nation are disproportionately black or brown, the groups' legitimate demands are inevitably racialized and the colorblind construct soon implodes.

A national solidarity to combat structural racism must be catalyzed by public policy and, as a result, must be color-conscious. If we are to stave off the threat to our country, bind together to hold the state accountable, and create a truly inclusive United States, we have to understand that racism harms every citizen, but also that it harms each of us in distinct and peculiar ways that are not responsive to colorblind, blanket remedies. Because national solidarity seeks to hold the state accountable for insufficiently addressing racism and at times sanctioning it altogether, public policy becomes the means by which the demands of the citizen are met.

Undoing structural issues requires the same instruments of policy that erected them in the first place. As appellate judge John Wisdom wrote of desegregation and racial equality, "The Constitution is both colorblind and color conscious." It is colorblind when it comes to the equal protection clause that forbids discrimination on the basis of race, he argued. "But the Constitution is color conscious to prevent discrimination being perpetuated and to undo the effects of past discrimination. The criterion is the relevancy of color to a legitimate government purpose."[19] Colorblindness may be an ideal morality for an ideal society, but in an imperfect world with a jagged history, accounting for the role race plays in people's lives is the only way to ensure justice does not skip over those who have been denied a fair shake. Solidarity champions color-conscious policies as the most effective weapon to battle structural racism.

There are material gains to be realized by deliberately addressing issues in a color-conscious fashion instead of a colorblind or class-based one. Politicians routinely champion "rising tide lifts all boats" policies because of their political expedience and perception of ultimate fairness in giving everyone the same thing regardless of specific needs. But these sorts of colorblind approaches do not address the disparity between racial groups. Fair public policy aimed at reducing suicide or opioid use that does not consider the specifics of the white rural population that disproportionately suffers from these problems will be less effective if it is not color-conscious. Similarly, studies of maternal mortality rates show that black women are more likely to die in childbirth than white women, and those differences hold steady across class: rich black women and poor black women die at three or four times the rate of rich white women and poor white women, respectively.[20] A class-based or colorblind policy that targets maternal mortality is a worthy endeavor, but it will leave the racial disparity entirely unaddressed. The gap between the black and white experiences with maternal mortality and suicide are outcroppings of structural racism's effects on our society and require solutions that account for race. Problems that are not colorblind are not solved by measures that are.

Color-conscious policies are needed to manufacture the conditions most conducive to national solidarity and the remission of racial inequality. Racism in the United States did not arise from evil in the hearts of men. Instead, as historian Ibram X. Kendi has argued, racist ideas emanate from racist policies.[21] When a state grants racism a foothold and entrenches it in policies advantageous to the national interest instead of to the humanity of its citizens, racist ideas about those harmed usually crop up to justify their unfair and unequal treatment. Countering racism, then, requires policies that acknowledge race to facilitate the American idea that is fully inclusive of all citizens. Juliet Hooker asserts that political and civic solidarities are racialized in that they occur much more readily in homogenous communities, and the only way to "transcend the limits established by racialized solidarity" is to have citizens in diverse societies "learn to 'see' the other as such while simultaneously envisioning him or her as a fellow citizen."[22] Policies that see race do not just integrate black Americans into standing notions of who and what is American, which defaults to white citizens. Rather, they spark the evolution of Americanism by integrating white citizens and citizens of color into an advanced version of the American idea that is closer to the Promise. Color-consciousness forces us all to see an American as something other than white, just as the Civil War compelled the public to see enslaved black people as citizens and the Civil Rights Movement nudged the nation to see black people as equals deserving of justice. Color-conscious policies led these transformations.

The American system of governance is actually well suited to reacting to a minority population's policy demands when it deems this in the national interest. Whereas France's centralized government proves less capable of addressing the concerns of minority populations, federalism in the United States weakens our national government relative to France's but also gives it an advantage in instituting color-conscious antidiscrimination laws. The federal government is massive and provides oversight for nearly every aspect of our society, but governance occurs at multiple levels, which, in turn, fragments power across municipal, local, state, and federal levels. At each tier, legislation is hardly ever specific enough to address every issue that arises, so executive branches create administrative rules and regulations to fill the gaps. These government mandates, however, can be unclear, change too frequently, and are often enforced in uneven and fragmented ways, features that cause governance to appear weak.[23] But sociologists Frank Dobbin and John Sutton argue that this uncertainty creates a peculiar kind of strength that leverages the government's ability to set norms through policy but delegates power to local levels that are better positioned to engage disaffected communities and oversee compliance.[24] In other words, our more distributive, less centralized style of governance allows multiple debates to occur simultaneously in various places that eventually shape a national consensus on policy with substantial input or influence from minority communities.

Because of the United States' historical foundations, our politics and policies developed alongside the evolving state of race relations. Our democratic systems were originally structured to accommodate the institution of slavery, the rights of states and localities to enforce racial codes to police newly freed black Americans, and Jim Crow laws and racial segregation in public spaces, thereby, according to political scientist Robert Lieberman, causing American social policy in the early twentieth century to "reproduce racially structured imbalances linking white workers to a newly national welfare state while leaving African Americans disproportionately attached to discriminatory local structures of power."[25] But by the mid-twentieth century, civil rights activists began concerted and organized lobbying at the White House, battled racism in the courts, moved north where their votes changed local politics, and protested with visible and emotional demonstrations to access constitutional rights, all of which contributed to the transformation of American politics, policies, and eventually society. Our political institutions evolved with race relations.

The Civil Rights Movement's combination of local and national political strategies that leveraged colorblind and color-conscious appeals proved extraordinarily effective. The yearlong Montgomery bus boycott in Alabama was a local event that made colorblind appeals to the Constitution and color-conscious appeals to city ordinances. When President Eisenhower deployed the U.S. Army's 101st Airborne to escort nine black students in Little Rock, Arkansas, to integrate a local high school, he was enforcing a Supreme Court ruling over the intransigence of a state government. Constitutional amendments and sweeping federal legislative reforms during the John F. Kennedy and Lyndon Johnson presidential years ensured local issues like voting, working, and housing had color-conscious protections provided by the institutional colorblindness the Constitution demands. These examples illustrate how race policy in the United States begins with colorblind appeals for equal treatment and protection but turns toward color-conscious policies as minority communities are engaged and their specific challenges are addressed. Lieberman has argued that the combined local orientations of our political institutions and traditional black American politics "paved the way for political strategies that led to the construction of a powerful antidiscrimination enforcement regime."[26] Whereas the centralization in France permits the government to wipe the word *race* from its constitution and forbid the collection of its peoples' racial data, American race policy is shaped by an ongoing set of local negotiations and practices enabling incremental change that takes root more quickly and establishes new societal norms.

Clearly, in the nation's best moments, color-consciousness is pumping vigorously through our veins. Any hope we have of leaving the United States and the American idea better than the versions we inherited rests on our ability to see each other as racially different but civically similar. Whereas other sizable nations and societies have not managed to create multiracial bonds of solidarity, the United States is uniquely positioned—and challenged—to do so as a result of its history, its demographics, its system of governance, and the present threat of racism and its catalytic effect on the inequality, political polarization, and public disunity that hang over our heads like the Sword of Damocles. For us to meet the moment requires embracing the differences that usually divide us and deriving from them the strength that can sustain us.

PART IV

A Path Toward
National Solidarity

If I read the temper of our people correctly, we now realize as we have never realized before our interdependence on each other; that we cannot merely take but we must give as well; that if we are to go forward, we must move as a trained and loyal army willing to sacrifice for the good of a common discipline, because without such discipline no progress is made, no leadership becomes effective.

We are, I know, ready and willing to submit our lives and property to such discipline, because it makes possible a leadership which aims at a larger good. This I propose to offer, pledging that the larger purposes will bind upon us all as a sacred obligation with a unity of duty hitherto evoked only in time of armed strife.

With this pledge taken, I assume unhesitatingly the leadership of this great army of our people dedicated to a disciplined attack upon our common problems.

—Franklin D. Roosevelt, First Inaugural Address, March 4, 1933

CHAPTER 9

National Solidarity as the Right Response to Racism

The vast majority of Americans today are descended from people who struggled mightily against some set of odds just to get a glimpse of the Promise and a shot at the Dream. We carry in our national character the stories of those who came before us, whether native, immigrant, or enslaved. The distinct lessons their lives and experiences impart can fashion us all into better people and the United States into a better place. Black America is no exception—the best of America can be found in its indomitable spirit, a strain of which exists in every American and the people from whom they came.

The lesson that black America has for the nation is discernible in the lives of its ordinary citizens. Superlative citizenship, group solidarity, and the trickling down of democratic inclusion when moral claims are paired with the national interest are pillars that provide structural support for the concept of national solidarity. They are to be found everywhere—on sleepy side streets in small-town America, in crowded metro areas where opportunity is gathered amid bustling downtowns, at community convenings full of citizens and denizens negotiating terms with governance councils and resident associations, and in the halls of power where policies and programs are devised that will determine whether we move toward the Promise together or scatter from it in factions hell-bent on shaping the United States to their liking.

The nation's mettle and commitment to its principles are routinely tested, in some periods more than others. The 1960s were a time of such disruption. There were assassinations, hot and cold wars, and transformational laws that sought to unmake some of the unconstitutional civil rights infringements that were crafted out of thin air and from the thinnest of thinking. The decade began with the presidential election between Senator John F. Kennedy and Vice President Richard Nixon, a historic election on a number of fronts. It was the first election in which fifty states participated, the first in which candidates debated live on national television, and the first in which the sitting president was ineligible to run again because the Twenty-Second Amendment, passed in 1947, limited presidential tenure to two terms. And it was the last election in which Jim Crow was legally permitted to run roughshod over the ideals that Americans were supposed to hold dear. Kennedy won, but his presidency was cut short by an assassin's rifle on November 22, 1963, leaving Vice President Lyndon Baines Johnson to lead the nation through a time of heartache and turmoil.

In his first address to a joint session of Congress, just five days after Kennedy was taken, Johnson told a mourning legislature and public that the best way to honor the fallen president was "the earliest possible passage of the civil rights bill for which he fought so long."[1] He issued a clarion call to action: "We have talked long enough in this country about equal rights. We have talked for one hundred years or more. It is time now to write the next chapter, and to write it in the books of law." Strong and comprehensive legislation was needed to plug all the holes Jim Crow had poked in the Constitution so that, as Johnson went on to say in words tinged with national solidarity, "we can move forward to eliminate from this Nation every trace of discrimination and oppression that is based upon race or color. There could be no greater source of strength to this Nation both at home and abroad."Just over seven months later, the landmark Civil Rights Act of 1964 passed with bipartisan support, dealing yet another blow to the sanctioned discrimination that lingered despite major steps like the desegregation of the military and the federal workforce in 1948 and *Brown v. Board of Education* in 1954.

The national solidarity that one would expect to follow a major national tragedy like a presidential assassination, however, remained elusive. In the wake of Kennedy's death, three-fourths of Americans believed the nation had learned a lesson about the importance of civic forbearance and understanding and the destructiveness of hate and intolerance, but nearly half reported being worried about the future of the country and its ability to manage race relations.[2] Amid the nation's grief and the ensuing passage of a historic civil rights statute, black voters were still being excluded from the electoral process. In one Louisianan parish in 1964, black Americans were forced to get a perfect score on a thirty-question logic exam before they were permitted to vote, given just ten minutes to complete a test filled with brainteasers such as "Write every other word in this first line and print every third word in same line, but capitalize the fifth word that you write."[3] Elsewhere in the nation, hopeful black voters first had to pass oral exams, like the young man in northern Georgia who reported being escorted into a room where a jar of corn, a mushmelon, a cucumber, and a bar of soap rested on a table. He was asked questions that the administering poll worker did not even have answers to: "How many kernels of corn in the jar? How many seeds in the melon? How many bubbles in the bar of soap?"[4] Episodes like this further demonstrated that because national solidarity was unrealized, the Promise, too, remained out of reach for all.

Looking to make the case that national solidarity, racial equality, and democratic inclusion were not only in the nation's interest but essential to the Promise, President Johnson returned to the halls of Congress on the evening of March 15, 1965, to champion a new law that would protect the right of every American to vote, no matter "his color or race, his religion or the place of his birth."[5] But in the historic speech that followed, Johnson did something much grander—he called on the nation's better angels and its highest principles. In the course of making a straightforward policy argument, he sought to expand the nation's conception of American citizenship to be fully inclusive of the country's black sons and daughters. In one of the most powerful speeches ever given by an American president—one grounded in the nation's mythology while simultaneously calling out its hypocrisy—Johnson spoke to the essence of the Promise and its direct link to black America. "Rarely in any time does an issue lay bare the secret heart of America itself. Rarely are we met with a challenge . . . to the values and the purposes and the meaning of our beloved nation," he said, continuing, "The issue of equal rights for American Negroes is such an issue."

President Johnson was no dyed-in-the-wool racial progressive. It was an open secret that behind closed doors he occasionally used vulgar epithets when referring to black Americans. He rose to the vice presidency by virtue of being a savvy Texas Democratic senator who Kennedy believed would help win the White House by appealing to conservative voters in Southern states. And yet, as president, Johnson recognized that racism against black Americans was harming U.S. national interests abroad, was at the heart of domestic unrest in cities across the country, and presented a political opportunity for the party that was able to expand the electorate through black enfranchisement. For his actions in implementing a series of historic, revolutionary laws, he will go down as one of the greatest presidents on civil rights in American history, perhaps second only to Abraham Lincoln. Indeed, an analysis of black newspapers over the course of more than a century found that black editorialists considered Johnson the best president on civil rights and race relations by a wide margin.[6]

Lyndon Johnson's address to Congress that night, aptly titled "The American Promise," sought to reframe the question of racial

equality as not only an issue of national concern, but one that threatened the very nature of what America is and would define its existential purpose. "A century has passed since the day of promise. And the
promise is unkept." Noting black citizens' historic quest for equality
and full citizenship mirrored the same spirit that inspired a young
nation to declare its independence nearly two centuries earlier, he
declared, "The real hero of this struggle is the American Negro. His
actions and protests, his courage to risk safety and even to risk his
life, have awakened the conscience of this Nation ... He has called
upon us to make good the promise of America. And who among
us can say that we would have made the same progress were it not
for his persistent bravery, and his faith in American democracy."

Channeling the high-mindedness of the nation's principles and
aspirations in his now-famous oration, Johnson called the nation
to account: "Should we defeat every enemy, should we double our
wealth and conquer the stars, and still be unequal to this issue,
then we will have failed as a people and as a nation." He went on,
"There is no Negro problem. There is no Southern problem. There
is no Northern problem. There is only an American problem." That
American problem remains, and the answer to it that Johnson etched
into the record remains the same: national solidarity. The reforms
of the sixties wounded structural racism, but they did not slay it.
The Promise has still not yet been fully realized. Now it is our turn
to write the next chapter of our shared country, to make our mark
for the ages.

NATIONAL SOLIDARITY MEANS many different things to different
people. Its most common usage in modern times is in the titles of
political parties and agendas within various nations, such as Peru's
National Solidarity Party and eponymous programs in Mexico and
Afghanistan. But its most common interpretation is as a synonym for
national unity—that is, when the people of a nation feel connected

to one another. In this way, national solidarity is perceived to be strongest when the public reports a deep sense of national pride or in the face of severe calamity like terrorist attacks, pandemics, or natural disasters that fuel compassion and sympathy for their fellow citizens. But these uses and interpretations of national solidarity do not capture the meaning, depth, or characteristics required to combat the effects of racism in the United States. Solidarity required for this work must be much thicker.

National solidarity is the political unity of a people demanding, on moral and principled grounds, that the state address wrongs suffered by some of its members so that the rights and privileges prescribed in the social contract are equally available to all. Social contract theory states that people within a society explicitly or tacitly agree to adhere to a set of moral and political obligations and normative behaviors.[7] Thus, when it comes to the relationship between a nation and its people, the social contract—essentially an article of faith that evolves over time—defines the expectations of our government and responsibilities of citizenship.

National solidarity, then, obligates one citizen to another to work toward national viability, accessibility to the fullness of citizenship, and the state's adherence to its responsibilities. It is not the basic pride of being a citizen, unconditional and uncritical patriotism, or a willingness to excuse the nation's shortcomings for the sake of unity and peace. Rather, it is an instrument used to constrain the actions of a geopolitical entity chasing its interests when such things are inimical to the obligations it has to the people. It is the citizenry's moral oversight of a state's amoral interests and behavior.

National solidarity is what happens when people come together to hold their country accountable. It does not require that deep connections and affection exist between every citizen; it simply means each person respects the other's equality and recognizes that his or her equality is tied to the government's protection of it for all its people. It understands that when the state permits the rights of some citizens to be unjustly abridged, the country fails everyone, undermines the things it is supposed to stand for, and must answer and make amends for its shortcoming. It is the only power the people can successfully wield over their country to make sure it does what it is supposed to on issues of racial justice and morality.

Racism is not just the primary threat to the American idea; it also complicates the formation of national solidarity. Studies of racial and ethnic diversity in the United States help make the point: solidarity is higher in homogenous places like South Dakota, and interracial trust is challenged in heterogenous locales like Los Angeles.[8] The civic and political components of national solidarity are more difficult to establish among diverse peoples, especially when the relationship is characterized by a history of oppression and intergroup conflict that has threatened the society's stability. Civic solidarity pertains to the relationship between citizens within a state and between the state and the people, and political solidarity is when people unite in response to a specific injustice.[9] National solidarity blends the two, bringing people together in a just cause to hold the state accountable. And because the cause is overcoming the effects of racism, the thing that makes national solidarity hard to form is also thing that can no longer thrive once national solidarity is established.

Generally, civic solidarity becomes possible when diversifying societies create a more inclusive concept of who the "we" is.[10] Evolving the "we" identity can occur by promoting a common allegiance to shared principles, prioritizing a national culture or identity, or embracing people's differences and their unique contributions to the shared culture or identity.[11] Political solidarity brings together democratic strangers—people with shared citizenship in a democracy who experience it differently and have no other connection to one another aside from membership in the same nation-state—with the intent of expanding the "we" on moral grounds.[12] National solidarity benefits from the two—employing a shared culture and sounding a moral call to action, double-knotting citizens in pursuit of the Promise.

If successful in creating national solidarity, the United States has the potential to accomplish something unprecedented. When leaders and pundits of all ideological stripes refer to America as an experiment, it is an acknowledgment that the nation we are attempting to build has no predecessor but remains within the realm of the possible. The most common advice to succeed in this operation—while keeping the patient in good humor—is simply to put aside racial differences and cling to the American identity alone, or to just treat the rights and privileges of citizenship as infinite resources that are enjoyed by all in abundance and require sacrifice by none. Both suggestions are not only incorrect; they are impossible. National solidarity is only achievable when racial group distinctions are embraced instead of wished away, when the source of national identity is grounded in shared ideals and principles, when the people accept the expansion of the "we" to be more inclusive, and when there is a recognition that the benefits of solidarity are realized only when the people are committed to each other and a cause. We will all gain from its presence, but it asks something of everyone. It requires civic acceptance, forbearance, and sustained public will. America is possible, but it is hard as hell.

The goal of national solidarity is to redirect the focus of racism from the competition between different racial groups to the state's breach of the social contract with its people. It expands our conception of "we" and establishes the power to hold the state accountable when it reneges on its obligations. It employs a referential system of moral beliefs that sacralize equality, liberty, and justice. Where other types of solidarity may come undone when the thread of racial diversity is pinched and pulled through, national solidarity remains intact because it deliberately targets the thing that threatens the others—racism.

Think of it in this way: A solidary group that fights for vaccinations will not succumb to a measles outbreak—they are immune to it because they have been vaccinated against it. But if the group does become infected with the virus, it demonstrates that its members did not share a real commitment to the cause and were not truly in solidarity. Thus, national solidarity fashioned as such is resilient to racial conflict because it weakens the racial group competition that too many political and economic elites leverage to underdeliver on the nation-state's obligation to the people.

The thing takes work. National solidarity is difficult to create, but it is not beyond grasp. It is solidarity that sits at the intersection of the civic and political, the moral and material, the individual and nation-state. It relies on national mythology, identity, and interests. Though it is not infallible, impervious to erosion, or unimpeachable, it is capable of managing the effects of racism in the United States and protecting America and the Promise for future generations.

A FEW MINUTES BEFORE the East Coast's midnight on November 4, 2008, Republican presidential candidate and Arizona senator John McCain ascended a stage erected on the grounds of the Biltmore Hotel in Phoenix, the sprouting tops of towering palm trees framing the assembled crowd and banners emblazoned with stars trailing gold into the sky draped at each corner of the gathering. With his wife and running mate in tow, he delivered a measured and respectful address as a pendent American flag served as the backdrop on the night America elected its first black president.

Just over a minute into it, McCain looked the past and the present in the eye, saying, "This is an historic election, and I recognize the special significance it has for African Americans and for the special pride that must be theirs tonight," and going on to note that work remains even "though we have come a long way from the old injustices that once stained our nation's reputation and denied some Americans the full blessings of American citizenship."[13] In one of the nation's most important rituals—political concessions that precede the peaceful transition of power as the will of the people is carried out—McCain had no problem extolling the virtues of America through a color-conscious, civil religious lens while congratulating President-elect Barack Obama on winning the White House.

The next thing McCain said turned out to be a shooting star for me: "A century ago, President Theodore Roosevelt's invitation of Booker T. Washington to visit—to dine at the White House—was taken as an outrage in many quarters." To hear, on this night, the story of how my name came to be—a story about the dinner that inspired millions of disenfranchised black Americans, including my paternal great-grandparents, Will and Annie—lit a fire in me. In the months following the election, I scoured the internet and history books to learn every detail I could about Booker T. Washington's visit, feeling deep in my soul that there was more to the story and that history held something else for my family.

Of my grandparents' generation, only my maternal grandmother, Orrie Bell Lee, was alive on the night a black man won the presidency. She would have been thrilled to cast her vote and see history in the making, but dementia pressed her down and covered her eyes, refusing her a joy she hardly would have been able to fathom in her best days and when her faith was at its peak. This is an irony about historic moments long in the making—those who would appreciate them most are often robbed of the pleasure. How I wish she, and all my grandparents and those before them, could have seen their faith and perseverance bear fruit, symbolized by a black family in the White House. Election night in 2008 set the wheels in motion for the events that occurred three years later over the span of just a few months: I would carry my family story into Obama's Oval Office, and I would say a final goodbye to my grandmother.

The election night speeches of Obama and McCain were a duet in national solidarity. Obama asked Americans to "summon a new spirit of patriotism; of service and responsibility where each of us resolves to pitch in and work harder and look after not only ourselves, but each other."[14] In acknowledging his and Obama's opposing policy views, McCain made one thing clear: "Whatever our differences, we are fellow Americans. And please believe me when I say no association has ever meant more to me than that." Obama tied the Promise to our solidarity, declaring, "Tonight, we proved once more that the true strength of our nation comes not from the might of our arms or the scale of our wealth, but from the enduring power of our ideals: democracy, liberty, opportunity and unyielding hope." And McCain replied by explicitly naming it, concluding with, "I call on all Americans . . . to not despair of our present difficulties but to believe always in the promise and greatness of America, because nothing is inevitable here."

Many Americans saw Barack Obama's victory as a symbolic exorcism of the demons lingering from the nation's original sin. With the burden lifted, the nation's path to a colorblind society seemed cleared and paved to lead us into a post-racial existence. It did not happen—overcoming racism was never going to be that easy or straightforward. And the reaction to his presidency, with clear racial lines of demarcation between those who viewed him favorably and those who held negative opinions of him and his wife, further demonstrated how much work remains to be done in the United States. And yet, Obama's victory was a sign that the nation had struck another blow in the match against racism, not because the American people ignored the color of his skin, but because we saw that he and his family were black and he won *anyway*. National solidarity does not require that we no longer see race; it asks us to see each other's racial differences and still obligate ourselves to one another. The fulfillment of the Promise is not the erasure of difference; it is the acceptance of it. National solidarity is the means to make it so.

WHAT NATIONAL SOLIDARITY LOOKS LIKE in practice and how it is exercised is far from straightforward if the national solidarity of the sort America needs has not been seen. Fortunately, just as many groups in the multiracial and multiethnic United States have lessons the nation can learn from and apply, black America has a specific history with racism and solidarity that the country would be wise to heed. National solidarity can be constructed in response to the racism that fuels the hyperpartisanship, economic inequality, and strongman populism that is presently roiling the country. And to do so, it must provide citizens with the means to demonstrate their commitment to equality and justice, to each other, and to holding the nation accountable for delivering and protecting the Promise.

The same pillars that buttress black solidarity are suitable for the national version to be adopted by Americans: superlative citizenship, a call to civic engagement and political unified commitment, and the strategic use of national interests to encourage inclusion to trickle down.

Superlative citizenship for national solidarity concerns one's role in society, one's relationship with fellow citizens, and one's relationship with the nation. The former two are captured in the concepts of civic virtue and civic friendship. Civic virtue can be summed up as displays of the "excellences of citizenship," for which there is no absolute standard.[15] For example, some citizens may view participation in the political process by voting as "excellences of citizenship," while others would offer that disruption of the political process—through protest, for example—is the more virtuous approach, particularly if it or actors in it are deemed corrupt or unjust. When it comes to national solidarity, however, civic virtue primarily refers to those actions citizens take to close the gap between who a people say they are and who they actually are, addressing the misalignment between our principles, our mythology, and our practices.[16] It asks a simple question: Do we live our creed?

Whereas civic virtue is an individual aspiration, civic friendship requires community. A few years ago, Princeton professor Robert George and Harvard professor Cornel West engaged in a public discussion about political polarization and how people who disagree politically must be able to engage one another with respect and compassion. George stated, "Civic friendship is an absolutely indispensable condition of self-government . . . If you don't have civic friendship, disagreements turn us into enemies, and you cannot sustain a republic among people who regard themselves as each other's enemies."[17] Definitions of *civic friendship* abound. But most seem to generally point to a relationship between citizens based on equality, respect, a willingness to engage and understand one another, and compassion. It is the civic version of the Golden Rule: treat others as you would like to be treated. It does not require the full-throated acceptance of every person and all their beliefs and practices; it simply suggests that there is a common area of belief among all people who desire a politically just society that is sufficient to establish solidarity and social unity.

Similarly, trickle-down citizenship—leveraging the national interest to advance civil rights protections and racial equality—has utility for national solidarity. Researchers have long chronicled the role that the security threats posed by the Soviet Union during the Cold War played in creating conditions more conducive to the dismantling of Jim Crow's laws and racist societal norms. The spate of racial progress in America from the late 1940s through the late 1960s was not the sole product of a sudden surge of national morality. Rather, it was seen as a necessary step to disarm Soviet attacks on the American narrative identity and our system of democratic governance.[18] Similarly, national solidarity will not be born or expanded as a result of a wave of moral epiphanies cascading nationwide. Rather, it will require a pairing with a material national interest to bring it about. Just as with black solidarity, the objectives of national solidarity will be achieved as a byproduct of the pursuits of an amoral geopolitical entity.

Racism, in and of itself, has proved to be a strong-enough force to pry apart the Union. But over the course of the nation's history, it has buried itself in other issues that are sufficiently concerning and appropriately sized to command the nation's attention. That is, racism is often deemed too large, too intractable, and too much of an evil for any batch of political programs to undo. The nation embarked on civil war, passed constitutional amendments, and acted in every branch of government to declare racial discrimination un-American and illegal, and yet, it persists—in a lesser form, certainly, but it persists nonetheless. But things racism feeds—economic inequality, hyperpartisanship, illiberal populism—seem snack-sized next to the far-reaching effects and impacts on life chances that racism produces in the United States.

From Progressive Era measures in the early twentieth century to the New Deal legislation of the 1930s, policy reforms tackled the problem of economic inequality and led to its dramatic reduction over the next four decades—a period that economists have termed the Great Compression. On the score of the hyperpartisanship that has only intensified over the last few decades, there is no shortage of regulatory or statutory proposals to stem the tide, including reforming the campaign finance system and fundamentally transforming the election process to vitiate gerrymandering, party primaries, and two-party, winner-take-all elections. And should these steps be taken, the pillars on which illiberal populism is erected will be too weak to bear its weight. But what is the law that will undo racial hierarchy and inequality? What is the suite of regulatory reforms that will finally lay racial discrimination to rest? They do not exist. If the United States solves economic inequality, overcomes the divisiveness of partisan politics, and reimagines its liberal democracy, but does not address racial injustice and inequality, the Promise will remain out of reach and America will remain at risk.

National solidarity requires a deeper understanding of how the United States settles on threats that require a response. Returning to the civil rights and Cold War example, the easy answer suggests that the Soviet nuclear arsenal presented a sufficient threat to the nation's existence and left us no choice but to use every tool at our disposal to avoid war and build alliances to help us prevail should conflict occur. The racial progress realized in this period could be viewed as providing evidence to nations trapped on the Cold War battlefield that the United States was the better and more principled partner. But the Soviet attack on the United States' hypocrisy—professing to be a democracy that champions individual liberty while enforcing state-sanctioned racial discrimination and turning a blind eye to racial violence—was an existential threat to U.S. security. Further, the advent of television captured the violence administered by the state against peaceful civil rights marchers, providing visual evidence of the inconsistency of American principles. In other words, there were simultaneous foreign and domestic threats to the national narrative that disrupted the U.S. sense of self and the image it broadcast to the world. This occurrence was not a mere inconvenience that paled in comparison with physical threats; it was just as dire and calamitous to the nation's interest and well-being as armed conflict.

A state's sense of its identity is immensely consequential—this point cannot be overstated. International relations scholars refer to this as a state's ontological security, which is bound up in its identity, history, autobiography, and mythology. It suggests that these geopolitical entities are motivated to ensure the security of their self-identity because it confers stability, ritual, and agency in their interactions with the world and their people. Political scientist Brent J. Steele has written that if states were to ignore these types of security threats, "their sense of self-identity would be radically disrupted, and such a disruption is just as important to states as threats to their physical security."[19]

Consider it in this light: The September 11 terrorist attacks certainly presented a threat to the United States' physical security. But their most serious threat was to the nation's identity as a military and economic superpower—thus the attacks on the Pentagon and World Trade Center—and its sense of exceptionalism, two attributes that are central to the American identity.[20] The attacks removed the certainty that the American way of life was unassailable as they suddenly placed citizens' sense of safety into doubt, crashed into symbols of our economic and military power, and attempted to rebrand the principles of freedom and liberty as national vulnerabilities. The wars waged in Afghanistan and Iraq were less about ensuring the United States' physical security and more concerned with restoring the nation's sense of certainty and identity by relying on the things that characterize them—military and economic power. In 2005, President George W. Bush justified the actions as fighting for "the cause of freedom that once again will destroy the enemies of freedom."[21] The War on Terrorism was enacted to restore the ontological security of the United States, reaffirming its self-identity as the defender of liberty whose free and equal citizens are safe, secure, and prosperous.

Trickle-down citizenship contributes to the establishment of national solidarity by identifying the material costs of racial inequality and pairing them with the defining of racism as an ontological security threat. In this way, it leverages the national interest to work toward the goal of a more racially just and equal society. If we cannot rely on the moral argument alone to disrupt our society and make it more inclusive and fairer, trickle-down citizenship assertively identifies the security costs of failing to act. This line of thinking is not supposition—it is behind a number of actions the United States has taken, including advancing civil rights, making certain declarations of war, and the expanding the social safety net. The work of citizens is to make clear the threat that racism poses to our self-narrative, the instability it fosters in our republic, and the role that national solidarity plays in restoring the sense of certainty in the United States and the American way of life.

On the final measure of the model black solidarity provides, the example of how to meld civic and political solidarities has been made clear. But there is another dimension that has utility: though national solidarity does not require social solidarity to exist, it is a feature of black solidarity that may be useful in building the nation-wide effort. Social solidarity is about group membership—even when that membership is imposed—and cohesion, entailing obligations expressed in established customs, laws, and social mores.[22] For example, families, victims of natural disasters, and survivors of violent crimes often experience a strong sense of social solidarity. Clearly, given the historical and contemporary role that race has played in the lives of black Americans, a crystallized social solidarity emerges.

Americans have a version of this that is often activated when its security is threatened by foreign nations or groups; terrorists have targeted Americans simply because of their nationality. Notes of it were apparent in 2020, when the coronavirus pandemic reached our shores and when outrage at the killing of George Floyd filled our streets. And it is certainly the sort of solidarity felt among military personnel when scattered together across the globe. Social solidarity can work to remove the racial connotation typically associated with the name American and expand it such that it refers to group membership based on a shared culture and set of principles. The evolution of the "we" benefits from the group cohesion and belongingness that the title *American* should confer, demonstrated by a commitment to each other through customs and mores.

National solidarity modeled on the successful solidarity exercised by black Americans challenges the existence, premise, and power that racism has in our nation. It requires actions at the individual, group, and national levels. It highlights the threat that racism poses to our self-identity and ontological security. And it can create a cohesion among citizens that feeds the virtue, friendship, obligations, and willingness to sacrifice for the democratic strangers that we call fellow citizens. Most of all, it coats multiracial coalitions with a resilience that makes them less susceptible to attempts at exploiting racial division—the very thing it was created to overcome.

*   *   *

ONE UNAVOIDABLE ISSUE concerning national solidarity lingers: perhaps a nation-state is too big for solidarity. Political theorists have often contemplated the question of whether the size of a nation prohibits true connections among its people, especially if it is a democratic republic and its people are diverse. The city-state was Plato's and Aristotle's preferred unit for a republic because, as renowned theorist Robert Dahl has characterized it, a modest city is of "human dimensions" and of an appropriate scale where "citizenship would be close to friendship . . . where human relations are intense rather than bland, and where the eternal human quest for community and solidarity can be wholly satisfied."[23] Even the term *citizen* is based on Latin and Anglo-Norman French words that meant "city."

Scholars have noted that a country as populous, geographically expansive, and complex as the United States is predisposed to the problems of large democratic nations: a public dissatisfied with its government, a nation slow to respond to the will of its people, and a lack of civic trust between social groups.[24] Political scientist Karen Remmer cites the difficulties that size presents nations in "creating a sense of community, fostering social capital and civic engagement, enforcing norms of citizenship responsibility, and lowering the costs of political activity."[25] For all the benefits of a large republic that James Madison laid out in "Federalist No. 10" in November 1787—a natural resilience to a majority faction monopolizing power, coupled with its economic and security advantages[26]—the factors that lead to national solidarity are harder to establish because of the nation's sheer size.

To deal with this complication, a critically important feature of national solidarity is that it does not require the daily maintenance of bonds of kinship with 325 million Americans simultaneously organized toward the oversight and ceaseless surveillance of a massive system of government. Solidarity exercised in smaller environs is not antithetical to a national version; rather, it is the building block that permits a more comprehensive solidarity to be constructed. National solidarity is most tangible in neighborhoods and communities across the country, such as when a multiracial cohort protests the wrongful death of a citizen or leaps into action to save a local school or community center. The motivation for national solidarity is to ensure the Promise reaches to all corners of the country, but the actions of national solidarity are exercised within the social and civic reach of individuals and groups. The U.S. system of federalism not only requires change to be realized in our nested form of government, but it makes change possible because it does not require ordinary Americans to have superhuman reach and influence. It is the sum of localized efforts, processes, and institutional efforts that gives national solidarity its valence. It does not require 325 million people to act in unison and on one accord; it requires only that they believe in the same principles and work toward the same end.

Admittedly, national solidarity is an abstract concept and can be hard to pin down. Definitions, models, and examples are helpful, but solidarity is most clear when it is felt and acted on. For Americans to create national solidarity, it is necessary to understand its pillars—superlative citizens, trickle-down citizenship, and political and civic solidarities—and the conditions most conducive to its formation: the American civil religion, racism framed as a crime of the state, and the importance of color-consciousness. But public policy is where structures meet enduring change. And so, if it is to be, national solidarity needs a program of action, one that fosters the development of the pillars, cultivates the conducive conditions, and can be applied at every sociopolitical level from local communities to the national systems of democracy.

A Conclusion

Creating National Solidarity

In the months and years following the 2008 election night speeches from Senator John McCain and President-elect Barack Obama, I learned lots about the October 1901 dinner between President Teddy Roosevelt and Booker T. Washington. The dinner was a singular event, but it embodied and engaged the rich debate about the nation's history and potential, the contentious issue of race in the United States, the presence of faith and malice among the American people, and the centrality of the Promise to the nation's ultimate well-being. Every so often in my on-again, off-again curiosity, I would come across some interesting new detail. By 2011, I was selected for promotion to the rank of commander in the U.S. Navy, was beginning to question whether military service was my life's purpose and the best thing for my family, and was waiting for a sign on what my next professional and personal moves should be. And it was then, for some reason I could not quite pinpoint, that one detail of the dinner stuck with me—a room in the White House.

On the evening of October 16, 1901, Booker T. Washington arrived at the White House to dine with President Theodore Roosevelt and the first family. As he waited in the Blue Room—an oval salon with blue satin drapery and a nineteenth-century French chandelier where presidents typically receive guests—he knew this historic occasion was possible only because it was politically expedient. Roosevelt arranged the dinner to discuss Southern politics and seed advantages in the region for his 1904 presidential nomination, "not for any racial purpose," as historian Robert J. Norrell writes, "but as a convenience for himself and a courtesy to Washington for helping him with [political] appointments."[1] Though the dinner came to represent "an embrace of racial equality by the most powerful white man and the most powerful black man in the United States," neither man intended that to be the message.[2] Instead, Washington, a superlative citizen, recognized the opportunity to use the president's self-interest as a means to help his view of equal citizenship trickle down to more black Americans, displaying a commitment to group solidarity in the process. He walked out of the Blue Room to meet the president, they shared pleasantries and a meal, and the two retired to talk politics.

On a whim undoubtedly influenced by the 2008 election and the story of my name, I decided to apply for the White House Fellowship, created by President Lyndon Johnson in 1964 and billed as the nation's most prestigious program for leadership and public service. In the summer of 2011, I was selected for the fellowship, and, a few weeks after it began, received an invitation to the White House's Halloween reception for military families. Nearly 110 years to the day—and in a moment eerily reminiscent of the October 1901 dinner invitation that had so inspired my great-grandparents Will and Annie Johnson—my family and I arrived at the White House to meet the president and first lady, and waited in the Blue Room for their entrance. In that instant, the connection to history rushed over me in a wave—as if fate had orchestrated a reenactment with the first black president, a reality even Will and Annie would scarcely have been able to imagine. I introduced President Obama to my family, he thanked us for our service, and as quickly as the moment arrived, it passed. We stayed at the reception for a couple of hours, dining on finger foods, talking with staffers in costume, and even helping a magician with a trick to close out his show for the first family and all those gathered. As we left and headed home, my family's American story seemed to be coming full circle.

About two weeks later on Veterans Day, I made the trek to the southwest corner of Georgia to visit my last surviving grandparent, Orrie Bell, the ninety-six-year-old granddaughter of a man born into slavery. Dementia had long robbed us of her distinctive personality, infectious laugh, and sharp wit, and I felt a sudden sense of urgency to see her. The woman who was once a voracious reader, earning a degree in her eighties and penning encouraging letters to me, had grown weary; when my aunt asked what happened to her love of reading, she had answered, "One day it just got up and left me." The visit was an emotional one—she was only fully present with my aunts and me for a lucid minute or two at a time—age would whisk her away just as soon as we got comfortable. In one of her final moments of clear thinking during that visit, she looked squarely into my teary eyes and said, "I'm proud of you." Those would be the last words she would ever say to me; she died a few short months later, the red clay of Georgia serving as the ceremonial carpet that ushered her into the stars above.

I did not know it then, but the first shoot of this book found daylight the following March in the White House. In the final meeting the fellowship cohort would have with President Obama, we spent an hour discussing current policy issues in the Eisenhower Executive Office Building, and then he invited us into the Oval Office to show us some of the office's artifacts and history. In the room that day, I caught a fleeting glimpse of the Promise. Gathered at the seat of power in the world's most powerful nation, a diverse group of Americans—different races, different ethnicities, different genders, and different religions—contemplated how to make the nation stronger and more unified. Our home states spanned the country, from California and Utah to Florida and Maine. We were military officers and public health experts, lawyers and investment bankers, and leaders in education and nonprofits. We were center-right and solidly left of center, gay and straight, and the products of childhoods from across the socioeconomic spectrum. And we brought all these differences to a shared American identity, a shared belief in the Promise, and a shared understanding that the United States must take on racial inequalities to be true to its ideals. Civil religion's pantheon was on display—a bust of King, a portrait of Lincoln, the "Resolute" desk, first placed in the Oval Office by Kennedy in 1961—and the Roosevelt Room was just across the hall. National solidarity was there, in the air.

Behind a door that opened to the president's private study was a picture of Teddy Roosevelt holding the reins of a stubborn horse and trying to lead it up a hill—a metaphor for a president doing his level best to lead a nation to a better tomorrow. After Obama explained how the picture was sent to him, a classmate mentioned that I had been named after Roosevelt. Preparing to share my family's story with the president in the West Wing of the White House was surreal. Family I never met envisioned moments like these decades before most of the country could ever conceive of them, and I do believe that they, too, caught a glimpse of the Promise from the heavens. "Well, Mr. President, I am Theodore Roosevelt Johnson, III, and my great-grandparents so believed in the promise of America . . ."

DURING THE QUEST to establish a free and independent republic, and with good and moral intentions at heart, founding father John Jay took some liberties with the facts. It was especially evident after state representatives convened in a stuffy room in the Pennsylvania State House in the summer of 1787 to replace the Articles of Confederation in the hopes of giving the young nation renewed meaning. Once the U.S. Constitution emerged from that Philadelphian heat, the public had to be convinced that it was indeed the right course, and the delegates returning to their states had to be encouraged not to lose their nerve when defending it at home. The public was swayed to support the new body of law by the compelling arguments made in Thomas Paine's *Common Sense*. But the case for ratification was made anew to the delegates and voters, in New York especially, through *The Federalist Papers*, a collection of essays by John Jay, Alexander Hamilton, and James Madison. Their writings were the eighteenth-century version of a public relations media blitz, and Jay put a positive, if inaccurate, spin on the argument in favor of the Constitution.

Jay was a wealthy New Yorker who came to be a staunch advocate for slavery's abolition, the governor of New York, and the first chief justice of the Supreme Court. He recognized early on in the fight to ratify the Constitution the inconvenient truth that continues to plague the nation today: it is difficult to get a diverse group of people to trust one another. Jay suspected a homogenous society would be more pliable and amenable to the project of national unity, so he set out to convince the people recently ordained as American of their oneness.

In "Federalist No. 2," published in late 1787, Jay made clear that the future of the United States depended primarily on the Union, a sentiment that captured the prevailing ideology of those who supported the newly drawn Constitution. He famously argued that a union between the states was possible and preferable because "Providence has been pleased to give this one connected country to one united people—a people descended from the same ancestors, speaking the same language, professing the same religion, attached to the same principles of government, very similar in their manners and customs."[3] Making this grand and demonstrably false claim required that Jay ignore Native Americans, enslaved black people, white immigrants, and numerous other groups that led to multiple ancestries, languages, religions, cultures, and customs being present among the nascent nation's residents.

Though Jay set about creating a sense of obligation among American citizens by fabricating the source of their connection, his instinct that national unity was contingent on people finding commonalities with their fellow citizens in order to reach a goal beneficial to them all was right. He believed a diverse people simply could not pull off solidarity unless they were united against "the danger which immediately threatened the [union] and more remotely the [cause of liberty]." Similarly today, the attempt to wash away our differences by focusing only on the qualities that unite us is an unnecessary step toward solidarity when a real danger threatens the American idea and the well-being of the republic. We can be different and united—the value of the American experiment is contingent on the truth of this proposition.

The work before each of us is to make our Union more perfect by not treating the racial tensions in our citizenry and the racial discrimination in our systems as unfortunate but inconsequential relics of a bygone era. We agree that our government is not as responsive as it should be to the problems that we care about most— we are not satisfied with our healthcare costs, our public schools, our infrastructure, the tax code, and a host of other policy questions that the government has failed to make significant progress on in decades. We agree that partisan politics and the politicians that leverage them are intentionally pitting Americans against one another, miring the country in the muck and passing out rakes to the public to move it around instead of clearing it out. And yet, when structural racism is pointed out as a linchpin threat to the Promise, the nation collectively yawns and uses its next breath to argue over racism's existence, character, purveyors, victims, and effects. Meanwhile, those with political and economic power are serviced most by a beneficent government, stoking and presiding over the bickering while the nation's largesse paves their paths with ever-increasing levels of prosperity.

Perhaps if the impacts of racism were felt as the sudden onset of a widespread calamity, we would be incentivized to act in the way we respond to threats from foreign nations and international adversaries. But structural racism has little of the sudden horrors associated with armed conflict. It does not replicate slavery's brutality, the lethal hypocrisy of Jim Crow, or the instantaneous deaths of thousands as in the attack on Pearl Harbor or the terrorist attacks on September 11—and when the ugliness is explicit and visible, it is reduced to an insensitive act committed by a flawed individual or group that is misunderstood at best or an example of rare racists at worst. Only occasionally does an event capture the sustained attention of a restless nation. Instead, structural racism is more evident when the landscape is surveyed, and perspective reveals the hierarchy that becomes apparent across socioeconomic indicators. Unfortunately, slow-moving disasters are less likely to marshal national action; there is a reason that the Civil War took eight decades to occur over an issue debated at length during the Founding Era.

But we do not have to wait to take action against the harms that racism commits against citizens of every race and ethnicity or the damage it does to the American idea. Indeed, we cannot afford to wait much longer. Leaving the threat racism poses unattended only feeds the destructive partisanship, economic inequality, and illiberal populism that present peril in their own right. Successfully addressing this monumental and defining challenge would mean black Americans would finally enjoy equal protection of the law and a version of citizenship that is not bounded by the color line. It would mean the anxieties white Americans feel that are fueling rampant drug use, dramatic increases in suicides, and tolerance of divisive strongmen politicians can be tamped down and addressed. It would mean the experiences of people of color in the United States do not have to be boiled down to a black-and-white binary but instead can be a richer contribution to the unique texture and culture of America. And it would mean the material losses we all experience as those with power divide us and dole out crumbs to pacify parts of the public will be seen for what they are: state graft at the expense of the people.

The experience of black people in the United States illustrates that John Jay did not have to be pessimistic about the ability of diverse peoples to unify and find solidarity in a cause. The first black Americans were not the product of the same ancestors with the same language and culture. Instead, they were a new creation that Providence conceived from the peoples of more than a dozen present-day West African nations who had different ancestors, languages, religions, cultures, and customs. The creation of the black American is proof that in the face of harm and danger, dissimilar people can establish bonds of kinship and obligation to one another in the course of fighting for a shared goal as sacred as survival and liberty. It is one of the earliest instances of proof that the American experiment was worth the endeavor and that the Promise was possible.

Black America has also learned from its very specific history that racism is an existential threat to the American idea and has proved how it endangers the stability of the United States. It recognized, much as the founding fathers did, that the nation's prosperity was intimately linked to the ability of its people to find unity. From the earliest of their days on the North American continent, black Americans have struggled without ceasing to access the equality and rights that the nation's founding documents promised: serving in the military, rebelling against repressive regimes, migrating to new sections of the nation, instituting political and economic strategies, enduring physical violence and infringements of unalienable rights, and checking every box of the responsibilities of citizenship even when the attendant rights and privileges were denied—all just to demonstrate being worthy of the Promise and compatible with the American way of life.

National solidarity takes these lessons from this group of Americans and applies them to citizenry writ large. It recognizes that, as political theorist Danielle Allen has written, "when [distrust of one's fellow citizens] pervades democratic relations, it paralyzes democracy; it means that citizens no longer think it sensible, or feel secure enough, to place their fates in the hands of democratic strangers."[4] This makes us more susceptible to exploitation by the political elites who, as George Washington warned in his 1796 Farewell Address, would "enfeeble public administration [and] agitate the community with ill-founded jealousies and false alarms, kindling the animosity of one part against another."[5] To guard against these occurrences, national solidarity requires that democratic strangers develop civic friendships wherein they obligate themselves to one another and take a unified stance against the state's breach of the social contract for their mutual material and social benefit.

The American civil religion provides the belief system and ritualistic acts of solidarity, strengthening the tendons within the citizenry that help the democratic muscle move the bones of the republic. It gives national solidarity moral, public, and ideological dimensions that make it especially sturdy to resist the lazy but effective appeals to racial divisions that typically cramp, strain, and tear the connections between citizens. With this unifying force in place, national solidarity can leverage the strength derived from color-conscious conceptions of the Promise and be brawny enough to take on the state, which bears responsibility for the historical and contemporary presence of racism in the United States.

Ultimately, if racism was manufactured from governmental policies that at first sanctioned racial oppression and then did not do enough to punish violations of the foundational American ideals, then perhaps it can be combatted by a national solidarity manufactured by programs and policies that unite the people. Such an undertaking is necessarily difficult and large, but it is the best hope of a nation in need of renewal and a return to first principles.

JUMP-STARTING THE CREATION of national solidarity will require a concerted effort by Americans to demand sweeping and transformational changes to government and pursue innovative undertakings that create conditions for civic friendships to form. It operates in adherence to a prevalent maxim, one that permeates this book and public policy scholarship: be hard on structures and easy on people.

A comprehensive list of actions that would ensure a system of governance more responsive to average citizens and deeper connections between citizens of different races would be long, but if we are serious about uniting and heading off racism, the following changes would be important.

Democracy Reform

Americans are not happy with our government, and for good reason; it is far more responsive to economic elites and organized business interests that wield far more influence on government policy than the average citizen does. Three in four of us believe our trust in the government has been shrinking, and nearly two-thirds believe this lack of trust is to blame for making problems harder to solve. When asked about the need for reform, most Americans agree that democracy works well, but more than 60 percent think it is time for significant changes in our government's fundamental design and structure.[6] This accords with the views of some thinkers from the Revolutionary generation, like Thomas Jefferson, who said that each generation has "a right to choose for itself the form of government it believes most promotive of its own happiness . . . so that it may be handed on, with periodical repairs, from generation to generation, to the end of time."[7] The United States has not seen sweeping transformational reforms to its democracy since the civil rights era. To further contain the menace of racial inequality, our generation needs to improve our systems of democracy.

The major thrust of democracy reform should focus on two broad objectives: facilitating citizens' increased political participation and reducing the amount of partisan gamesmanship occurring in our elections. One of the most straightforward ways to do the former is to make voter registration and the process of voting easier. Research from the Brennan Center for Justice has shown that millions of Americans are turned away because of registration issues, such as being purged from voter rolls for not participating in previous elections or because of name misspellings on state records—millions of Americans whose voices are not heard in local, state, and national elections.[8] And millions more are purged from states' voter registration rolls, often in error and in a racially disproportionate manner.[9] Automatic voter registration is an increasingly popular reform that registers eligible Americans to vote when they interact with government agencies or upon turning eighteen, allowing those who do not wish to be registered to opt out. Since 2016, sixteen states and the District of Columbia have implemented automatic voter registration measures. A recent study from the Knight Foundation found that of the approximately 40 percent—or 100 million—of eligible Americans who did not vote in the 2016 presidential election, 5 million of them cited registration issues as the primary reason.[10]

Moreover, 8 percent of all nonvoters, including 15 percent of registered voters who chose not to participate, cited lack of time as the reason for not voting.[11] Reform measures that ease the process of voting—expanded early voting periods and increased use of mail-in ballots—have been shown to increase voter participation, as in Colorado, where voting by mail raised overall turnout, and participation by eighteen- to twenty-four-year-olds increased by more than 12 percent in a midterm election.[12] And because the partisan and ideological leanings of nonvoters mostly resemble those of voters, there is no inherent political advantage for either side in increasing voter participation. Further, concerns that making voting easier would lead to increased voter fraud are unfounded, as research has shown that "an individual is more likely to be struck by lightning than that he will impersonate another person at the polls."[13]

To address the latter challenge of political parties rigging election rules in their favor, campaign finance and gerrymandering reforms are essential. In the 2010 landmark case *Citizens United v. Federal Elections Commission*, the Supreme Court ruled that restricting corporations' contributions to political campaigns was an infringement of their free speech rights. Because corporations tend to hold more wealth than individuals, their larger donations can translate into more speech and more influence on elections and policy outcomes than most Americans have. Though *Citizens United* alone did not revolutionize the world of campaign finance, constitutional law professor Justin Levitt makes the point that the case "has provoked such a strong reaction because it stands for a series of opinions that, together, allow the potential for corporate speech to overwhelm a democratic system built to serve individual voters."[14] The end result is that a third of political spending in the 2016 federal election came from .01 percent of Americans, and 96 percent of Americans blamed money in politics for political dysfunction.[15] Electoral reforms—like public financing of elections so that the donations of small donors are amplified by supplemental government funding, or requiring donors to disclose their political spending to remove the influence of dark money and anonymous giving—can mitigate the influence of big money on our democratic system.

Similarly, politicians often draw legislative districts to bake in electoral advantages that allow them to hold on to power even if they do not receive the majority of the vote in any given election. For example, in Wisconsin, Republican legislators devised a map that allowed them to win 60 percent of seats in the state assembly by winning just 48 percent of the popular vote.[16] Democrats are guilty, too, as seen in states like Maryland, where a challenge to its map made it all the way to the Supreme Court. The most commonly cited reform to combat this is to have independent commissions placed in charge of drawing maps and using metrics like the efficiency gap, a measure created by law professor Nicholas Stephanopoulos and political scientist Eric McGhee to assess how fairly distributed the population is across districts, as a means of public oversight. And though the Supreme Court refused to intervene and compel states to consider reforms, Chief Justice John Roberts acknowledged that "such gerrymandering is incompatible with democratic principles."[17]

Democracy reforms that expand the electorate, increase civic engagement, and hold politicians' feet to the democratic fire would all serve to lay the groundwork for national solidarity. Steps taken to restore Americans' faith in the processes, institutions, and systems of democracy help address the political corruption and outsize influence of special interests, which 77 percent of Americans believe are especially important to reduce.[18] Complicating Americans' access to voting and sifting our collective voice through campaign donations and district lines drawn from an easel of unfairness degrades our democracy and citizens' sense of trust in the government. Nearly 40 million Americans say the main reason they do not vote is because either they think their votes do not matter, they believe the system is too corrupt, or they dislike the candidates the flawed system attracts.[19] National solidarity hinges on the ability of citizens to participate in the polis, on the citizenry's capacity to hold sway over elected officials, and on the responsiveness of the state to the public. A more participatory democratic system signals a shared investment in the nation and harnesses civic virtue, thereby creating conditions more conducive to the formation of this solidarity.

Deliberative Democracy

More citizens voting and accountability of politicians may help create a more responsive system, but that is not enough to create solidarity. People's trust in the government is important, but 70 percent of us believe trusting each other is more important to solving societal problems than having confidence in the government, and nearly two-thirds of us say that trust is shrinking.[20] The dual aims of restoring faith in our government and each other require an increasingly engaged and interactive citizenry.

In addition to increased civic participation, deliberative democracy offers a supplemental means to achieve civic engagement, improve the chances of enacting policies responsive to the public, and create stronger connections among the people. This form of democracy is generally defined as one where "free and equal citizens (and their representatives) justify decisions in a process in which they give one another reasons that are mutually acceptable and generally accessible, with the aim of reaching conclusions that are binding in the present on all citizens but open to challenge in the future."[21] In essence, it is a style of governance that requires genuine deliberation and consensus agreement, not just a preponderance of votes, for decisions to be made and implemented.

It can take many forms, but its basic principles are that participants should be willing to talk and listen to all sides with civility and respect, they should be representative of the larger public and see one another as equals, and the discussion should be informed and informative.[22] Scholars have argued that "the goal of deliberative forums is to help participants develop an opinion informed by relevant facts, expert information, and an understanding of multiple perspectives held by others in their community," and that the "process encourages citizens to engage in a structured discussion on polarizing issues."[23] Think of it as a town hall or caucus where the outcome of the discussion is an agreement that becomes law or an enforceable rule. This process further integrates the people into the system of checks and balances, while demanding they talk to and negotiate with one another to exercise this power.

Deliberative convenings are new to neither societies in general nor the United States in particular. The Athenians of ancient Greece encouraged citizen participation in political deliberation: Thucydides wrote in the seminal tome *History of the Peloponnesian War* that "our ordinary citizens, though occupied with the pursuit of industry, are still fair judges of public matters," and "instead of looking on discussion as a stumbling block in the way of action, we think it an indispensable preliminary to any wise action at all."[24] And certainly, the framers of the Constitution believed in deliberative politics as demonstrated by their Philadelphia sequester in the summer of 1787 and the checks and balances they baked into our republic. But most of the nation's democratic deliberation to date occurs with restricted participation, either by having a narrow construction of who qualifies as a citizen, and so leaving the political discussion to representatives of the people instead of the people themselves, or by prioritizing winning over building consensus.

In a nation as large and diverse as the United States, coming up with practical schemes to implement deliberative democracy is a difficult but not impossible undertaking. Generally speaking, it begins with a random selection of citizens to consider some issue, similar to how juries are selected today but without the voir dire gaming that often attends the process. The immediate concern is whether the average American citizen is up to, or even interested in, the task. After all, we have long been labeled an anti-intellectual country that does not value rigorous debate and prefers to take our information with a heavy dose of entertainment.[25] Just one in four of us can name all three branches of government, and a third cannot name a single one, while only 37 percent can name their congressional representative, and more than one in three cannot list a single right protected by the First Amendment.[26] Moreover, at a time when partisan fever is running particularly high, citizen deliberation may simply devolve into sophomoric shouting matches where beating each other is more important than solving a problem.

But when issues are considered without political party representatives as the arbiter of the final decision, citizens are freer to express their beliefs in a manner unmoored from party affiliation and support for specific candidates. We do not have to guess about this point; it is clear in direct democracy referenda that occur at the local and state levels. For example, when a measure was considered in Florida that would reinstate the voting rights of former felons, it passed in equal measure in counties won by Donald Trump and Hillary Clinton in 2016.[27] And though nearly 90 percent of black voters support Democratic presidential and congressional candidates, 60–40 splits are not uncommon when a range of issues are considered via direct democracy referenda.[28] Outcomes such as these point to the capacity and willingness of Americans to break from polarizing partisan allegiances and examine policy measures on their merits.

The task at hand, then, is to provide the requirement and the means for citizens to engage in deliberative democracy. Undertaking such a program nationally at the outset is a daunting task and may be a bridge too far as a first step. Therefore, deliberative democracy should begin in communities, localities, and municipalities so that the public is engaging on the most salient and consequential decisions that will impact their daily lives. A locality-first approach not only builds on the system of federalism the framers of the Constitution instituted, but it also aligns with the thinking of Plato and Aristotle, who identified the city as the optimal size for governance and the maintenance of relations among the citizenry.

Local government efforts to install deliberative democracy are already underway in places like Pittsburgh and Cambridge, Massachusetts. In order to increase civic participation, the City of Pittsburgh partnered with Carnegie Mellon University to develop a program for citizen-driven deliberative forums, employing it for decisions ranging from selecting a new chief of police to creating strategies to combat socioeconomic disparities.[29] The City of Cambridge conducts participatory budgeting, a tool of deliberative democracy wherein members of the community study the issues and advise the local government on spending decisions and local projects. After its third year of utilizing this process, local officials found that civic engagement expanded, participation by underrepresented groups was good but could be improved, and all citizen participants reported better connections to their neighbors and the city government.[30]

Ideas abound for how a more citizen-led, deliberative form of democracy could be exercised nationally. Political scientists Bruce Ackerman and James Fishkin have proposed instituting a Deliberation Day, a two-day national holiday during which citizens would be paid to engage in group discussions on issues, meet and pose questions to candidates for various offices, listen to candidate debates, and interact with party officials.[31] Law professor Ethan Leib believes a citizen-populated fourth branch of government should be created, staffed with citizens randomly chosen from jury pools who would provide a deliberative democratic check on the other branches.[32] But a federal system based on deliberative democracy is not necessary for the nation to reap its benefits. Implementation at the local level and the lessons learned from those efforts can serve as a foundation for expanded application of deliberative democracy for state and federal governance; citizens engaging one another in their communities across the country is more important than the establishment of a national process for deliberation. Local-level civic engagement can have national-level impacts that facilitate a broader solidarity.

The actual method of carrying out deliberative democracy is an open question; there is no rigid set of guidelines for how it must be done. Political scientist Mark Button and historian Kevin Mattson undertook a yearlong study of deliberative democracy case studies and reached the following conclusions: deliberation is not a standardized process and must be tailored to the setting in which it is to occur; the connection between deliberation and democracy will require that we rethink the latter because we have become too accustomed to deferring to representatives; and deliberation challenges the instrumental view of politics and becomes an experiment of imagination.[33] The process will need to be suited to the specific task at hand, from the administration of municipal issues to revisions of federal statutes or rules. And it will need to account for the regional, cultural, and political differences of the citizens engaged in the process. But most importantly, Button and Mattson saw evidence that the process "can provide citizens with an opportunity for building a common democratic culture," an outcome that facilitates national solidarity.

Deliberative democracy is far from a cure-all to all that ails us. There is no guarantee that the process and determinations will result in significant improvements in policy outcomes. But, as Mattson has noted elsewhere, "we must be honest that deliberation needs to be an end in itself, something that citizens should cherish for its own sake."[34] Solidarity requires that we emerge from our cliques and engage in good faith with one another. As the American idiom goes, freedom is not free; it requires our time, resources, energies, talents, and commitment. Outsourcing the maintenance of our society to a system that is not responsive to our concerns does not build bridges—neither the actual ones the nation needs nor the social ones solidarity requires.

A Program of National Service

Three sociologists conducted a study on the best ways to build solidarity and proposed a theory of reciprocity from their findings. In a society where people are dependent on one another, social exchange—the reciprocal transfer of goods or resources, material and nonmaterial, such as physical products and services, time and attention, prestige and respect, or information and advice[35]—typically occurs with direct or indirect reciprocity. In the former, two people provide value to each other; whereas in the latter, the benefit you receive from one person is passed on in some manner to a third person, and the original giver eventually receives a benefit by virtue of living in a mutually dependent society.[36] They reference the work of fellow sociologist Peter Ekeh, who argued that direct exchanges are characterized by low levels of solidarity and trust, self-interested actors who perpetually question the fairness of their interactions, and a quid pro quo mentality; conversely, indirect exchanges create actors with a more collective orientation and high levels of solidarity and trust.[37]

They found that in societies where people contribute to the common good without expectation of direct reward or compensation for their contribution, they build communal solidarity characterized by trust, positive feelings, social unity, and feelings of commitment. Volunteers for charitable organizations, citizens engaged in civic processes like working at polling stations, and groups devoted to community service, for example, often attest to how their endeavors create deeper connections to others and to their communities. An important caveat, however, exists: when inequality and power imbalances are present, incentives and normative constraints may be necessary to encourage wider participation in these social exchanges and the desired outcomes.

Increasing these sorts of generalized social exchanges is central to fostering national solidarity, especially for a nation whose civic health could be improved. One of the more commonly offered recommendations to accomplish this is to establish a program of national service. Conservative and progressive think tanks, politicians, and service-oriented nonprofit organizations alike have echoed the call for an expanded national service requirement, to compel or encourage young Americans to practice civic altruism with the primary goal being interactions with others with whom they would not typically engage. Such a program encourages the indirect exchanges in a mutually dependent society in hopes it will create and strengthen connections among citizens. Political scientists Cecilia Hyunjung Mo and Katharine Conn note that numerous studies have found national service can "trigger healthier sympathies and soberer ideas" and result in "heightened social awareness, increased amity toward the community they service, reduced reliance on stereotypes about marginalized groups, and higher appreciation for diversity and tolerance."[38] The basic premise is that contact with other groups helps overcome preconceived notions and any sense of threat, facilitating the intergroup trust that is essential for solidarity in multiracial societies.

The path from national service to solidarity, however, is not an easy one. As the history of the United States suggests, increased contact between groups does not always or inevitably lead to improved relations. Indeed, it has often led to increased competition, tensions, discrimination, and violence—such as when 6 million black Americans migrated out of the South in the twentieth century only to be met by unenthusiastic white citizens and immigrants who resented the job competition, political disruptions, and housing fights. The conditions and context of the contact are essential in determining which outcome—conflict or comity—results.

The military is typically cited when the advantages of national service are discussed because it is the most respected institution in the country and it brings together Americans from all backgrounds and unites them in a common cause.[39] It is also an example of how contact can lead to different outcomes. Mo and Conn cite studies that show the desegregation of the military led to more positive racial attitudes between white and black servicemembers the more they deployed together.[40] But once back in segregated towns and cities, black and white veterans were relegated to their positions in the nation's social hierarchy and subject to the disparate treatment by the government and the public that resulted. The advantages of intergroup contact have a limited radius and half-life; if it is not properly maintained or is overcome by divisive social forces, the benefits are lost. Thus, a properly administered program of national service, as part of a larger multifaceted effort to establish national solidarity, would create a more enduring sense of trust and unity among the nation's democratic strangers.

Proposals for national service have come in many forms, from service programs that provide some incentive, such as grants or student loan deferments, to a mandatory two-year period of service established by federal law. Precedents for the various approaches exist in the United States, including legal mandates like military conscription and incentivized options like Franklin Roosevelt's Civilian Conservation Corps, John F. Kennedy's Peace Corps, and Bill Clinton's AmeriCorps. Community-level programs have also been in place for some time and are increasingly becoming part of secondary-education programs: service learning is incorporated into the curriculum and graduation requirements in high schools across the country. Moreover, national service is popular with Americans—it is one of the few areas that Democrats and Republicans agree on in approximately equal measure.[41] Voters say that such a program would be good for citizens and the nation, have deep interest in participating, and believe the cost would be worth the benefits gained.

Yet a significant distinction exists: 80 percent of voters favor a system of voluntary national service, while 71 percent oppose mandatory national service.[42] Some corners of the polity fear that a mandatory national service program is a socialist undertaking to have young citizens do the bidding of political elites; others argue that such a program would violate the Thirteenth Amendment, which outlaws slavery and indentured servitude except as punishment for a crime.[43] Three ways to implement such a national service program would likely survive a constitutional challenge: tie service requirements to an incentive or sanction, merge a service requirement with the extant military draft framework, or establish a federally mandated national service requirement on every American.[44]

Politically, the first of the three is likely the only tenable option—a program of national service will likely need to be voluntary and incentivize participation through both material benefits, like student-loan forgiveness and job training, and normative social behavior where respect and prestige are granted to participants. Using sanctions, such as disqualification from federal work or loans for those who do not participate, as is presently the case for men who do not register with Selective Service, is far less popular.

One thing is certain: it is difficult to build national solidarity in a country where housing, schools, and social circles remain heavily segregated. Democratic strangers do not develop civic friendship by never interacting and avoiding each other altogether. A program of national service focused as much on citizens' connections as on service-centric outcomes can, therefore, begin to break down the walls. Given that much of the United States is sorted geographically and socially by race and class, neighborhood- or community-level-only service will not create the necessary connections to Americans sufficiently different from us. Analysis of hundreds of studies has shown that intergroup contact reduces prejudices by decreasing anxieties toward other groups, increasing empathy with their members, and increasing knowledge about other groups to dispel stereotypes and caricatures.[45] The benefit to the creation of national solidarity is pretty clear: if Americans do not interact and work together for a common national good, we are unlikely to develop the bonds needed to take on the challenges ahead and those in front of us today. National service alone is insufficient; it must occur alongside Americans whom we would not typically encounter or engage with.

A program of national service would need to be voluntary, provide enticements for participation, and ensure one's service takes place in a new environment with a diverse cohort. The "uneasy tension between moral individualism and civic obligation" that resides in the American psyche suggests service must be a choice that benefits individuals through both material and reputational gains.[46] Any program that does not help participants accrue a specific kind of social capital would likely lead to disproportionate representation by economically disadvantaged groups, thereby undercutting potential societal benefits.

Further, participants must also be given flexibility on the nature of their service, whether focused on public health, the environment, education, infrastructure, or any number of disciplines. But beyond the choice to serve and the general field of service, actual assignments should be prescribed to ensure program participants serve in cohorts and locales that provide exposure to a representative sample of America. Oversight, either by a government entity or independent commission, will be necessary to ensure the right mix of talents, classes, races, projects, and sites are maintained so that intergroup contact and indirect social exchanges occur. And while the program should be open to Americans of all ages, the focus should be on younger Americans so that exposure to their fellow compatriots happens in formative years. A survey of more than one hundred studies of civic service shows it results in positive effects on participants, institutions, beneficiaries, and communities across a range of fifteen different indicators.[47] National service—properly administered, managed, and led—is essential to making conditions ripe for national solidarity.

Civic Education

When concerns are raised about Americans' lack of trust, civility, and knowledge, the need for more civic education is the go-to remedy cited so frequently that the recommendation has begun to feel a bit trite. It is hard to argue against the premise that if the country did a better job of educating American children in the rights and duties of citizenship, we would have a more engaged and informed citizenry more capable of working toward the common good as adults. Yet it is also difficult to draw a straight line from Americans knowing who their congressional representative is to a nation ready to establish bonds of solidarity across race, class, and region. Studies of civic education programs reveal more of this paradox: while these programs can reduce political inequality by providing younger

Americans the ability to engage more effectively with politics, the communities most in need of them are often not well positioned to make the programs successful, and the benefits accumulate in those sections of society already enjoying an advantage.[48] To address this pitfall and help build national solidarity, the concept of civic education must be expanded beyond its current understanding.

Civic education is most often associated with school curricula focused on basic knowledge like the branches of government, the nation's founding documents, and voting rules. But a more enduring and broadly construed version of it exists in what the ancient Greeks termed *paideia*, which refers to the self-development and educational pursuits that prepare a member of the society to be an asset to family and community alike.[49] The civic education that will foster national solidarity is less measurable on standardized testing and more aligned to *paideia*. Broadly speaking, civic education should refer to "all the processes that affect people's beliefs, commitments, capabilities, and actions as members or prospective members of communities."[50] It is the education in how to be a productive citizen with a sense of what a well-ordered republic can and should accomplish.

Harvard professor Danielle Allen's concept of participatory readiness is a contemporary construction of *paideia* and much closer to meeting the present needs of the nation. Allen notes that most articulations of education concern preparing students for economic competitiveness, and the increased focus on college and career readiness has come at the expense of the civic. Participatory readiness, then, is the preparation for civic and political life as well as all the areas in which we hope to prosper, including our interpersonal relationships, our communities, and our professions.[51]

Civic education, in Allen's construct, is about preparing for civic and political life, where *civic* "suggests public action undertaken through approved venues and within the confines of longstanding public agendas," and the more charged term *political* "invokes approved actions such as voting and holding office, but it also suggests protest action, activism, and advocacy."[52] It comprises "three developmental pillars: verbal empowerment, democratic knowledge, and a rich understanding of the strategies and tactics that undergird efficacy."[53] Civic education readies citizens to give voice to their experiences and ideas, provides the ability to bond with and relate to others in the shared society, and prepares civic agents to use the primary civic and political instruments to engage effectively.

Though its ability to transform a nation remains to be seen, there is little doubt that civic education is lacking in the United States and needs to be reinvigorated if we are to have any hope of creating national solidarity and fulfilling the Promise. And young Americans agree: two-thirds of them think schools and colleges should prepare students to be informed voters, but less than one in three schools offers stand-alone civics courses.[54] Scholars have argued that providing civic education to the youth population is especially advantageous for creating a critical-thinking citizenry with a culture of civic engagement, particularly in diverse societies, and this is most easily done through the school system.[55] The learning, however, must necessarily go beyond the classroom to include and account for the learning that takes place in the public sphere and the counterpublic spaces where the American culture and way of life are learned. And civic education must also be a lifelong learning endeavor—one never ages out of needing civic education. Because our society is always changing, the ways to maintain one's civic and political agency are always evolving. Strong democracies need an active citizenry that does not delegate its civic duty, and civic education is central to a democratic person's agency.

The effort to build national solidarity will require a civic education that offers far more than baseline knowledge about government structure, pared down lessons about the American civil religion and its undergirding mythology, or best practices about active citizenship. Those things are important, certainly, but a richer civic education must teach a fuller accounting of the nation's history to include the flaws and hypocrisies that characterize it. Some have taken any criticism of the United States or its historical figures to be an assault on the American idea itself and a personal affront to those who believe in its core principles. But civic education should be fashioned and received in the spirit of the famous quote from renowned writer James Baldwin: "I love America more than any other country in the world, and, exactly for this reason, I insist on the right to criticize her perpetually."[56] Education that truly reckons with the nation's history not only serves to give citizens a better sense of its shortfalls, the experiences of others, and facts to refute the historical opinions of those with ulterior motives, but it also provides an opportunity to highlight the nation's trajectory of progress and instill a sense of pride in the generations of Americans who fought to bring the nation closer to the Promise.

Moreover, there are real threats to our systems of democracy that require an educated and savvy citizenry to think critically about civic, political, and electoral matters. For example, it is widely known that Russia attempted to interfere in the presidential election of 2016 and spread racist tropes on social media in order to depress black American turnout and activate cultural anxieties in white Americans. While we do not know the exact extent to which such tactics were successful, millions of American citizens were fooled by, and actively contributed to the dissemination of, Russian misinformation intended to damage faith in our democracy and in our candidates for president.[57] Further, decades of political science scholarship demonstrate that voters rely primarily on certain markers, such as political party or candidate affect, and less on more critical and time-consuming assessments of a candidate's policy proposals and leadership abilities. Civic education makes citizens smarter and more astute.

Most importantly, civic education is essential to the other needed actions and initiatives—democracy reform, deliberative democracy, and national service—that can help manufacture solidarity

across lines of race and class. Though instituting it will not solve
the nation's issues alone, leaving the lack of civic education unaddressed will only contribute to the growing divisions in our society.
The Education Center proposes that every civic education program should be inquiry-based to help draw out students' particular
experiences and ideas, interdisciplinary to show the various ways
civic engagement plays out, and empowering to give citizens confidence to take action.[58] Such programs can be available in the school
system, community colleges, and civic institutions like libraries
and churches to ensure a wide reach and easy accessibility by the
citizenry. Further, the relationship between civic education and
the other recommended actions is symbiotic: they, too, are part
of the delivery system. Fundamental reforms to our civic institutions, processes, and modes of engagement are not only educative
through increased participation, but they also establish normative
behaviors and constraints that make civic laggards subject to social
sanction and reputational costs.

As we are all civic agents, we must also be perpetual students
of civic education. In this way, we learn how to wield our rights to
compel government action; establish connections to one another
through better understanding and a shared, inclusive history; and
facilitate building bonds of solidarity.

A Transformative Figure

Sound arguments to address daunting challenges are rarely enough
to win the day in getting such significant reforms and programs as
described above implemented. Even if the public is supportive of
such measures, the movement will need a champion. Abolition and
the Civil War needed Frederick Douglass and Abraham Lincoln; the
antitrust crowd and recovery from the Great Depression had the Roosevelt presidents, Teddy and Franklin; the women's suffrage movement
needed Mary Church Terrell and Elizabeth Cady Stanton; and the

Civil Rights Era required both Martin Luther King, Jr., and Lyndon Johnson. The policies that resulted from those transformational periods, clearly necessary and long overdue, would not have seen the light of day if not for the force of personality and stubborn insistence of those transformational figures. Establishing national solidarity to take on structural racism, however, is a larger and more complicated task. It has the potential to fundamentally reshape the nation and finish the work begun by transformative undertakings like the Revolutionary War, the Civil War, the Suffrage Movement, and the New Deal. This will require more than a powerful advocate; to paraphrase the famous Bonnie Tyler song from 1984, it needs a hero(ine).

Political scientist Scott Edwards has argued that the United States has always been partial to hero worship, and it is almost impossible to think about the founding of the country or the narrative around restoring the Union in the mid-nineteenth century apart from the idea of the hero.[59] The pantheon of the American civil religion is essentially an ode to national heroes, each having created, saved, or restored the nation in their time. They serve as embodiments of the good achieved as well as exemplars of the best of us. In a sense, Americans needed heroes as they provided a glimpse of the more perfect citizen who helped construct a more perfect Union.

In his treatise on heroes, the philosopher Jean-Jacques Rousseau wrote, "The Hero does not always perform great actions; but he is always ready to do so if needed and shows himself to be great in all the circumstances of his life."[60] Rousseau believed they must work primarily for the benefit of others, must have both virtue and vice as they make heroism within reach of the average person, and must display a courage and strength of soul that places social utility above naked self-interest.[61] Indeed, as Edwards suggests, for the nation not to need a hero "is to lose a quality essentially American." All these things are clearly evinced in the monomythic structure—or "hero's journey"—featured in much of the nation's historical and civil religious narratives.

Yet, the call for a transformative figure to marshal America toward national solidarity may feel a bit quixotic. The grace extended to leaders of the founding era and the Civil War generation would be quite hard to come by for leaders in the present-day United States; even King, inarguably seen as an American hero today, was widely despised just before his death by many Americans. Institutions, whose leaders are often self-cast or perceived to be a sort of hero, are declining in importance in American life. The citizenry's diminished faith in politics and government negatively impacts the admiration the earlier generations had for the political and military leaders of their eras. There is also a sense that "gotcha" politics and the speed of information and judgment means that political heroes have little chance of emerging today because they are torn down at every turn and granted no time or space for redemption.[62]

Moreover, unlike movements of the past, recent mass-based movements—like Black Lives Matter, the Tea Party, and Occupy Wall Street—have been flat enterprises that resist identifying organizational leaders who speak for the collective. These trends, bundled with the rise of a social media that propagates cynicism at light speed, have complicated the path for a would-be hero while also accelerating the path to celebrity. Studies show a potential outcome of this evolution is "younger people tending to choose heroes known for their talents, physical skills, and celebrity status," while "older people tend to favor moral heroes."[63] Edwards argues that our passion for the traditional hero has passed, and that while trying times may create favorable conditions for one to emerge, "what is necessary and sufficient to produce them is a popular mood favorable to hero-hood." The national mood, in the estimation of many scholars, is no longer interested in a hero. And yet, as others suggest, "a system without heroes diminishes us all."[64]

It remains true, however, that the nation's best moments have had a transformative figure, or figures, at the helm. The renowned historian Anna Julia Cooper said in 1892, "The great, the fundamental need of any nation, any race, is for heroism, devotion, sacrifice; and there cannot be heroism, devotion, or sacrifice in a primarily skeptical spirit."[65] Given our national history, we are unlikely to find the motivation to refashion our society without a consummate American making the popular case for the need for action. When asked what makes someone a hero, more than three in four Americans cite doing the right thing regardless of personal consequences, while two-thirds believe a willingness to risk personal safety to help others, perseverance, composure in a crisis, overcoming adversity, and changing society for the better are all important qualities of heroes.[66]

Social scientists Scott T. Allison and George R. Goethals have deeply researched the dynamics of hero selection and found that heroes provide scripts for beneficial social behaviors and energize us by promoting moral improvement and growth.[67] Further, they note that our needs and motives determine who we ultimately select as a hero.[68] The question, then, is whether the nation will recognize its need for a transformative figure—not to help specific groups win political battles or prevail over others, but to bring Americans closer together, bring the nation closer to the Promise, and bring structural racism to its knees through the power of example and the implementation of principled and inclusive public policy.

This transformative figure would have a personal story that bridges the existing national mythology to the future iteration wherein our narrative is one of progress instead of perfection at our origin. She or he will be capable of making a compelling case to Americans of all races that racism exploits divisions within the citizenry for the primary benefit of the relatively small cadre of those who hold power. She or he will be a walking testament to the advantages of an inclusive democracy and the harm caused by an exclusive one. She or he will champion the American civil religion while demonstrating that our society's imperfections are not proof of its infeasibility. She or he will illustrate how democratic strangers can becomes civic friends. And this transformative figure will help Americans across the color line see their fates as linked. This is a tall order, but Cooper's words in her day remain relevant today: "The Hour is now—where is the (wo)man?" It is not possible to know if this transformative figure will emerge and be noticed in the moment, or if she or he will be appreciated only posthumously for bringing about national solidarity and taking us a step closer to the Promise. Perhaps she will champion the cause and compel the nation to act, or maybe he will leverage some crisis or event and nudge us in the proper direction. Whichever it is, this figure is needed—the American people follow leaders with charisma and ideas in a time of need, not ideas alone.

THE UNITED STATES IS BARRELING ALONG as nations do, weathering growing and shrinking economies, international conflicts, and the ebbs and flows of domestic politics. The American idea, however, is in danger.

In many ways, the idea has never *not* been in danger. Since the nation's inception, the principles the nation clings to for dear life have been under assault by the very forces that created them. The United States is just doing what is in the nature of nation-states—chasing its security, its interests, and more prosperity. But America is in a battle for its life—either it beats back racial hierarchy and its offspring, or it succumbs to the selfishness and hypocrisy that extinguish the pilot light of liberal democracy. The Promise cannot long endure alongside a citizenry that permits its racial diversity to be exploited as a source of division while political and economic elites fashion the country in a manner most advantageous to them. If we do not find the solidarity to compel the state to reform, then, in the closing words of John Jay in "Federalist No. 2," the American idea "will have reason to exclaim, in the words of the poet: 'FARE-WELL! A LONG FAREWELL TO ALL MY GREATNESS.'"

A greatness that grasped the heights of human possibility but ultimately tumbled into the doldrums of human frailty.

We, the people, are the moral characters and agents capable of
preserving the Promise and making the Union more perfect in the
process. There is no one else to do it on our behalf. We need not stum-
ble around in the dark waiting for destiny to direct our steps until we
trip by happenstance over national solidarity. We can manufacture it
through the making of demands on our government and commitment
born of a recognition that our fates as Americans are linked across
lines of color and class. And we know what solidarity in response to a
long-term and slow-moving catastrophe looks like, thanks to, among
others, black people who have forced the United States over time, and
often against its will, to be more American. When the storm clouds
of injustice covered black America, its people—with a spirit that is
America in its essence—managed to find the sun and the stars. That
energy is born of the same stuff and from the same place as the force
that has propelled people of all races and from all sets of circumstances
to find and continually fight for a home in the United States and a
place in America. The black experience is particular, but it is not alone.
The nation would do well to learn lessons from its people, and this
can be done only if we are willing to accept one another as Americans
with our differences and perspectives fully intact.

This is a lot. Racism is a wicked problem. There is no easy way
through it or away from it. If left to fester, it will ultimately consume
the nation and us along with it. The remedy—national solidarity—
demands a level of honesty, commitment, and forbearance that can
feel unnatural to American sensibilities grounded in individualism,
self-determination, and a bootstrapping work ethic. But as the writer
George Packer chronicled in a look at the forces threatening our
civic cohesion, we must recognize that injustice is lethal; "that, in a
democracy, being a citizen is essential work; that the alternative to
solidarity is death."[69] We have the value system, the blueprint, and
the hazard ahead begging us to act—all that remains to be seen is

if we also have the necessary courage and strength of soul. Either we devise a way to achieve national solidarity, or our chapter in history will be a fable about the ephemerality of multiracial liberal democracies and the naivete about human nature.

In a book chronicling the debates and events that led to the signing of the Declaration of Independence and the creation of the Unites States, the acclaimed historian Pauline Maier wrote that our founding document had become akin to a religious scripture that has been reimagined throughout its existence. The founding fathers planted a seed of liberty in fertile soil interspersed with clay that was vile, and that act alone is worthy of praise. But as any farmer knows, you can plant whatever seed you like, but you do not get to dictate how, when, or if the life it harbors springs forth. And should fortune smile upon it, once it has burst through and tasted the rising and setting sun, it has a life of its own.

Maier believed, "[The Declaration] was what the American people chose to make of it, at once a legacy and a new conception, a document that spoke both for the revolutionaries and their descendants, who confronted issues the country's fathers had never known or failed to resolve, binding one generation after another in a continuing act of national self-definition."[70]

Whatever the future of the United States holds, we have our say in what its next iteration will be. The nation cannot allow racial revanchism to plug our ears and mute the tolling of liberty's bell that we have been charged to heed. The work ahead is substantial; nature—human and otherwise—is not easily tamed. But the prospect of constructing a national solidarity, of finally managing the effects of racism and proving the possibility and viability of a multiracial democracy, is too important to abandon. As Representative John Lewis articulated in an article published posthumously, offering his final words to the country from beyond the grave, "Ordinary people with extraordinary vision can redeem the soul of America . . ."[71]

*   *   *

A NAMELESS ENTRY on a U.S. census form epitomizes the current choice before Americans and the United States. Though the narrative arc of the presidential name my paternal great-grandparents gifted to the family seems quintessentially American, it is the missing name in my maternal lineage that is more apt.

Hoping to learn more about the cast of ancestral characters that the Sisters, including my grandmother Orrie Bell, told the family about back on that June afternoon in 1999 thick with Georgia's humidity, I turned to the National Archives. This institution enshrines the sacred texts of our civil religion—the Declaration of Independence, the Constitution, the Bill of Rights—and houses decades of census records. Before the Civil War, enslaved black Americans were recorded on census forms only by age and sex—no names.

Guided by the Sisters' oral history, I found the nondescript listing of an eight-year-old black boy in the 1850 U.S. Census Slave Schedule. He was owned by the same family in the Sisters' telling that lived in the same place where I had spent summers on my grandparents' farm avoiding fire ants, chasing fireflies, and going to church with strong-willed folk on fire for the Lord. Over three censuses, I traced his evolution from an unnamed enslaved child into an American citizen with the right to vote. By 1870, the United States recognized him as William "Bill" Humphrey, my great-great-grandfather, who appears in the census free of the Fain family name of his enslavers. Instead, as had also occurred in my paternal lineage, Bill unilaterally renamed himself to demonstrate kinship to his now-freed Humphrey siblings scattered from southwest Georgia to north-central Florida.

Similarly, the earliest citizens of the United States unilaterally decided to rename themselves. By the time of the nation's founding, the word *America* had come to mean the New World, and residents of the colonies were often referred to as British Americans or

English Americans. Our country announced itself to the world in the Declaration of Independence, opening with, "The unanimous Declaration of the thirteen united States of America"—the *united* appears in lowercase with capitalized *States* and *America* throughout the document. Since our inception, we have chosen to be called *Americans*, and the world today refers to citizens of the United States and the nation itself as such, often to the chagrin of the more than half a billion people outside the United States who live in the Americas. In choosing this name, the nation-state's first generation associated themselves with their vision of the possibilities the New World represented—the right to "institute new Government" and provide "new Guards for their future security" so that a country could be born that recognizes human equality and the attendant inalienable rights. America became the name of a nation of Promise.

But ideas cannot administer governance; only people within systems can. The United States became that governing entity, one that has often fallen short of the Promise imbued in the America that trails its title. The United States of America may be the official name of our country, but the United States and America are not synonymous. The geopolitical nation-state known as the United States is not the Promise; it is governed by its interests, even when they are antithetical to the Promise, as history has shown. In this regard, it is important that we have chosen *American* for ourselves and not *United Statesmen*. Whether the founding generations did so purposely or not is less important than our recognition today that our value and purpose are most defined by the American idea.

The natural inclination of nation-states is to do what is in their best interests, but the natural tendency of people who call themselves Americans must be to do what is right and just in accordance with their professed ideals. For all the nation's shortcomings over the course of its relatively short life, the tremendous progress it has realized is the result of Americans insisting it be more perfect. The work of real Americans is to compel the United States to ensure security and prosperity, not as ends unto themselves, but solely as a means to permit equality and liberty to exist unmolested.

The moniker American is not the exclusive possession of the overzealous who drape themselves in the national flag and lather their words with clichés ripped from the civil religious canon, often investing themselves in the items of Americana more than in the principles of America and the people who constitute it. Rather, the purest form of America is found in the evolving lot who have helped the United States endure and occupy the mantle as the oldest constitutional democracy by fighting for incremental progress over the generations. We Americans are imperfect, succumbing at times to passions and self-interest, as fallible humans are wont to do, but our aim is straight: making the Promise more real and more accessible.

National solidarity is the means to push the United States to protect America. It is an investment in the state such that the returns benefit the people. It is how we demonstrate our civic kinship to our fellow American sisters and brothers scattered from sea to shining sea. It is how we earn our title and remain worthy to pass it and its charge to the next version of us. If we are to be truly American, national solidarity is the means by which is must be so.

Whether we meet the challenge or not, we will inscribe our mark for posterity and for the annals of history. When the stars begin to fall, we get to decide if they are falling out of the sky as the Promise collapses on itself, or if they are finally falling into place behind the brightness of a new day and the unmistakable declaration that America will be.

Acknowledgments

This is a book without a beginning. It is impossible to pinpoint the exact moment when the idea for it, or the core arguments in it, suddenly came to be. It is not the product of a burning question or earworm of a concept that I could not shake. Instead, it sort of came together over a lifetime—little puzzle pieces littered throughout my personal, professional, and academic experiences that were impossible to fit together without a visual of the end product. In the midst of growing racial tensions and in the months after embarking on a mid-career reinvention, just after putting the finishing touches on a military career and a doctoral degree, the book was suddenly there, brought forth and nurtured by so many who have generously offered their time, talents, and unconditional support. This work only exists because of those who have helped, inspired, and convinced me that I could do the thing that has just been done.

A book is not a project for the overextended. It requires time and space and solitude to think and experiment and chase ideas down rabbit holes knowing full well that today's obsession is likely to meet tomorrow's delete button. Because of the Brennan Center for Justice, which took a chance on me and my nontraditional career path, I had the room to be curious and to let the project breathe. It is impossible to recognize all my colleagues there who, over the last three years, have encouraged me and sharpened my thinking, but there are some who I simply must call by name. I owe a debt of gratitude to John Kowal, who stacked all the odds in my favor to pull this project off and who provided much sage counsel as we commiserated about writing our respective manuscripts. To Michael Waldman, L.B. Eisen, Mike German, Wilfred Codrington, and Jen Weiss-Wolf, thank you for all the guidance and conversations on the book-writing process and for keeping the spark alive when the ordeal felt so daunting. Thanks to Kim Thomas, Wendy Weiser, Spencer Boyer, Alan Beard, Ruth Sangree, Taylor Doggett, Alex Cohen, the whole D.C. office crew, and fellows who have helped me in ways big and small. An especial thanks to Tony Butler and Isabella Dominique, who read an early version of the manuscript in its entirety and offered incredibly thoughtful comments and edits. And a heartfelt thanks to my fellow Southerner Abigail Godwin for all the morning and midday conversations that made long writing days much more bearable, and to Lauren Seabrooks for such a careful and considered reading of the book—line by line and in between the lines—to ensure it did not sacrifice the truth-telling for the bridge-building.

I am forever indebted to New America and its Fellows Program for the invaluable role it played in transforming a germ of an idea into a compelling book proposal. Anne-Marie Slaughter, Tyra Mariani, Awista Ayub, Matthew Davis, Mark Schmitt, Lee Drutman, Peter Bergen—thank you for the doors you opened, the steadfast encouragement, the clarifying conversations, and collegiality over the last five years. Marcia Chatelain and Emefa Agawu, thank you for the care you took with your read of the manuscript and the suggestions that followed. And to Samieleen Lawson and Veronica Mooney, who always had a smile and reassuring words—I cannot thank you enough.

I was equipped to undertake this project because of the education and training provided by Northeastern University's College of

Professional Studies, which taught me how to create new knowledge from an open question, dissecting ideas to the nth degree along the way. When this book was in its infancy, the college invited me back to campus to give an expanded talk—it was an invaluable exercise, the fruit of which is clearly evident in these pages. Thanks to Dean Mary Loeffelholz, to Doctor of Law and Policy program staff, and particularly to professors Neenah Estrella-Luna and Dan Urman. The doctoral journey is a difficult one, but my classmates in Cohort VIII made it enjoyable and rewarding. More important than the credential, however, are the lifelong friendships I formed in the course of earning it—I am so thankful for Noradeen Farlekas, Keenan Davis, and especially Joni Beshansky for her dear friendship and unconditional support.

Writing a book can sometimes feel like being stranded on an island with nothing but jumbled ideas and a collection of badly written paragraphs to keep you company. In those times, conversations—about the book, about life, or about nothing at all—are a welcome reprieve from the solitary pursuit of writing something you hope will be of consequence. Here, there are so many people to recognize: Carole Bell and our weekly Write Club conversations when the manuscript was little more than a blinking cursor on an empty screen; Karen Mills Taylor and Hope Copeland for sharing your stories and allowing them to appear in these pages; David Moore and Stefanie Sanford for your careful and attentive read of the manuscript, and the many conversations around your dining room table with thoughtful women and men from across the ideological spectrum; Janice Johnson-Dias, Anthony Thomas-Davis, Leah Wright Rigueur, Rakia Clark, Kajuana Killings, Wambui Munge, Nicole Collier, and Rima Mandwee for both the short and the extended chats at various points along the way that were always rejuvenating.

There are not enough words to express how eminently grateful I am to my agent, Gail Ross, and my editor, George Gibson. When my proposal seemed to be stuck and my confidence waning, Gail rescued the project, and within weeks of our initial lunch on a late spring afternoon in D.C., she found a home for it at Grove Atlantic. Her wisdom and knowledge of the industry quietly impart confidence to her writers, and this book is a direct result of her particular brand of Midas touch. I am so fortunate to have the red ink of George Gibson's editorial pen all over this manuscript. He believed in this book and clearly saw its potential from the first reading of the proposal, undeterred by its unorthodox layering of memoir, academic theory, historical and political analysis, and essayistic argumentation. His kind and gentle tightening of the vise got words and ideas from me that would not have been possible otherwise, finding the exact places where less is more and where more is needed. Thank you, George.

There are some people and institutions that are so part of your constitution that it is impossible to imagine life without them. I am blessed beyond measure for the nearly thirty-year friendship of Darren Allison, who has taught me friendship. And during a crucial stretch of my teenage years, the friendship of Darrell Skinner and Julious Pulley led to some of my most treasured memories and experiences. The God-fearing men and women of Bethlehem Baptist Church in Raleigh, North Carolina—people I have known since back when it was the "little church on the hill"—shaped me in ways that I have only grown to appreciate more and more over time. Hampton University was a godsend for reasons that I cannot articulate well but feel deep in my soul. The Omega Psi Phi Fraternity, Incorporated, gave me confidence for life, helping me outdo myself. And though this book is the culmination of a lifetime of observations and experiences, the courage necessary to undertake and complete the project blossomed during my year as a White House Fellow. I could not have asked for a better class of fellows to bond with, learn from, and grow alongside than the Class of 2011–2012.

It feels wholly inadequate to attempt any sort of recognition of my family and friends here. What they mean to me cannot be captured in words and could never express the depth of my love and gratitude. Despite all my faults and shortcomings, they have loved me anyway—accepting me as I am for who I am. To my mother and father, your love and many sacrifices are beyond compare; thank you from the depths of my soul. To my siblings—Kim Battle, Jennifer Shank, and Travis Johnson—who bring out the best version of me and are the only people on the planet who can crumple me to the floor in laughter, I truly love y'all, as well as my extended siblings Travis B., Jonathan, and Cierra, and my nieces and nephews. For all my aunts and uncles and Team A, B, and C cousins—who have in one way or another been a second set of parents and siblings—thank you. I only wish that my paternal grandparents, Theodore and Louisa Johnson, who both passed on before I was born, and my maternal grandparents, Bobby and Orrie Bell Lee, who filled my formative summers with love and life lessons, were here—especially the Humphrey Sister Orrie; how she would have loved to hold this volume in her hands.

Lastly, but most importantly, to my wife and boys: for their love, patience, unrelenting faith, and devotion to our tight-knit unit. While staring into the endless abyss of a laptop screen trying to punch out compelling prose, I missed many movie nights and short family excursions and silly antics around the dinner table. But recalling any one of the several bad jokes told in our home or scrolling through pictures from family vacations or dropping everything to see you play or stealing away for quiet moments or emerging from the writing funk to smiles and encouraging words—all these joys renewed and strengthened me to complete the thing. This book is as much yours as it is mine—I hope I've made you proud.

Notes

An Introduction: Race and Solidarity in the United States

1   "Papers of Dr. James McHenry on the Federal Convention of 1787," *American Historical Review* 11, no. 3 (1906): 618.

2   NBC News–SurveyMonkey Poll Results, May 29, 2018.

3   Carrie Dann, "Poll: More Voters Acknowledge Symptoms of Racism but Disagree about Its Causes," NBC News, July 21, 2020, https://www.nbcnews.com/politics/meet-the-press/poll-more-voters-acknowledge-symptoms -racism-disagree-about-its-causes-n1234363; and Pew Research Center, *Race in America*, April 2019.

4   Georgetown University Politics Civility Poll, GU Politics press release, October 23, 2019, http://politics.georgetown.edu/press-releases/ civility-press-release-oct-2019/.

5   Federal Bureau of Investigation, *Hate Crime Statistics, 2018*, Fall 2019, https:// ucr.fbi.gov/hate-crime/2018/topic-pages/victims.

6   Language adopted from Langston Hughes, "Mother to Son," from *The Collected Works of Langston Hughes* (Columbia: University of Missouri Press, 2002).

7   Gallup News Service, *U.S. Future and Trade*, June 2018.

8   Carol Graham, "Why Are Black Poor Americans More Optimistic Than White Ones?," Brookings Institution, January 30, 2018, https://www.brookings.edu/articles/why-are-black-poor-americans-more-optimistic-than -white-ones/.

9   Pew Research Center, *The Public, the Political System and American Democracy*, April 2018.

10 From the Diary of Charles Francis Adams, April 18, 1861, quoted in Doris Kearns Goodwin, *Team of Rivals: The Political Genius of Abraham Lincoln* (New York: Simon and Schuster, 2005), 352; and David O. Stewart, *The Summer of 1787: The Men Who Invented the Constitution* (New York: Simon and Schuster, 2007), 206.

11 This formulation was informed by Sally J. Scholz, *Political Solidarity* (University Park: Pennsylvania State University Press, 2008).

12 Danielle Allen, "Charlottesville Is Not the Continuation of an Old Fight. It Is Something New," *Washington Post*, August 13, 2017, https://www .washingtonpost.com/opinions/charlottesville-is-not-the-continuation -of-an-old-fight-it-is-something-new/2017/08/13/971812f6-8029-11e7-b359 -15a3617c767b_story.html.

13 Plessy v. Ferguson, 163 U.S. 537 (1896).

14 As quoted in Alexander P. Lamis, *The Two-Party South*, 2nd expanded edition (New York: Oxford University Press, 1990).

15 E.Y. Harvey, letter to the editor, *Metropolis* (Jacksonville), October 29, 1901, quoted in John K. Severn and William Warren Rogers, "Theodore Roosevelt Entertains Booker T. Washington: Florida's Reaction to the White House Dinner," *Florida Historical Quarterly* 54, no. 3 (1976): 310.

16 James Vardaman, editorial, *Greenwood Commonwealth*, January 10, 1903, quoted in Edmund Morris, *Theodore Rex* (New York: Random House, 2002), 203.

17 James Brown Scott, Galliard Hunt, and James Madison, *The Debates in the Federal Convention of 1787: Which Framed the Constitution of the United States of America* (New York: Oxford University Press, 1920), 585.

18 As recounted in W.E.B. DuBois, *The Souls of Black Folk* (New York: Penguin Books, 1995), 269.

Chapter 1: The Primary Threat to America

1 Russell Goldman, "Did Obama Go Too Far with Race Remark?," ABC News, July 23, 2009.

2 CNN, *Opinion Research Poll*, August 4, 2009, i.cdn.turner.com/cnn/2009/ images/08/04/rel11a.x.pdf.

3 Jamelle Bouie, "The Professor, the Cop, and the President," *Slate*, September 21, 2016, https://slate.com/news-and-politics/2016/09/the-henry-louis-gates -beer-summit-and-racial-division-in-america.html.

4 Astead Herndon, "How Trump's Brand of Grievance Politics Roiled a Pennsylvania Campaign," *New York Times*, March 15, 2019, https://www.nytimes. com/2019/03/15/us/politics/trump-white-voters-politics.html.

5 Robert P. Jones and Maxine Najle, "American Democracy in Crisis: The Fate of Pluralism in a Divided Nation," PRRI, February 22, 2019, https://www

.prri.org/research/american-democracy-in-crisis-the-fate-of-pluralism-in
-a-divided-nation.

6   As reported in Robert P. Jones, "Self-Segregation: Why It's So Hard for
     Whites to Understand Ferguson," *The Atlantic*, August 21, 2014, https://
     www.theatlantic.com/national/archive/2014/08/self-segregation-why-its
     -hard-for-whites-to-understand-ferguson/378928/.

7   Don Gonyea, "Majority of White Americans Say They Believe Whites Face
     Discrimination," NPR, October 24, 2017.

8   Nikki Graf, "Most Americans Say Colleges Should Not Consider Race or
     Ethnicity in Admissions," Pew Research Center, February 25, 2019, https://
     www.pewresearch.org/fact-tank/2019/02/25/most-americans-say-colleges-
     should-not-consider-race-or-ethnicity-in-admissions/.

9   Frank Newport, "Most in the U.S. Oppose Colleges Considering Race in
     Admissions," Gallup, July 8, 2016, https://news.gallup.com/poll/193508/
     oppose-colleges-considering-race-admissions.aspx.

10   University of Chicago with the Associated Press–NORC Center for Public
     Affairs Research, *GenForward Survey*, October 2016, http://genforwardsur-
     vey.com/assets/uploads/2016/12/GenForwardEarlyOctober2016Toplines_
     Final.pdf.

11   Peter King town hall video recording, produced by NowThis News (@
     nowthisnews), October 25, 2016, https://twitter.com/nowthisnews/sta-
     tus/1055516339119538176, 1:28.

12   Erica Frankeberg, "What School Segregation Looks like in the US Today,
     in 4 Charts," *The Conversation*, July 19, 2019, https://theconversation.com/
     what-school-segregation-looks-like-in-the-us-today-in-4-charts-120061;
     Algernon Austin, "The Unfinished March," Economic Policy Institute, June
     18, 2013, epi.org/publication/unfinished-march-overview.

13   Ryan D. Enos, "A World Apart," *Boston Review*, November 1, 2011.

14   Barack Obama, reelection speech, November 7, 2012.

15   Paul Ryan, Speaker address, March 24, 2016.

16   Mary Church Terrell, "What It Means to Be Colored in the Capital of the
     U.S.," speech delivered to the United Women's Club of Washington, D.C,
     October 10, 1906.

17   William Jay, *The Life of John Jay with Selections from His Correspondence* (New
     York: J. and J. Harper, 1833), 181–82.

18   Jonathan Elliot, *The Debates in the Several State Conventions of the Adoption
     of the Federal Constitution, Vol. 3 (Virginia)* (Washington, DC: United States
     Congress, 1827), 452.

19   Thomas Jefferson, *Autobiography*, https://avalon.law.yale.edu/19th_century/
     jeffauto.asp.

20 David O. Stewart, *The Summer of 1787: The Men Who Invented the Constitution* (New York: Simon and Schuster, 2007), 196.

21 Stewart, *Summer of 1787*, 197.

22 Stewart, *Summer of 1787*, 197.

23 Alexis de Tocqueville, *Democracy in America* (Chicago: University of Chicago Press, 2000), 326.

24 Abraham Lincoln, "A Letter from President Lincoln.; Reply to Horace Greeley," *New York Times*, August 24, 1862.

25 Abraham Lincoln, "Annual Message to Congress—Concluding Remarks," December 1, 1862.

26 Plessy v. Ferguson, 163 U.S. 537 (1896).

27 Harry S. Truman, "Special Message to the Congress on Civil Rights, February 2, 1948," *Public Papers of the Presidents of the United States: January 1 to December 31, 1948* (Washington, DC: United States Government Printing Office, 1964), n. 20.

28 Lyndon B. Johnson, "Address on Voting Rights to Joint Session of Congress," March 16, 1965.

29 Martin Luther King, Jr., "The Other America," delivered at Stanford University on April 14, 1967.

30 Larry Rivers, "Dignity and Importance: Slavery in Jefferson County, Florida—1827 to 1860," *Florida Historical Quarterly* 61, no. 4 (1983): 425.

Chapter 2: The Veiled Threats Exposed

1 Dred Scott v. Sandford, 60 U.S. 393 (1857).

2 Pew Research Center, *The Public, the Political System and American Democracy*, April 2018.

3 John Wagner and Scott Clement, "'It's Just Messed Up': Most Say Political Divisions Are as Bad as in Vietnam War Era, Poll Shows," *Washington Post*, October 28, 2017, https://www.washingtonpost.com/politics/its-just-messed-up-most-say-political-divisions-are-as-bad-as-in-vietnam-era-poll-shows/2017/10/27/ad304f1a-b9b6-11e7-9e58-e6288544af98_story.html.

4 Wagner and Clement, "'It's Just Messed Up.'"

5 Pew Research Center, *Partisanship and Political Animosity in 2016*, June 2016.

6 Emily Badger and Niraj Chokshi, "How We Became Bitter Political Enemies," *New York Times*, June 15, 2017, https://www.nytimes.com/2017/06/15/upshot/how-we-became-bitter-political-enemies.html.

7 Lilliana Mason, *Uncivil Agreement: How Politics Became Our Identity* (Chicago: University of Chicago Press, 2018), 101.

8 Kimberly Amadeo, "Income Inequality in America," *The Balance*, June 25, 2019, https://www.thebalance.com/income-inequality-in-america-3306190.

9 Lawrence Mishel and Jessica Schneider, *CEO Compensation Surged in 2017*, Economic Policy Institute, August 16, 2018, https://www.epi.org/files/pdf/152123.pdf.

10 Lawrence Mishel and Julia Wolfe, "Top 1.0 Percent Reaches Highest Wages Ever—Up 157 Percent Since 1979,"Working Economic Blog, Economic Policy Institute, October 18, 2018, https://www.epi.org/blog/top-1-0-percent-reaches-highest-wages-ever-up-157-percent-since-1979/.

11 Martin Gilens and Benjamin I. Page, "Testing Theories of American Politics: Elites, Interest Groups, and Average Citizens," *Perspectives on Politics* 12, no. 3 (2014): 565.

12 Raj Chetty, "Improving Opportunities for Economic Mobility: New Evidence and Policy Lessons," in *Economic Mobility: Research and Ideas on Strengthening Families, Communities and the Economy*, ed. Federal Reserve Bank of St. Louis and the Board of Governors of the Federal Reserve System (United States, 2016), 37.

13 Raj Chetty, David Grusky, Maximilian Hell, Nathaniel Hendren, Robert Manduca, and Jimmy Narang, "The Fading American Dream: Trends in Absolute Income Mobility Since 1940," *Science* 356, no, 6336 (2017): 1.

14 Commission on Industrial Relations, *Industrial Relations: Final Report and Testimony*, Vol. 8 (Washington, DC: Government Printing Office, 1916), 7659.

15 Barack Obama, "Remarks by the President on the Economy in Osawatomie, Kansas," December 6, 2011.

16 Michael Kruse, "Trump Reclaims the Word 'Elite' with Vengeful Pride," *Politico*, November–December 2018, https://www.politico.com/magazine/story/2018/11/01/donald-trump-elite-trumpology-221953.

17 William A. Galston, "The Populist Challenge to Liberal Democracy," *Journal of Democracy* 29, no. 2 (2018): 10, https://www.journalof democracy.org/articles/the-populist-challenge-to-liberal-democracy/.

18 Benjamin R. Tillman and Daniel Murray Pamphlet Collection. *The Race Problem: Speech of Hon. Benjamin R. Tillman of South Carolina . . . in the Senate of the United States, February 23–24.* [Washington, DC: s.n., 1903], https://www.loc.gov/item/91898597/.

19 Francis Butler Simkins, *Pitchfork Ben Tillman: South Carolinian* (Baton Rouge: Louisiana State University Press, 1944), 171.

20 Pew Research Center, *The Partisan Divide on Political Values Grows Even Wider*, October 2017.

21 See, for example, Joel Olsen, "Whiteness and the Polarization of American Politics," *Political Research Quarterly* 61, no. 4 (2008): 704–18.

22 Nicholas Valentino and Kirill Zhirkov, "Blue Is Black and Red Is White? Affective Polarization and the Racialized Schemas of U.S. Party Coalitions" (paper, Midwest Political Science Association, Chicago, April 2018).

23 Raj Chetty, Nathaniel Hendren, Maggie R. Jones, and Sonya R. Porter, "Race and Economic Opportunity in the United States: An Intergenerational Perspective" (paper, Equality of Opportunity Project, Cambridge, MA, March 2018).

24 Derived from U.S. Census Bureau, Current Population Survey, 1968 to 2018 Annual Social and Economic Supplements; Janelle Jones, "The Racial Wealth Gap: How African-Americans Have Been Shortchanged Out of the Materials to Build Wealth," Working Economics Blog, Economic Policy Institute, February 13, 2017, https://www.epi.org/blog/the-racial-wealth-gap-how -african-americans-have-been-shortchanged-out-of-the-materials-to-build -wealth/.

25 Eric Morath and Soo Oh, "Black Workers' Pay Increases Are Lagging Behind," *Wall Street Journal*, April 17, 2019.

Chapter 3: Superlative Citizenship

1 The story of Jehu Grant is told through his pension letter and corroborating letter. See Jehu Grant, "Pension Statement," in *The Revolution Remembered: Eyewitness Accounts of the War for Independence*, ed. John C. Dann (Chicago: University of Chicago Press, 1968), 26–28.

2 Michael Lee Lanning, *African Americans in the Revolutionary War* (New York: Kensington, 2000), 177.

3 Andrew Jackson, *First Annual Message to Congress*, December 8, 1829.

4 See, for example, Samuel L. Perry and Andrew L. Whitehead, "Christian America in Black and White: Racial Identity, Religious-National Group Boundaries, and Explanations for Racial Inequality," *Sociology of Religion* 80, no. 3 (Autumn 2019): 277–98; Rhys Williams, "Religion and Place in the Midwest: Urban, Rural, and Suburban Forms of Religious Expression," in *Religion and Public Life in the Midwest: America's Common Denominator*, ed. Philip Barlow and Mark Silk (Walnut Creek, CA: AltaMira, 2004), 187–208; Robert P. Jones, *The End of White Christian America* (New York: Simon and Schuster, 2016); and Joshua T. Davis, "Funding God's Policies, Defending Whiteness: Christian Nationalism and Whites' Attitudes Towards Racially-Coded Government Spending," *Ethnic and Racial Studies* 42, no. 12 (2019): 2123–42.

5   Michael Tesler, "To Many Americans, Being Patriotic Means Being White," *Washington Post*, October 13, 2017, https://www.washington post.com/news/monkey-cage/wp/2017/10/13/is-white-resentment -about-the-nfl-protests-about-race-or-patriotism-or-both/.

6   Pew Research Center, "What It Takes to Truly Be 'One of Us,'" February 2017.

7   Robert P. Jones and Daniel Cox, "Most Americans Believe Protests Make the Country Better; Support Decreases Dramatically Among Whites if Protesters Are Identified as Black," PRRI, 2015, http://www.prri.org/research/ survey-americans-believe-protests-make-country-better-support-decreases -dramatically-protesters-identified-black/.

8   Rhys Williams, "Civil Religion and the Cultural Politics of National Identity in Obama's America," *Journal for the Scientific Study of Religion* 52, no. 2 (2013): 243.

9   Pew Research Center, "What It Takes."

10 John Gramlich, "What Makes a Good Citizen? Voting, Paying Taxes, Following the Law Top List," Factank, Pew Research Center, July 2, 2019, https://www .pewresearch.org/fact-tank/2019/07/02/what-makes-a-good-citizen-voting -paying-taxes-following-the-law-top-list/.

11 J.J. Mulhern, review of *Defining Citizenship in Archaic Greece*, ed. Alain Duploy and Roger Brock, *Bryn Mawr Classical Review*, March 14, 2019.

12 Evelyn Brooks Higginbotham, *Righteous Discontent: The Women's Movement in the Black Baptist Church, 1880–1920* (Cambridge, MA: Harvard University Press, 1993): 186.

13 Higginbotham, *Righteous Discontent*, 187.

14 Paisley Jane Harris, "Gatekeeping and Remaking: The Politics of Respectability in African American Women's History and Black Feminism," *Journal of Women's History* 15, no. 1 (2003): 212–20.

15 W.E.B. DuBois, "The Talented Tenth," from *The Negro Problem: A Series of Articles by Representative Negroes Today* (New York: J. Pott and Company, 1903).

16 Booker T. Washington, Atlanta Exposition Address, September 18, 1895.

17 Byron D'Andra Orey, "Explaining Black Conservatives: Racial Uplift or Racial Resentment?," *Black Scholar* 34, no. 1 (2004): 20.

18 Tehama Lopez Bunyasi and Candis Watts Smith, "Do All Black Lives Matter Equally to Black People? Respectability Politics and the Limitations of Linked Fate," *Journal of Race, Ethnicity and Politics* 4, no. 1 (2019): 180–215.

19 Fredrick C. Harris, "The Rise of Respectability Politics," *Dissent*, Winter 2014, https://www.dissentmagazine.org/article/the-rise-of-respectability-politics.

20 Randall Kennedy, "Lifting as We Climb," *Harper's Magazine* 331, no. 1985 (2015): 24.

21 James Weldon Johnson, "Lift Ev'ry Voice and Sing," 1905.

22 Benjamin R. Tillman, quoted in Edmund Morris, *Theodore Rex* (New York: Random House, 2002), 55.

23 Lisa D. Cook, Trevon D. Logan, and John M. Parman, "Distinctively Black Names in the American Past," *Explorations in Economic History* 53C (2014): 64–82.

24 Ralph Ellison, *Shadow and Act* (New York: Random House, 1964), 150.

25 Ellison, *Shadow and Act*, 149.

26 Michael Dennis, "The Idea of Citizenship in the Early Civil Rights Movement," *Citizenship Studies* 9, no. 2 (2005): 181–203.

27 Ronald R. Krebs, "The Power of Military Service," in *Fighting for Rights: Military Service and the Politics of Citizenship* (Ithaca, NY: Cornell University Press, 2006), 17.

28 Maury Feld, *The Structure of Violence; Armed Forces as Social Systems* (Sage, 1977).

29 Frederick Douglass, *What the Black Man Wants: Speech of Frederick Douglass at the Annual Meeting of the Massachusetts Anti-Slavery Society at Boston*, 1865.

30 Alan Gilbert, *Black Patriots and Loyalists Fighting for Emancipation in the War for Independence* (Chicago: University of Chicago Press, 2012), viii.

31 Lauren McCormack, *Black Sailors in the United Sates Navy During the War of 1812* (Boston: USS Constitution Museum, 2011).

32 Elsie Freeman, Wynell Burroughs Schamel, and Jean West, "The Fight for Equal Rights: A Recruiting Poster for Black Soldiers in the Civil War," *Social Education* 56, no. 2 (February 1992; revised and updated in 1999 by Budge Weidman): 118–20.

33 Gerry J. Gilmore, "African-Americans Continue Tradition of Distinguished Service," United States Army, February 2, 2007, https://www.army.mil/article/1681/african_americans_continue_tradition_of_distinguished_service.

34 See the Medal of Honor recipient database at https://themedalof honor.com/.

35 Keith D. McFarland, ed., *The Korean War: An Annotated Bibliography*, revised 2nd edition (New York: Routledge, 2010).

36 Military OneSource, *2018 Demographics: Profile of the Military Community*, Department of Defense.

37 Robert A. Geake and Loren M. Spears, *From Slaves to Soldiers: The 1st Rhode Island Regiment in the American Revolution* (Yardley, PA: Westholme Publishing, 2016).

38   Vincent Mikkelsen, "Coming from Battle to Face a War: The Lynching of Black Soldiers in the World War I Era," 2007, ProQuest Dissertations and Theses.

39   For examples of these leaflets and use in conflict, see Herbert A. Friedman, "Race as a Military Propaganda Theme," *Psywar*, December 7, 2008, https://www.psywar.org/race.php; and Theodore R. Johnson, "How American Racism Aids Our Adversaries," *Washington Post*, September 17, 2017, https://www.washingtonpost.com/news/made-by-history/wp/2017/09/17/how-american-racism-aids-our-adversaries/.

40   James G. Thompson, letter to the editor, *Pittsburgh Courier*, January 31, 1942.

41   This high school is where I met Hope Copeland. Our conversation about her life and experiences took place over a couple of days in December 2018.

42   Coretta Scott King, as quoted by Barbara Williams-Skinner in Coretta Scott King, *My Life, My Love, My Legacy* (New York: Henry Holt, 2017), 330.

Chapter 4: Inclusion Trickles Down

1   Renee Romano, "No Diplomatic Immunity: African Diplomats, the State Department, and Civil Rights, 1961–1964," *Journal of American History* 87, no. 2 (September 1, 2000): 569.

2   Jennifer Erdman and JoAnn Robinson, "'Eyes of the World': Racial Discrimination Against African Dignitaries Along Maryland Route 40 During the Kennedy Administration" (thesis, Morgan State University, May 2007).

3   *Life*, "Big Step Ahead on a High Road," December 8, 1961, 32.

4   "Envoy Says Race Policies Damage US," *Washington Post*, May 13, 1961, as quoted in Jennifer Erdman, "'Eyes of the World': Racial Discrimination Against African Dignitaries Along Maryland Route 40 During the Kennedy Administration," 2007, ProQuest Dissertations and Theses.

5   *Life*, "Big Step Ahead on a High Road," 32.

6   Romano, "No Diplomatic Immunity," 569.

7   *Life*, "Big Step Ahead on a High Road," 34.

8   *Life*, "Big Step Ahead on a High Road," 36.

9   Erdman, "'Eyes of the World,'" 53.

10   George Collins, "Everybody Eats but Americans," *The Afro-American*, September 2, 1961.

11   Iris Marion Young, "Polity and Group Difference: A Critique of the Ideal of Universal Citizenship," *Ethics* 99, no. 2 (1989): 250–74.

12   Kenneth M. Stampp, "To Make Them Stand in Fear," in *A Turbulent Voyage: Readings in African American Studies*, ed. Floyd Windom Hayes, 3rd edition (New York: Rowman and Littlefield, 2000), 277–78.

13 Heike Paul, "E Pluribus Unum? The Myth of the Melting Pot," in *The Myths That Made America: An Introduction to America* (Bielefeld, Germany: transcript Verlag, 2014).

14 Paul, *The Myths That Made America*, 259.

15 Annie Nova, "A $1,000 Emergency Would Push Many Americans into Debt," CNBC, January 23, 2019.

16 William Jennings Bryan, "Speech Concluding Debate on the Chicago Platform at the Democratic National Convention," Chicago, Illinois, July 9, 1896.

17 Will Rogers, "And Here's How It All Happened," *St. Petersburg Times*, November 26, 1932.

18 W.R. Sorley, "The Morality of Nations," *International Journal of Ethics* 1, no. 4 (1891): 427–46.

19 Scott Bixby, "Donald Trump Releases His Healthcare Plan in Campaign Statement," *The Guardian*, March 2, 2016.

20 Barack Obama, "A Just and Lasting Peace" (Nobel Lecture, Oslo, Norway, December 10, 2009).

21 John F. Kennedy, "The Presidency in 1960," January 14, 1960.

22 Ronald Reagan, Inaugural Address, January 20, 1981.

23 Theodore Roosevelt, "The New Nationalism," August 31, 1910.

24 Peter Moore, "Overwhelming Opposition to Reparations for Slavery and Jim Crow," YouGov, June 2, 2014.

25 Brent J. Steele, *Ontological Security in International Relations: Self-Identity and the IR States* (New York: Routledge, 2008); and Azuolas Bagdonas, "The Practice of State Apologies: The Role of Demands for Historical Apologies and Refusals to Apologize in the Construction of State Identity" (PhD dissertation, Central European University, 2010).

26 Apologizing for the Enslavement and Racial Segregation of African-Americans, H.R. 194, 110th Congress (2008).

27 A Concurrent Resolution Apologizing for the Enslavement and Racial Segregation of African Americans, S.Con.Res.26, 111th Congress (2009).

28 See Theodore Parker, "Of Justice and Conscience," in *The Collected Works of Theodore Parker*, vol. 2, *Sermons-Prayers*, ed. Frances Power Cobbe (London: Trubner, Ludgate Hill, 1879), 48.

Chapter 5: Black Solidarity

1 Mary J. Ferguson, *The Hebron Cross: An African American's Family Life During Twentieth Century Marlboro County, South Carolina* (Pittsburgh: Lauriat Press, 2019), 83–84.

2   A Southern White Woman, "Experiences of the Race Problem," *The Indepen-
     dent ... Devoted to the Consideration of Politics, Social and Economic Tendencies,
     History, Literature, and the Arts* (1848–1921) 56, no. 2885: 590.

3   Tommie Shelby, *We Who Are Dark: The Philosophical Foundations of Black
     Solidarity* (Cambridge: Harvard University Press, 2005), 202.

4   Shelby, *We Who Are Black*, 13.

5   Mara Ostfeld, "Unity Versus Uniformity: Effects of Targeted Advertising
     on Perceptions of Group Politics," *Political Communication* 34, no. 4 (2017):
     530–47.

6   Marilynn B. Brewer, "Social-Identity, Distinctiveness, and In-Group Homo-
     geneity (Perceptions of Group Variability)," *Social Cognition* 11, no. 1 (1993):
     150–64.

7   W.E.B DuBois, "Of Our Spiritual Strivings," in *The Souls of Black Folk*
     (New York: Penguin Books, 1995); Paul Laurence Dunbar, "We Wear the
     Mask," in *The Complete Poems of Paul Laurence Dunbar* (New York: Dodd,
     Mead, 1913), https://www.poetryfoundation.org/poems/44203/we-wear
     -the-mask.

8   Karen Mills, Esquire (now Karen Taylor), in conversation with the author,
     March 2019.

9   Richard D. Harvey, Rachel E. Tennial, and Kira Hudson Banks, "The Devel-
     opment and Validation of the Colorism Scale," *Journal of Black Psychology* 43,
     no. 7 (2017): 740–64.

10   Tayler J. Mathews and Glenn S. Johnson, "Skin Complexion in the Twenty-
     First Century: The Impact of Colorism on African American Women," *Race,
     Gender, and Class* 22, no. 1–2 (2015): 248–74.

11   David A. Bositis, "Blacks and the 2012 RNC," Joint Center for Political and
     Economic Studies, 2012.

12   Bositis, "Blacks and the 2012 DNC."

13   Associated Press–NORC Center for Public Affairs Research, *The February
     2018 AP-NORC Center Poll*, February 2018.

14   Hannah Gilberstadt and Andrew Daniller, "Liberals Make Up the Largest
     Share of Democratic Voters, but Their Growth Has Slowed in Recent Years,"
     Pew Research Center, January 17, 2020.

15   Tasha Philpot, *Conservative but Not Republican: The Paradox of Party Identifica-
     tion and Ideology Among African Americans* (New York: Cambridge University
     Press, 2016).

16   Hannah Hartig and Abigail Geiger, "About Six in Ten Americans Support
     Marijuana Legalization," Pew Research Center, October 8, 2018.

17   EducationNext, *2018 EducationNext Poll*, https://www.educationnext
     .org/2018-ednext-poll-interactive/.

18 Tatishe Nteta, "United We Stand? African Americans, Self-Interest, and Immigration Reform," *American Politics Research* 41, no. 1 (2013): 147–172.

19 Zoltan Hajnal, "Black Class Exceptionalism: Insights from Direct Democracy on the Race Versus Class Debate," *Public Opinion Quarterly* 71, no. 4 (Winter 2007): 560–87.

20 Giles Oakley, *The Devil's Music: A History of the Blues* (New York: Da Capo Press, 1997).

21 Michael Dawson, *Behind the Mule: Race and Class in African-American Politics* (Princeton, NJ: Princeton University Press, 1994), 57–58.

22 Dawson, *Behind the Mule*, 76.

23 Melissa Victoria Harris-Lacewell, *Barbershops, Bibles, and BET: Everyday Talk and Black Political Thought* (Princeton, NJ: Princeton University Press, 2004), 12.

24 Taeku Lee, *Mobilizing Public Opinion: Black Insurgency and Racial Attitudes in the Civil Rights Era* (Chicago: University of Chicago Press, 2002).

25 Ismail White and Chryl Laird, *Steadfast Democrats: How Forces Shape Black Political Behavior* (Princeton, NJ: Princeton University Press, 2020), 15, 26.

26 Ismail White, Chryl Laird, and Troy D. Allen, "Selling Out? The Politics of Navigating Conflicts Between Racial Group Interest and Self-interest," *American Political Science Review* 108, no. 4 (2014): 786.

27 United States House of Representatives, Creation and Evolution of the Congressional Black Caucus, https://history.house.gov/Exhibitions-and-Publications/BAIC/Historical-Essays/Permanent-Interest/Congressional-Black-Caucus/.

Chapter 6: Finding Civil Religion

1 Robert N. Bellah, "Civil Religion in America," *Daedalus* 96, no. 1 (1967): 1–21.

2 Jean-Jacques Rousseau, *The Social Contract: And Discourses* (New York: E.P. Dutton, 1920).

3 Richard T. Hughes, "Civil Religion, the Theology of the Republic, and the Free Church Tradition," *Journal of Church and State* 22, no. 1 (January 1980): 75–87.

4 Hughes, "Civil Religion," 76.

5 Philip Gorski, *American Covenant: A History of Civil Religion from the Puritans to the Present* (Princeton, NJ: Princeton University, 2017).

6 N.J. Demerath and Rhys H. Williams, "Civil Religion in an Uncivil Society," *Annals of the American Academy of Political and Social Science* 480 (1985): 154; Marcela Cristi, *From Civil to Political Religion: The Intersection of Culture, Religion, and Politics* (Waterloo, ON: Wilfrid Laurier University Press, 2001).

7   J. Milton Yinger, *Sociology Looks at Religion*, 1961. (London: Macmillan)

8   Rhys Williams, "Civil Religion and the Cultural Politics of National Identity in Obama's America," *Journal for the Scientific Study of Religion* 52, no. 2 (2015): 242.

9   George Washington, First Inaugural Address, April 30, 1789.

10   Martin Luther King, Jr., "Letter from a Birmingham Jail," in *Why We Can't Wait* (New York: Penguin Press, 1964), 84.

11   Ronald Reagan, "Remarks on Signing the Bill Making the Birthday of Martin Luther King, Jr., a National Holiday," November 2, 1983.

12   Barack Obama, "Eulogy for John Lewis," as published in *The New York Times*, https://www.nytimes.com/2020/07/30/us/obama-eulogy-john-lewis-full -transcript.html, July 30, 2020.

13   Abraham Lincoln, Gettysburg Address, November 19, 1863.

14   Martin Luther King, Jr., speech delivered at Mason Temple (Church of God in Christ Headquarters), Memphis, TN, April 3, 1968.

15   John F. Kennedy, Inaugural Address, January 20, 1961.

16   Anna Julia Cooper, "The Ethics of the Negro Question," Session of Friends' General Conference at Asbury Park, NJ, September 5, 1902.

17   Joseph Campbell, *The Hero with a Thousand Faces* (Princeton, NJ: Princeton University Press, 1968).

18   Bellah, "Civil Religion in America," 42.

19   Ronald Reagan, First Inaugural Address, January 20, 1981.

20   Gorski, *American Covenant*, 32.

21   There is a debate about whether flag prints on clothing are violations of the Flag Code. In the past, a shirt with the American flag on it, for example, was considered to be disrespectful. See the story of Abbie Hoffman, as here: https://www.racked.com/2017/7/3/15879778/american-flag -clothes-code. More recently, however, some have argued shirt prints are acceptable and only clothing made from an actual flag is deemed unacceptable, as seen here: https://www.legion.org/flag/questions-answers/91517/ it-permissible-wear-item-clothing-looks-united-states-flag.

22   Mike Garafolo (@MikeGarafolo), "He's actually done it all preseason. No one noticed. First time in uniform was last night," Twitter, August 27, 2016, 4:34 a.m., https://twitter.com/MikeGarafolo/status/769498231243993088.

23   Colin Kaepernick, Postgame Remarks, at "Colin Kaepernick Explains Why He Sat during National Anthem," *NFL News*, August 26, 2016, https:// www.nfl.com/news/colin-kaepernick-explains-why-he-sat-during-national -anthem-0ap3000000691077.

24   Drew Brees, as quoted in Mike Triplett, "Drew Brees 'Wholeheartedly' Disagrees with Colin Kaepernick's Method of Protest," ESPN, August 29,

2016, https://www.espn.com/blog/new-orleans-saints/post/_/id/23063/drew-brees-wholeheartedly-disagrees-with-colin-kaepernicks-method-of-protest.

25   Ryan Wilson, "Esiason on Kaepernick Sitting: 'It's About as Disrespectful as Any Athlete Has Ever Been,'" CBS Sports, August 31, 2016, https://www.cbssports.com/nfl/news/esiason-on-kaepernick-sitting-its-about-as-disrespectful-as-any-athlete-has-ever-been/.

26   *All Things Considered*, "The Veteran and NFL Player Who Advised Kaepernick to Take a Knee," NPR, September 9, 2018.

27   Robert Segal, "The Myth-Ritualist Theory of Religion," *Journal for the Scientific Study of Religion* 19, no. 2 (June 1980): 173–85.

28   Speech of Hon. James H. Hammond, of South Carolina, On the Admission of Kansas, Under the Lecompton Constitution: Delivered in the Senate of the United States, March 4, 1858, Washington, D.C., 1858.

29   Cristi, *From Civil to Political Religion*, 8.

30   Cristi, *From Civil to Political Religion*, 58.

31   Gorski, *American Covenant*, 2, 3.

32   Ephesians 6:12.

33   Gorski, *American Covenant*, 2.

34   Gallup, "Religion," news.gallup.com/poll/1690/religion.aspx.

35   Michael Lipka and Claire Gecewicz, "More Americans Now Say They're Spiritual but More Religious," Pew Research Center, September 6, 2017.

36   Grace Davie, "Believing Without Belonging: Is This the Future of Religion in Britain?," *Social Compass* 37, no. 4, 455–69.

37   Mark Oppenheimer, "Examining the Growth of the 'Spiritual but Not Religious,'" *New York Times*, July 18, 2014.

38   Orestes P. Hastings, "Not a Lonely Crowd? Social Connectedness, Religious Service Attendance, and the Spiritual but Not Religious," *Social Science Research* 57 (2016): 63–79.

39   Andrew R. Murphy, "Civil Religion for a Diverse Polity," *Political Power and Social Theory* 22 (2010): 234.

40   Gorski, *American Covenant*, 174.

Chapter 7: Racism Is a Crime of the State

1   Gabrielle Berman and Yin Paradies, "Racism, Disadvantage, and Multiculturalism: Towards Effective Anti-racist Praxis," *Ethnic and Racial Studies* 33, no. 2 (2010): 214–32.

2   David Newman, *Sociology: Exploring the Architecture of Everyday Life, Brief Edition* (Los Angeles: Sage, 2006).

3   Alicia Lukachko, Mark L. Hatzenbuehler, and Katherine M. Keyes, "Structural Racism and Myocardial Infarction in the United States," *Social Science and Medicine* 103 (2014): 42–50.

4   Janelle Jones, "The Racial Wealth Gap: How African-Americans Have Been Shortchanged out of the Materials to Build Wealth," Working Economics Blog, Economic Policy Institute, February 13, 2017, https://www.epi.org/blog/the-racial-wealth-gap-how-african-americans-have-been-shortchanged-out-of-the-materials-to-build-wealth/.

5   Aaron Glantz and Emmanuel Martinez, "For People of Color, Banks Are Shutting the Door to Homeownership," *Reveal*, February 15, 2018.

6   Lisa Rice and Deidre Swesnik, "Discriminatory Effects of Credit Scoring on Communities of Color," *Suffolk University Law Review* 46 (2013): 935–966.

7   Zillow Group, *Consumer Housing Trends Report 2018*, https://wp.zillowstatic.com/38/ZGReport2018_Download-a27213.pdf.

8   Office of Policy Development and Research, *Housing Discrimination Against Racial and Ethnic Minorities 2012*, Department of Housing and Urban Development, https://www.huduser.gov/portal/Publications/pdf/HUD-514_HDS2012.pdf.

9   John C. Donovan, Richard E. Morgan, Christian P. Potholm, and Marcia A. Weigle, *People, Power, and Politics: An Introduction to Political Science*, 3rd ed. (Lanham, Maryland: Rowman and Littlefield) 1993.

10 David Kauzlarich, Christopher Mullins, and Rick Matthews, "A Complicity Continuum of State Crime," *Contemporary Justice Review* 6, no. 3 (2003): 241–54.

11 Penny Green and Tony Ward, *State Crime: Governments, Violence and Corruption* (Sterling, VA: Pluto Press, 2004).

12   Robert N. Bellah, "Civil Religion in America," *Daedalus* 134, no. 4 (2005): 53.

13 Hampton University, Department of Freshman Studies, University 101 course description.

14 Michael Tesler, *Post-Racial or Most-Racial? Race and Politics in the Obama Era* (Chicago: University of Chicago Press, 2016), 88–90.

15 Michael Tesler, "The Spillover of Racialization into Health Care: How President Obama Polarized Public Opinion by Racial Attitudes and Race," *American Journal of Political Science* 56, no. 3 (July 2012): 696.

16 Kaiser Family Foundation in March 2013, as in James Hamblin, "What Is Obamacare?," *The Atlantic*, April 2, 2013.

17 Jonathan L. Metzl, *Dying of Whiteness: How the Politics of Racial Resentment Is Killing America's Heartland* (New York: Basic Books, 2019), 3.

18 U.S. Department of Agriculture, *Characteristics of Supplemental Nutrition Assistance Program Households: Fiscal Year 2017.*

19 Martin Gilens, *Why Americans Hate Welfare: Race, Media, and the Politics of Antipoverty Policy* (Chicago: University of Chicago Press, 1999).

20 Rachel Wetts and Robb Willer, "Privilege on the Precipice: Perceived Racial Status Threats Lead White Americans to Oppose Welfare Programs," *Social Forces* 97, no. 2 (2018): 793–822.

21 Emily M. Wager, "Inequality, Stereotypes, and Black Public Opinion: The Role of Distancing," University of North Carolina–Chapel Hill (paper under review).

22 U.S. Department of Agriculture, *Characteristics of Supplemental Nutrition Assistance Program Households: Fiscal Year 2018*, Report No. SNAP-19-CHAR, November 2019.

23 Alvin Chang, "More Affluent Neighborhoods Are Creating Their Own School Districts," *Vox*, April 17, 2019.

24 U.S. Department of Education, *Status and Trends in the Education of Racial and Ethnic Groups 2018* (Washington, DC: National Center for Education Statistics, 2019); and Lisette Partelow, Sarah Shapiro, Abel McDaniels, and Catherine Brown, "Fixing Chronic Disinvestment in K–12 Schools," Center for American Progress, September 20, 2018.

25 See Harry Holzer and David Neumark, "Are Affirmative Action Hires Less Qualified? Evidence from Employer-Employee Data on New Hires," *Journal of Labor Economics* 17, no. 3 (1999): 534–69; Sally Kohn, "Affirmative Action Has Helped White Women More Than Anyone," *Time*, June 17, 2013; and Victor Massie, "White Women Benefit Most from Affirmative Action—and Are Among Its Fiercest Opponents," *Vox*, June 23, 2016.

26 Herbert Blumer, "Race Prejudice as a Sense of Group Position," *Pacific Sociological Review* 1, no. 1 (March 1958): 3–7.

27 Hubert M. Blalock, *Toward a Theory of Minority-Group Relations* (New York: Wiley, 1967).

28 Allen E. Liska, *Social Threat and Social Control, SUNY Series in Deviance and Social Control* (Albany: State University of New York Press, 1992).

29 Martin Gilens and Benjamin I. Page, "Testing Theories of American Politics: Elites, Interest Groups, and Average Citizens," *Perspectives on Politics* 12, no. 3 (2014): 564–81.

30 Richard Reeves, *Dream Hoarders: How the American Middle Class Is Leaving Everyone Else in the Dust, Why That Is a Problem, and What to Do About It* (Washington, DC: Brookings Institution, 2017).

31 National Center for Health Statistics, *Drug Overdose Deaths in the United States, 1999–2015*, Center for Disease Control and Prevention.

32 American Foundation for Suicide Prevention, "Suicide Statistics," https:// afsp.org/about-suicide/suicide-statistics/.

33 Anne Case and Angus Deaton, "Rising Morbidity and Mortality in Midlife Among White Non-Hispanic Americans in the 21st Century," *Proceedings of the National Academy of Sciences* 112, no. 49 (December 2015): 15078–83.

34 Anne Case and Angus Deaton, "Mortality and Morbidity in the 21st Century," *Brookings Papers on Economic Activity* (2017): 397–476.

Chapter 8: Solidarity Is Not Colorblind

1 United States Naturalization Law of March 26, 1790, 1 Stat. 103 (1790).

2 James Truslow Adams, *The Epic of America* (Boston: Little, Brown, 1931; reprint, New York: Routledge, 2017).

3 Amy Ansell, "Colorblindness," *Encyclopedia of Race, Ethnicity, and Society* (New York: Sage, 2008), 320.

4 Ronald Reagan, "The President's News Conference of February 11, 1986," *Weekly Compilation of Presidential Documents* 22, nos. 1–15 (February 11, 1986): 212.

5 Ansell, "Colorblindness."

6 Parents Involved in Community Schools v. Seattle School District No. 1, 551 U.S. 701 (2007).

7 Uma Jayakumar and Annie Adamian, "The Fifth Frame of Colorblind Ideology: Maintaining Comforts of Colorblindness in the Context of White Fragility," *Sociological Perspectives* 60, no. 5 (October 2017): 912–36.

8 Letter posted by the French Embassy in the United States (@france intheus), "@TheDailyShow, @Trevornoah called the @FrenchTeam's World Cup win an 'African victory.' Read Ambassador @Gerard Araud's response," Twitter, July 18, 2018, 2:13 p.m., twitter.com/franceintheus/status/1019691552384352257.

9 Karina Piser, "France Doesn't See Race (Officially). A Blackface Performance Changed That," *The Atlantic*, June 11, 2019.

10 Sylvia Zappi, "Black Portrait of the Economic Crisis in the Suburbs," *Le Monde*, May 2, 2016.

11 Rokhaya Diallo, "France's Dangerous Move to Remove 'Race' from Its Constitution," *Washington Post*, July 13, 2018.

12 National Consultative Commission for Human Rights, *The Fight Against Racism, Anti-Semitism, and Xenophobia*, 2014.

13 Erik Bleich, "Race Policy in France," Brookings Institution, May 1, 2001, https://www. brookings.edu/articles/race-policy-in-france.

14 Arthur Acolin, Raphael Bostic, and Gary Painter, "A Field Study of Rental Market Discrimination Across Origins in France," *Journal of Urban Economics* 95 (2016): 49–63.

15   Robert C. Lieberman, "A Tale of Two Countries: The Politics of Color Blind-
     ness in France and the United States," *French Politics, Culture and Society* 19,
     no. 3 (Fall 2001): 32–59.

16   Plessy v. Ferguson, 163 U.S. 537 (1896).

17   Brief for Appellants in Nos. 1, 2 and 4 and for Respondents in No. 10 on
     Reargument, *Brown v. Board of Education of Topeka*, 347 U.S. 483 (1954).

18   Juliet Hooker, *Race and the Politics of Solidarity* (New York: Oxford University
     Press, 2009), 168.

19   United States v. Jefferson County Board of Education, 372 F.2d 836 (5th
     Cir. 1966).

20   Centers for Disease Control and Prevention, "Pregnancy Mortality Sur-
     veillance System," https://www.cdc.gov/reproductivehealth/maternalin-
     fanthealth/pregnancy-mortality-surveillance-system.htm.

21   Ibram X. Kendi, *Stamped from the Beginning: The Definitive History of Racist
     Ideas in America* (New York: Nation Books, 2016).

22   Hooker, *Race and the Politics of Solidarity*, 181.

23   John Sutton and Frank Dobbin, "The Strength of a Weak State: The
     Rights Revolution and the Rise of Human Resources Management
     Divisions," *American Journal of Sociology* 104, no. 2 (1998): 441–76.

24   Sutton and Dobbin, "The Strength of a Weak State."

25   Lieberman, "A Tale of Two Countries," 39.

26   Lieberman, "A Tale of Two Countries," 33.

Chapter 9: National Solidarity as the Right Response to Racism

1   Lyndon B. Johnson, Address to Joint Session of Congress, November 27,
     1963.

2   Paul B. Sheatsley and Jacob J. Feldman, "The Assassination of President
     Kennedy: A Preliminary Report on Public Reactions and Behavior," *Public
     Opinion Quarterly* 28, no. 2 (1964): 189–215.

3   See this test at the Jim Crow Museum of Racist Memorabilia at Ferris
     State University, available online at https://www.ferris.edu/HTMLS/news/
     jimcrow/question/2012/pdfs-docs/literacytest.pdf.

4   See the story of Clarence Gaskins in International Association of Machin-
     ists and Aerospace Workers, "Longtime Activist Honored by Connecticut
     Machinists," February 5, 2015, https://www.goiam.org/news/longtime-activist
     -honored-by-connecticut-machinists/; and Clarence Gaskins, "How Many
     Bubbles in a Bar of Soap?," interview by the Machinists Union, published
     August 30, 2016, https://www.youtube.com/watch?v=jd89W_p8Cr8.

5   Lyndon B. Johnson, "President Johnson's Special Message to the Congress:
     The American Promise," March 15, 1965.

6   Alvin B. Tillery and Hanes Walton, Jr., "Presidential Greatness in the Black
     Press: Ranking the Modern Presidents on Civil Rights Policy and Race Rela-
     tions, 1900–2016," *Politics, Groups, and Identities* 7, no .1 (2019): 71–88.

7   *Stanford Encyclopedia of Philosophy*, "Contractarianism," June 18, 2000 (sub-
     stantive revision March 15, 2017).

8   Robert D. Putnam, "E Pluribus Unum: Diversity and Community in the
     Twenty-First Century," *Scandinavian Political Studies* 30, no. 2 (June 2007):
     137–74.

9   This formulation was informed by definitions of *civic solidarity* and *political
     solidarity* in Sally J. Scholz, *Political Solidarity* (University Park: Pennsylvania
     State University Press, 2008).

10   Putnam, "E Pluribus Unum," 165.

11   Sarah Song, "Three Models of Civic Solidarity," in *Citizenship, Borders, and
     Human Needs*, ed. Rogers M. Smith (Philadelphia: University of Pennsylvania
     Press, 2011).

12   Hooker, *Race and the Politics of Solidarity*.

13   John McCain, 2008 Presidential Election Concession Speech, November 4,
     2008.

14   Barack Obama, 2008 Presidential Election Victory Speech, November 5,
     2008.

15   Frank Lovett, "Civic Virtue," in *The Encyclopedia of Political Thought*, ed. M.T.
     Gibbons (Hoboken, New Jersey: Wiley 2014).

16   Lawrence Blum, "Race, National Ideals, and Civic Virtue," *Social Theory and
     Practice* 33 no. 4 (October 2007): 534.

17   Robert George, as quoted in Jason Raia, "What We Can Learn About Civic
     Friendship from Ideological Odd Couple Cornel West and Robert George,"
     Philadelphia Inquirer, January 29, 2018.

18   Mary L. Dudziak, *Cold War Civil Rights: Race and the Image of American
     Democracy* (Princeton, NJ: Princeton University Press, 2000).

19   Brent J. Steele, *Ontological Security in International Relations: Self-Identity
     and the IR States* (New York: Routledge, 2008).

20   Noa Epstein, "Explaining the War on Terrorism from an Ontological
     Security Perspective," *MIT International Review*, Spring 2007, 12–19.

21   George W. Bush, "National Endowment for Democracy," October 6, 2005.

22   Sally J. Scholz, *Political Solidarity* (University Park: Pennsylvania State Uni-
     versity Press, 2008), 21.

23   Robert Dahl, "The City in the Future of Democracy," *American Political Sci-
     ence Review* 61, no. 4 (1967): 954.

24   Neil Gross, "Is the United States Too Big to Govern?" *New York Times*, May
     11, 2018.

25   Karen L. Remmer, "Political Scale and Electoral Turnout: Evidence from the Less Industrialized World," *Comparative Political Studies* 43, no. 3 (March 2010): 279.

26   James Madison, "Federalist No. 10," in *The Federalist Papers*, Congress.gov, https://www.congress.gov/resources/display/content/The+Federalist+Papers.

A Conclusion: Creating National Solidarity

1   Robert J. Norrell, "When Teddy Roosevelt Invited Booker T. Washington to Dine at the White House," *Journal of Blacks in Higher Education* 63 (2009): 73.

2   Norrell, "When Teddy Roosevelt Invited Booker T. Washington to Dine," 71.

3   John Jay, "Concerning Dangers from Foreign Force and Influence for the Independent Journal," in "Federalist No. 2," *Federalist Papers*, October 31, 1787.

4   Danielle S. Allen, *Talking to Strangers: Anxieties of Citizenship Since Brown v. Board of Education* (Chicago: University of Chicago Press, 2004), xvi.

5   George Washington, Farewell Address, September 19, 1796.

6   Pew Research Center, *The Public, the Political System and American Democracy*, April 2018, www.people-press.org/2018/04/26/9-the -responsibilities-of-citizenship/.

7   Thomas Jefferson, letter to Samuel Kercheval, Monticello, July 12, 1816.

8   Wendy Weiser, "Automatic Voter Registration Boosts Political Participation," Brennan Center for Justice, January 29, 2016, https://www.brennancenter .org/blog/automatic-voter-registration-boosts-political-participation.

9   Kevin Morris, Myrna Pérez, Jonathan Brater, and Christopher Deluzio, *Purges: A Growing Threat to the Right to Vote*, Brennan Center for Justice, July 20, 2018.

10   Knight Foundation, *The 100 Million Project: The Untold Story of American Non-Voters*, 2020.

11   Gustavo López and Antonio Flores, "Dislike of Candidates or Campaign Issues Was the Most Common Reason for Not Voting in 2016," Pew Research Center, June 1, 2017; and Knight Foundation, *100 Million Project*.

12   Gilad Edelman and Paul Glastris, "Letting People Vote at Home Increases Voter Turnout. Here's Proof," *Washington Post*, January 26, 2018.

13   Justin Levitt, *The Truth About Voter Fraud*, Brennan Center for Justice, November 9, 2007.

14   Justin Levitt, "Confronting the Impact of 'Citizens United,'" *Yale Law and Policy Review* 29, no. 1 (Fall 2010): 217–34.

15 Wendy Weiser and Alicia Bannon, eds., *Democracy: An Election Agenda for Candidates, Activists, and Legislators*, Brennan Center for Justice at NYU School of Law, 2018.

16 Michael Li, "Gerrymandering Meets the Coronavirus in Wisconsin," Brennan Center for Justice, April 8, 2020.

17 *Rucho v. Common Cause*, 588 U.S. ___ (2019).

18 NBC News–*Wall Street Journal Survey*, Study #18955, September 16–19, 2018, http://media1.snbcnews.com/i/today/z_creative/18955%20NBCWSJ%20 September%20Poll.pdf.

19 Knight Foundation, *100 Million Project*, 8.

20 Lee Rainie and Andrew Perrin, "Key Findings About Americans' Declining Trust in Government and Each Other," Factank, Pew Research Center, July 22, 2019, https://www.pewresearch.org/fact -tank/2019/07/22/key-findings-about-americans-declining-trust-in -government-and-each-other/.

21 Amy Gutmann and Dennis Thompson, *Why Deliberative Democracy?* (Princeton, NJ: Princeton University Press, 2004), 7.

22 Ed Cox, "Our Call for Action on Deliberative Democracy," RSA, July 4, 2018, https://www.thersa.org/discover/publications-and-articles/rsa- blogs/2018/07/our-call-for-action-on-deliberative -democracy.

23 Casey Canfield, Kelly Klima, and Tim Dawson, "Using Deliberative Democracy to Identify Energy Policy Priorities in the United States," *Energy Research and Social Science* 8 (2015): 184–89.

24 Thucydides, *History of the Peloponnesian War*, trans. William Smith (Harper and Brothers, 1836).

25 Kevin Mattson, "Do Americans Really Want Deliberative Democracy?" *Rhetoric and Public Affairs* 5, no. 2 (Summer 2002): 327–29.

26 Annenberg Public Policy Center of the University of Pennsylvania, "Americans Are Poorly Informed About Basic Constitutional Provisions," September 12, 2017; Nick Freiling, "Just 37 Percent of Americans Can Name Their Representative," May 31, 2017, https://www.haveninsights.com/ just-37-percent-name-representative.

27 Florida Amendment 4 Exit Polling, December 21, 2018, CNN, https://www .cnn.com/election/2018/results/florida/ballot-measures/1.

28 Zoltan Hajnal, "Black Class Exceptionalism: Insights from Direct Democracy on the Race Versus Class Debate," *Public Opinion Quarterly* 71, no. 4 (Winter 2007): 560–87.

29 Camille Morse Nicholson, *Leading the Way: Pittsburgh, PA*, Jefferson Center (website), April 4, 2017.

30 Marcia Mundt, *Participatory Budgeting Evaluation Report*, City of Cambridge, January 2017.

31 Bruce Ackerman and James S. Fishkin, *Deliberation Day* (New Haven, CT: Yale University Press, 2014).

32 Ethan J. Leib, *Deliberative Democracy in America: A Proposal for a Popular Branch of Government* (University Park: Pennsylvania State University Press, 2004).

33 Mark Button and Kevin Mattson, "Deliberative Democracy in Practice: Challenges and Prospects for Civic Deliberation," *Polity* 31 no. 4 (July 1999): 609–37.

34 Kevin Mattson, "Do Americans Really Want Deliberative Democracy?," *Rhetoric and Public Affairs* 5, no. 2 (2002): 327–29.

35 Jacob Dijkstra, "Social Exchange: Relations and Networks," *Social Network Analysis and Mining* 5, no. 60 (2015).

36 Linda Molm, Jessica Collet, and David Schaefer, "Building Solidarity Through Generalized Exchange: A Theory of Reciprocity," *American Journal of Sociology* 113, no. 1 (July 2007): 205–42.

37 Peter P. Ekeh, *Social Exchange Theory: The Two Traditions* (Cambridge: Harvard University Press, 1974).

38 Cecilia Hyunjung Mo and Katharine M. Conn, "When Do the Advantaged See the Disadvantages of Others? A Quasi-Experimental Study of National Service," *American Political Science Review* 112, no. 4 (2018): 721–41.

39 Lydia Saad, "Military, Small Business, Police Still Stir Most Confidence," Gallup, June 28, 2018, https://news.gallup.com/poll/236243/military-small-business-police-stir-confidence.aspx.

40 Mo and Conn, "When Do the Advantaged See the Disadvantages of Others?"

41 Franklin Project at the Aspen Institute, *Voters for National Service: Perspectives of American Voters on Large Scale National Service*, 2013.

42 Franklin Project, *Voters for National Service*.

43 Doug Bandow, "Mandatory National Service: A Bad Idea That Won't Die," *American Conservative*, August 8, 2019, https://www.the americanconservative.com/articles/mandatory-national-service-a-bad-idea-that-wont-die/.

44 Andrew Pauwels, "Mandatory National Service: Creating Generations of Civic Minded Citizens," *Notre Dame Law Review* 88, no. 5 (June 2013): 2597–626.

45 Thomas F. Pettigrew and Linda R. Tropp, "How Does Intergroup Contact Reduce Prejudice? Meta-Analytic Tests of Three Mediators," *European Journal of Social Psychology* 38, no. 6 (2008): 922–34.

46 James L. Perry and Ann Marie Thomson, *Civic Service: What Difference Does It Make?* (New York: Routledge, 2015), xv.

47 Perry and Thomson, *Civic Service*.

48 Kay Lehman Schlozmar, Henry E. Brady, and Sidney Verba, *Unequal and Unrepresented: Political Inequality and the People's Voice in the New Gilded Age* (Princeton, NJ: Princeton University Press, 2018).

49 Jack Crittenden and Peter Levine, "Civic Education," *Stanford Encyclopedia of Philosophy* (Fall 2018 edition), ed. Edward N. Zalta.

50 *Stanford Encyclopedia of Philosophy*, "Civic Education," December 27, 2007 (substantive revision August 31, 2018).

51 Danielle Allen, *Education and Equality* (Chicago: University of Chicago Press, 2016), 27–28.

52 Allen, *Education and Equality*, 33.

53 Allen, *Education and Equality*, 40.

54 Campbell Streator, "Young Americans Demand Civic Education—for Good Reason," *The Hill*, July 20, 2019.

55 Lonnie Sherrod, Constance Flanagan, and James Youniss, "Dimensions of Citizenship and Opportunities for Youth Development," *Applied Developmental Science* 6, no. 4 (October 2002): 264–72.

56 James Baldwin, *Notes of a Native Son* (Boston: Beacon Press, 1955), 9.

57 Computational Propaganda Research Project, *The IRA, Social Media and Political Polarization in the United States, 2012–2018*, January 23, 2019.

58 Education Development Center, "3 Ways to Improve Civics Education," August 29, 2018.

59 Scott Edwards, "Political Heroes and Political Education," *North American Review* 264, no. 1 (1979): 8–13.

60 Jean-Jacques Rousseau, *Discourse on the Virtue Most Necessary for a Hero* (University Press of New England [for] Dartmouth College, 1994).

61 M.W. Jackson, "Rousseau's Discourse on Heroes and Heroism," *Proceedings of the American Philosophical Society* 113, no. 3 (September 1989): 434–46.

62 Mark Triffitt, "Why Politics Today Can't Give Us the Heroes We Need," *The Conversation*, August 10, 2015.

63 Scott T. Allison and George R. Goethals, "Our Definition of 'Hero,'" University of Richmond, October 15, 2015.

64 Triffitt, "Why Politics Today Can't Give Us the Heroes We Need."

65 Anna Julia Cooper, "The Gain from a Belief," in *A Voice from the South* (Xenia, OH: Aldine Printing House, 1892), 297.

66 Harris Poll, "Many Americans Find Their Heroes in Family Members," November 6, 2014.

67 Scott T. Allison and George R. Goethals, "Hero Worship: The Elevation of the Human Spirit," *Journal for the Theory of Social Behaviour* 46, no. 2 (2016): 187–210.

68 Allison and Goethals, "Our Definition of 'Hero.'"
69 George Packer, "We Are Living in a Failed State," *The Atlantic*, June 2020.
70 Pauline Maier, *American Scripture: Making the Declaration of Independence*, 1st edition (New York: Knopf, distributed by Random House, 1997), 208.
71 John Lewis, "Together, You Can Redeem the Soul of Our Nation," *The New York Times*, July 30, 2020.

Index